Annabelle Sreberny is Professor of Global
and Director of the Centre for Media and Fil
of London. She is President of the Internatic
Communication Research. Her book *Small Media, Big Revolution.
nication, Culture and the Iranian Revolution* provides an analysis of the communication dynamics of the 1979 revolution, some elements of which were
repeated in the 2009 process.

Gholam Khiabany is Reader in International Communications in the
Department of Applied Social Sciences, London Metropolitan University.
He is the author of *Iranian Media: The Paradox of Modernity*.

'In a world where we are yet even to imagine the revolutionary potentials of the new media, Annabelle Sreberny and Gholam Khiabany's
Blogistan explores the expanding power of internet technology and the politics of discontent it has made possible in one of its most exciting testing
ground—the Islamic Republic of Iran. . . . the fact that the Islamic Republic
has just launched a "cyber-army" to combat the "soft war" that they believe
Iranian bloggers have launched against tyranny is a testimony to the timeliness
of this critical study. Annabelle Sreberny and Gholam Khiabany's judicious,
informed, sympathetic, and pathbreaking intervention announces a whole
new generation of scholarship in the field'
—Hamid Dabashi, Columbia University

'*Blogistan* is essential reading for anyone who wants to really comprehend
how the digital age looks beyond the west — in this case contemporary Iran
where a media world has been created that encompasses government control
and censorship, digital activism, politically savvy hacking, gendered concerns,
and serious parody, to name a few of *Blogistan's* topics. The intensity and
creativity that the authors discuss and analyze make it clear that this part of
the world is a lively and essential location for readers across disciplines, from
anthropology to media studies. Who knew that Persian was one of the most
frequently used languages on the internet? Once you read this book — by
two scholars with deep knowledge of the Iranian mediascape — none of this
will surprise you.'
—Faye Ginsburg, Director, Centre of Media, Culture and History, NYU

'Of all the locations where the "new media" are making their mark, none
has the capacity to engage like Iran does, and this remarkable study has both
exhilarating and sobering things to tell us about life in a post-revolutionary
state. Essential and engaging reading!'
—Toby Miller, University of California Riverside

Blogistan

The Internet and Politics in Iran

Annabelle Sreberny
and
Gholam Khiabany

I.B. TAURIS

LONDON · NEW YORK

Published in 2010 by I.B. Tauris & Co Ltd
6 Salem Road, London W2 4BU
175 Fifth Avenue, New York NY 10010
www.ibtauris.com

Distributed in the United States and Canada Exclusively by Palgrave Macmillan
175 Fifth Avenue, New York NY 10010

International Library of Iranian Studies, Vol 18

ISBN: 978 1 84511 606 4 (hb)
ISBN: 978 1 84511 607 1 (pb)

A full CIP record for this book is available from the British Library
A full CIP record is available from the Library of Congress

Library of Congress Catalog Card Number: available

Typeset in Bembo by MPS Limited, a Macmillan Company
Printed and bound in Great Britain by
TJ International Ltd, Padstow, Cornwall

Contents

List of Illustrations

Introduction

IN JUNE 2009, the Islamic Republic experienced a contested presidential election and a rapid and powerful popular mobilisation that used a range of digital technologies to organise and to get its message out to the world. This book provides the necessary background to understanding this unexpected and dramatic political movement. Written before the June events, it nonetheless explains the development of internet infrastructure, the shift of face-to-face politics to the internet and the possibilities and constraints on social change existing inside the Islamic Republic.

This is a book about blogging and about Iran. It is about the emergence of 'new' communications technologies, the practices that are invented around them and the meanings of these. It is also about a specific post-revolutionary country called Iran and the manner in which 'blogging' has become a shorthand for political expression, journalism by another name and social exploration in a milieu where such exploration is not particularly welcomed. The blogistan has become a space of contention between the people and the state. As the Islamic Republic of Iran tries to celebrate 31 years of the revolution, the promises and disappointments of that process are brought into focus once more. An exploration of blogging is a fascinating way of understanding the failures of that revolution, while the dynamics of the 'Green Movement' echo some of that earlier political process.

The phenomenon of Iranian blogging has been recognised for some time by Iranian political commentators, by international journalists and within the blogging community. Often, there is a sense of surprise: Oh, Iranians are computer literate? Sometimes there's a sense of paradox: But isn't Iran a repressive state? Others are dumbstruck by the idea that there are women bloggers. There's even an experimental video on the subject.[1] There is just a general sense of 'wow!'

Much of this is of course a response mediated by the limited and skewed representations of Iran by the Western press, which was especially one-sided during the latter part of President George Bush's presidency as the potential 'nuclear threat' was so provocatively hyped in the media. Just try a Google search for 'Iran's nuclear weapons' and it produces over 6 million hits, making a sociolinguistic fact even if the material or military reality is not completely proven. However, since November 2007, and the publication of the independent report by US intelligence on the weak development of an Iranian nuclear weaponising programme, the English media in the USA and the UK started treating readers to a number of stories 'humanising' Iran and its people, recognising their ski resorts, appreciating their food, even claiming 'that they are just like us' (Schuh, 2008). Following the election of a Democrat president with a Muslim middle name, Barack Hussein Obama, the mood thawed and his warm Norouz message for the Persian new year in March 2009 was an important symbolic gesture that did not go unnoticed, although by March 2010, relations with Iran seemed to be back to the same threatening stand-off with a new sanctions regime in the offing.

One of the analytic difficulties in trying to understand the contemporary Iranian political environment is the poverty of conceptual tools available. At gatherings of Iranians, many critics often lambast the regime as 'totalitarian'. Without entering into a complex analysis of whether this term was of any use before, it certainly does not work for contemporary Iran. While the state might be said to have totalising impulses, arrogating itself the right to interfere and control many arenas of sociocultural life that would be designated private elsewhere, it still remains the case that contemporary Iran is remarkably porous. Groups of tourists from around the world – albeit not as many as before – can be found in many cities. The Iranian diaspora moves in and out with comparative ease. Satellite TV provides hundreds of channels that offer a range of content, from news and political debate to everyday entertainment, serials and soaps to a remarkable array of Arab porn channels. Nor does its political structure emulate the centralisation and organisation of China, let alone of North Korea. It is not like those states. But neither is it a Western democracy.

Herein lies the paradox of contemporary cultural and political analysis that we try to keep at the forefront of this book. Iran is both like and not like 'us', the 'West', and in the explorations of what is and isn't alike, we learn something about Iran and Iranians and certainly something about ourselves, including our assumptions about others. In exploring blogging and the development of the infrastructure of information and communication technologies in Iran, we also critique some of the generally taken-for-granted attitudes about 'the internet and society' that fill countless volumes in media and cultural studies. The nature of Iranian society, its political and economic contexts, the concerns of its people, mean that access and use of the internet takes on a different hue than in the USA and the UK. Our aim throughout this book is to not only provide rich and detailed historical contextualisation of the material from Iran but also to situate those developments within the broader developments in new technologies worldwide and the debates these have provoked. We consider that the choice is not to examine either the general phenomenon or the particular case, but rather to situate the particular within the general and to explore what each has to say to the other.

Blogging is partly a function of access to new communication technologies, especially the internet. The first lesson to understand about the Iranian experience is that its internet development has all taken place after the revolution, within a very specific set of diplomatic, political, ideological, religious and cultural contexts. The Islamic Republic was established in 1979 after a comparatively short, popular but not overly bloody revolution. Thus, all developments in relation to the internet and cyberspace have occurred within a highly politicised post-revolutionary environment with Shi'ite Islam as the ideology of the dominant theocratic state.

Yet the central issue about the development of new media in Iran is not the obvious and crude divide between a 'traditional' and 'religious' state and 'modern' technology since that very state has, and many individual clergy have, adapted rapidly to the use of new information technologies as they have to many other technologies, including IVF treatments, kidney transplants, transgender surgery and nuclear physics. Indeed, much of the Iranian debate about the nuclear issue is driven by the intense and justifiable desire to participate in this area of scientific endeavour along with other advanced knowledge communities.

It is evident that many new communication technologies are effective tools for popular social mobilization. (Ithiel de Sola Pool, 1983; Jeremy Rifkin, 2000; Dan Gillmor, 2004). We do not have to embrace the entire debate about Web 2.0 as the new participatory Jerusalem. This all too often sounds as though there were no opportunities for participation before the digital age, to which most historical moments of profound political change (1776, 1789, 1871, 1917, 1989, etc.) give the lie (Annabelle Sreberny-Mohammadi and Ali Mohammadi, 1994). Yet it is evident that the spread of digital technologies and the increased ability to produce, share and mash-up content is challenging the 'old' media environment. The shift from professional media producers to the citizen journalist is creating consternation and debate everywhere (Gillmor, 2004; Downing, 1996; Allan and Thorsen, 2009). Democracies worry about the demise of professional journalism to bloggers, while strong states worry about ideological challenges that cannot be controlled. Yet control over channels of communications has been a major issue in Iran since the introduction of the first newspaper almost 150 years ago. The emergent press was a powerful vehicle for the demands for political reform that produced the Constitutional Revolution in 1905–11 (Ahmad Kasravi, 2006). 'Small media' including audio cassettes and leaflets were used to great effect during the 1979 revolution that produced the Islamic Republic (Sreberny-Mohammadi and Mohammadi, 1994). The internet has just become the newest site of contestation and the latest set of technologies to offer an alternative mode of communications to those directly controlled by the state.

The second tension is the centralising state's attempt to manage the slow development of the private sector in Iran and the inhibitions placed on entrepreneurial ICT activity in a field that has produced net millionaires in other parts of the world and where Iranians often excel; Farhad Nazem with Yahoo; Omid Kordestani at Google; Hussein Eslambolchi with AT&T Labs; Pierre Omidyar at eBay are just a few of the high-placed Iranians within the global IT sector. State control over the rapid spread of new communications technologies in Iran exemplifies its uneven economic development and the contradictory role of the state.

The communication industries are amongst the most rapidly growing sectors of the economy, and the adoption of new media in various forms is part of that expansion. Alongside the considerable expansion of Iranian media channels, popular desire for access to informal channels of communication and for greater cultural consumption show in the increasing use of satellite television, broadband and the internet as well as mobile phone technology, often used to share jokes as well as to organise activity. Thus, the astonishing rise and popularity of weblogs as a particular site of struggle is part of this broader diffusion of digital technologies under the Islamic Republic, technologies that really came into their own during the 2009 election process and its exhilarating and tragic aftermath.

So why are so many Iranians 'veb-be-logging'? Frequently, it is explained by reference to a repressive state. This, while true, cannot in itself account for the huge blogging community. If repressive state control alone were a sufficient cause then, for example, Chinese and Arab bloggers, and citizens of many other strong states, could and should proportionally outnumber Iranians. It's odd to construct the blogosphere as the index of repression, as if the latter 'produced' the former in a necessary and equal response. Equally, the existence of so many bloggers, voicing their opinions about a huge range of issues, is itself a limit condition to the extent and the meaning of 'repression' in Iran. This paradox, of one of the world's most prolific blogospheres existing within what is perceived as a highly authoritarian state must give pause for thought and a reworking of some taken-for-granted assumptions about the nature of the Iranian state and how it functions, as well as the role of contemporary forms of communication as challenges to centralised political power. But this dynamic also echoes two long-standing dynamics of Iranian history: comparatively early adoption and rapid engagement with new forms of communication and a consequent duet between the central state and the public over the use of these forms. Thus, when the state is feeling strong, communications flourishes, but if the state feels threatened, media is one of the first spheres to be closed down.

Better answers must lie at a second order of analysis, around a complex set of issues that include the legacy of a revolutionary political culture, the perception and experience of repression by citizens, culturally preferred modes of expressivity as well as the meaning and experience of the Iranian diaspora and a deeprooted Iranian cosmopolitanism.

The grounded, empirical nature of our work must thus also raise questions about easy generalities about new media phenomena and about the universalist assumptions to be found in much of the literature on the subject. For us, books about the 'internet and society' beg many questions about which 'society' is the subject and how that society arranges its internet infrastructure and access to it. Thus, this is also a work of comparative media analysis, asking questions about the generalisability of communications analysis and suggesting that all work on media technologies are strung between universalist and particularist elements and that the best kinds of analysis try to do justice to the tensions between the two.

This book also engages with the stalled binary of 'tradition' and 'modernity' that stalks so much writing about Iran. By examining the new media practices of the clergy and members of the Iranian political establishment, we seek to show the contemporaneity of Shi'ite Islam. All societies have internal tensions between the maintenance of practices seen as traditional and pulls to novelty by drivers of change. The key analytic issue is to be able to identify what these are and how they interact, not to stage an abstract encounter between abstract notions.

This book is not an extended list of Iranian bloggers. One such, a volume erroneously claiming all blogging is about 'resistance', can be found in Nasrin Alavi's (2005) work. Indeed, with an estimated 70,000 or more active bloggers, we do not even pretend to map and analyse them all. Web-crawler research by John Kelly of Morningside Analytics is beginning to map the Iranian blogosphere and, with the benefit of different temporal snapshots, to show its change over time. Some of the arguments in Chapter Two can be read as methodological engagements with internet research, including the difficulties of counting blogs and the assumptions of much of such research.

At the same time, the blogosphere does force some basic questions about the dynamics of political change in Iran. The US sanctions regime with its block on the provision of industrial and electronic spare parts to Iran has had quite the opposite effect from that intended, cutting off more people from internet access and thus quieting the internal voices of dissent and debate, indeed helping the censorial hand of the state. This is another indication of the in-utility of US policy under President Bush towards the 'Axis of Evil' and its feeble attempts to bring democracy in to Iran from the outside, while actually quashing the real green shoots of internal pressure for change. External policy has sometimes driven a wedge between the Iranian diaspora and internal voices, while the 'return' to Iran of the post-revolutionary children of its revolutionary generation is producing a genuinely new set of encounters, a phenomenon that is as yet poorly recognised. The changing relationships between Iranians inside and outside Iran, between the diaspora and its 'home', as well as the issue of language are explored in Chapter Six.

In many ways, blogging is a form of commentary – on daily life, on politics, on art. Commenting on blogging is simply a continuation of the same practice, an extended essay in intermedia commentary, the stuff of more and more of media content, of contemporary life altogether. But in Iran, the closure of many press titles meant the opening up of websites carrying news and editorials, while blogs contain new material not available within the regime-controlled channel. In Chapter Seven we take up the issue of blogging as intermedia commentary and the relations between the blogosphere and more 'professional' media outlets, to the extent of asking whether such a distinction is meaningful in Iran today and what the future is for professional journalism there.

So, in this book we try to do a number of things. We situate the growth of blogging within the expansion of the Iranian telecommunications sector as part of its rapid modernisation. We historicise the rise of Iranian blogging and attempt a categorisation of the kind and content of blogs. We examine bloggers as contemporary intellectuals, both religious and secular, and examine the real engagement of the religious establishment with new media technologies. We focus on the particular vibrancy of women bloggers, and examine an emerging trend of 'halfies' and diasporic Iranian bloggers who are articulating the 'inside' and 'outside' in novel ways. There are other specific communities of bloggers, including a vibrant gay blogosphere, Ahmadinejad's disavowal not withstanding. One of the questions that needs to be addressed is the balance between a 'virtual public sphere' and actual public space in Iran, whereby the former may actually function as a safety valve against the depredations on the latter, the lid on the pressure cooker blowing off with enormous force in June 2009. So we begin to extrapolate a theory about the meaning of Iranian blogging using a variety of conjunctural and cultural nodes.

And in the final chapter, that demanded inclusion, we provide a brief overview of the events of the summer of 2009, because the rest of the book helps to contextualise and explain those events. In the thirtieth year of the revolution that brought the Islamic Republic to power, a wave of public protest triggered by a 'stolen election' revealed not only the pent-up anger and frustration of predominantly young Iranians but also the widespread and sophisticated use of new communications technologies. Pundits around the world quickly proclaimed this was a 'twitter revolution', while YouTube and Facebook groaned with up-loaded videos, photographs and musical responses to the events. The mainstream media outside Iran had to rely upon countless 'citizen journalists' to provide them with news updates and images from a country from which they were unable to report themselves.

The story of this recent upsurge deserves to be told in great detail and we are in the process of doing just that (Sreberny and Khiabany, 2011/forthcoming). This book serves as background to help understand how so many Iranians are so technologically savvy and how the terrain of new communications technologies has had to take over from more traditional forms of face-to-face politics, both because these are very constrained and because this new generation has no experience of such political forms. The new social networks provide sites of encounter with others, places to share material that can be easily distributed and mashed-up into other content, and fora for debate. These are dynamic spaces of interaction and dialogue, and places for the development and practice of politics. This book provides the historical, political and technological background to understand these dramatic recent events that were impossible to predict yet, on further analysis, appear highly over-determined.[2]

We dedicate this book to the various generations of Iranians who have struggled for their rights and especially to the next generation, ours and everyone's 'children', glad in the hope they represent.

1 The Internet in Iran: Development and Control

CRITICAL ANALYSES of the internet in Iran face two theoretical positions, each loaded with a sense of historical inevitability. On the one hand, we have accounts of the 'digital exceptionalism' of the internet that overstate the role of new technologies in economy and society and suggest a decisive break with the past. The key assumption in this scenario is that the internet changes the very nature of social relations and promises a future of democratic participation. If this account regards technology as the dynamic force of society, its so-called opposite, 'Islamic exceptionalism', proposes that it is Islam that acts as the determining factor and the sole signifier in the realm of culture and communication. In this scenario, the totalities of production and social relations are declared an inadequate starting point for analysis of media and this paves the path for epistemological nativism which offer an all-encompassing, never-changing and uniform 'Islam' as the basis for the realities of communication in the region (Khiabany, 2010).

The Islamic Republic was established in 1979 after a rapid popular mobilization that produced a revolutionary outcome. Thus, all developments in relation to the internet and cyberspace have occurred within a highly politicised post-revolutionary environment with Shi'ite Islam as the ideology of the dominant theocratic state. Yet the central issue about the development of new media in Iran is not the obvious and crude divide between a 'traditional' state and 'modern' technology because that very state has, and many individual clergy have, adopted rapidly to the use of new information technologies. There are two more subtle lines of tension running through internet development in Iran. The first is the centralising state's desire to control expression in a 'new technology' environment that is highly conducive to widespread and popular participation. The Iranian state has been concerned about this issue for over a century and internet has just become the newest site of contestation and the latest technology to offer an alternative mode of communications to those directly controlled by the state.

The second is the centralising state's desire to orchestrate and manage the slow development of the private sector and the inhibitions placed on entrepreneurial ICT (information and communication technologies) activity in a field that has produced Net millionaires in other parts of the world. The rapid spread of new communications technologies exemplifies Iran's uneven development as well as the contradictory role of the state.

Despite these two fault lines, the recent period has seen the rapid emergence of the communication industry in Iran as one of the fastest growing economic sectors and various uses of 'new media' now constitute one of the most dynamic and vibrant politico-cultural spaces. Beside the expansion of Iranian media channels, popular desire for access to informal channels of communication and for greater cultural consumption show in the increasing usage of mobile technology and the internet as well as the astonishing rise and popularity of weblogs which have become a particular site of struggle.

Newspaper kiosk, Tehran

This chapter locates the expansion of the internet in Iran in its wider social context and examines the realities of digital divides and the fact that Iran is lagging behind some of its richer regional neighbours. By looking at the expansion of telecommunication facilities and infrastructure, it maps the modernising policies of the Iranian state and the emerging contradictions of its development process. We suggest that limited access and usage only tells part of a more complex story of communicative experiences in Iran. Internet use has started to challenge the state monopoly not only over long-distance telephone calls but also as a channel of political and cultural communication. Private capital is challenging the monopoly of the state as government policies slowly adapt to the marketisation and privatisation of the communication sector, while the broader national and international contexts make for an intriguing mix of internet and media developments.

Although the tools and technologies are universal and while the general development of the internet cannot be understood outside the broader operation of capital and state, the internet as a whole also cannot be understood outside of place. In the age of 'globalisation' and 'transnationalism', it is worth remembering that the politics and political actions, nevertheless, do take place in concrete 'places'. This is not to deny the broader concerns, and the place itself cannot be understood without reference to broader processes and how people are united by common histories, concerns and language. Therefore, as Masserat Amir-Ebrahimi (2005) rightly observes:

> In spite of claims to a 'universal' language, the internet is a new public space/sphere grounded in particular socio-cultural aspects of everyday life. Its cultural significance varies considerably from place to place according to people's diverse experiences, lacks, needs and aspirations. In democratic societies, cyberspace is often viewed as an 'alter' space of information, research and leisure that functions in a parallel or complementary fashion to existing public spaces and institutions. In countries where public spaces are controlled by traditional or restrictive cultural forces, however, the internet can take on varied signification. In Iran, where the public sphere is closely monitored and regulated by traditional and state forces, the internet has become a means to resist the restrictions imposed on these spaces. For people living in these countries, especially marginalized groups such as youth and women, the internet can be a space more 'real' than everyday life.

The first section of this chapter examines aspects of digital divides in relation to current debates about internationalising media and internet studies. It then presents aspects of the expansion of the Iranian communication industries and their rapid modernisation in recent years. It then examines the contradictions in the development of the internet in Iran, its competing interests and policies.

But first, some more detailed context is necessary.

A Brief Reprise of Contemporary Iranian History: Producing an Islamic Revolution

The Islamic Republic of Iran was, and remains, a contradictory entity. Brought into being in 1979 by a popular revolution that included diverse class and ideological components, the reins of state power were rapidly Islamicised to produce the world's only theocracy, with a *velayat-e-faqih* (supreme jurisprudent) as the religious head of an Islamic polity. Khomeini was, of course, the first, followed by Khamenei, the extant (2010) unelected leader.

However, alongside this system of religious leadership decided through the acclaim of the clergy exists a parallel modern political system of elections and formal political roles. All Iranians over 18 including women, who were enfranchised in 1963, elect a president as well as representatives to the *Majles*, the parliament. This political process is orchestrated by the over-arching Guardian Council that vets political groups and individuals and makes knowledge of Islam a strong criterion for inclusion. The general enfranchisement, growth of political campaigning, strength of political debate and public eagerness to participate mean that many analysts (Ashraf Ahmad and Ali Banuazizi, 2001; Said Amir Arjomand, 2000; Charles Kurzman 2001; Ali Ansari, 2006) acknowledge the dual political system and the existence of democratising elements in the polity. Iran certainly enjoys a much wider political field of participation and expression than most other regimes in the region, an argument made repeatedly in the face of possible US incursions. Rakshan Bani-Etemad's powerful film *Roozegar-e Ma, Our Time* (2002) is a vivid exploration of contemporary political desires and imaginative possibilities, when even young women feel able to run for the presidency (although not formally allowed). There have been long-standing and deep internal struggles for power between 'liberal reformers' and 'conservatives', between the appointed and elected elements, which became particularly acute after Khatami's reformist presidency and Mahmoud Ahmadinejad's election in 2005. In 2009, it was precisely the re-investment of energy in the democratic process, stimulated by televised debates, rallies and all the insignia of political campaigning, which produced such a stunned response, as if the very processes of participation had been finally rendered a sham.

Beyond this internal power struggle, other issues are also relevant. Iran experienced a bitter eight-year war with Iraq that produced colossal death, injury and destruction, including missile attacks on urban areas, and this remains a process not fully absorbed or worked through inside the Islamic Republic. One of the consequences of the war was the elevation of security over all other public matters. Another was the elevation of war veterans to social heroes and their rapid ascension up various socioeconomic ladders, including being parachuted into university places often without appropriate schooling and background. Many have subsequently become key figures in educational institutions and companies, thus assuring regime control and monitoring of these organisations. The quiet rise of the Islamic Revolutionary Guards Corps (IRGC), also known as Pasdaran, as political and economic beneficiaries of revolutionary mobilization and state privatization, is part of the same process. In September 2009, the IRGC acquired 51% of Telecommunication Company of Iran minutes after the company was privatised in a $5bn deal, the biggest in Iranian economic history. It is now estimated that the Guards control around one third of Iran's economy through various charitable foundations, subsidiaries and trusts.

The Islamic Republic has also experienced chronic economic crisis from its inception. It inherited financial problems from the previous government that were exacerbated by the devastating Iraq war and the economic liberalisation thereafter (Parvin Alizadeh, 2000). Indeed, probably one of the clinching reasons for the election of Ahmadinejad in 2005 was his promise to look after the poorer sections of Iranian society, including those in the provinces. But he has not delivered. Despite rising oil prices, which reached over $140 barrel in the summer of 2008, their highest ever, inflation is higher (estimated to be around 35 per cent), so that even banks offering savers interest rates of 20 per cent lag well behind. Housing – especially in Tehran – is unaffordable for many, with scores of properties lying empty, and the gap between rich and poor is opening wider, despite the rhetoric of the revolution to support the *mostazzafin* over the *mostakbarin*. Hojatol-eslam Rafsanjani, the second most powerful man in the entire history of the Islamic Republic, is one of the richest men in Iran, showing the embrace of capitalist economics by Islamic practitioners. An often-repeated nostrum in Tehran in the autumn of 2008 was that every ayatollah has an oil well in his pocket, '*chah-e naft to jib darand*'.

And yet the Islamic Republic manifests some unexpected and progressive policies in certain areas. There are needle exchange programmes for heroin users, advanced IVF treatments, readily accessible transgender surgery (although that is widely seen as way to literally erase homosexuality) and payment for kidney organ donations that maintains a supply of organs (and there is global debate about the ethics of such practices). However, there is also a lack of clear and coherent policies in other areas, including rather weak provision of welfare benefits and unemployment. Iran has a very youthful demographic, over 70 per cent of the population being under 30, that produces considerable pressure on university places, training and employment, yet its provision is inadequate to the demand. Migration into Tehran is high and not readily absorbed. The traffic in the capital is nightmarish (and poor in other cities also) and the pollution dangerous, with the media publicising health warnings on days with particularly poor air quality and the government frequently having to resort to closing schools. Thus, less than three decades after massive political and ideological change, a lengthy war and a myriad of unresolved social and economic issues, Iranians experience multiple challenges in everyday life as well as a volatile political atmosphere in which they struggle to be heard through print, broadcast or new media.

The diffusion of internet access and the adoption of new information technologies have to be seen within this context, which its users both interrogate and exacerbate.

The International Turn and Internet Studies

Any serious engagement with the current debate about internationalising media theory and internet studies undoubtedly needs to go beyond technological determinism and dismantle many of the pointless and simplified binary construction and 'either/or' versions of media, technology and culture. Downing (1996) helped to raise the alarm about how our knowledge of the media field is essentially based on experience and examples from the West, mainly from the USA, so now we witness a growing concern over 'Western bias' in media theory and its negative, parochial impact (McQuail, 2001; Curran and Park, 2000). Slowly the work of communication scholars from different regions other than Western Europe and the USA is coming to the fore, revealing some much needed comparative analysis and a burgeoning literature focusing on examples of media and society outside the Anglo-American experience. However, internationalising media theory should be and should mean more than a collection of articles on the state of media and communication in various parts of the world. While stepping out of a specific and hegemonic geographical area is important, it is not adequate or 'de-Westernising' as such. What is being 'de-Westernised', on what basis and why remain significant questions that need scrutiny and critical examination. While media theory is in desperate need to renew itself and break out of its geographical confines of the 'West', it also needs to move away from the culturalist assumptions that have entrapped much of the debate about international communication, including modernisation theory. We must avoid simply inverting the tradition/modern dichotomy so that we overvalue the 'traditional' and line up the commercial, rootless, banal and pre-packaged 'western' products against the 'authentic', 'organic' and deeply rooted cultures of the 'east'.

'Internet Studies' also throws up a number of further questions and debates about the entanglement between media and society. Two significant issues revolve around the problem of access/social inequality and the nature of political participation and whether the new media has solved, or is capable of solving, some of the old problems in these two areas. Undoubtedly the notion of 'internet' itself remains problematic, not least because the singularity of the 'internet', as Livingstone (2005) reminds us, suppresses the diversity of technologies imbedded in 'new media', not to mention the differential social and geographic access and the different policies and responses it has generated across the world.

A key concern and a fruitful line of research developed in recent years has been about 'digital divides' and differential access to new technologies. Moving beyond the simple statistics at both the national and international levels, the idea has evolved from a 'singular' digital divide to include questions of the quality of access, models of engagement and the diversity of content. Communication technologies by themselves cannot solve political, social, cultural and economic discrepancies within societies, nor can they be regarded as the engines of history. They do not teach literacy, are not education in themselves and cannot resolve the lack of clean water or electricity or food. Technologies are developed in historical societies and as such carry all the marks of their historical moment in their shapes, designs, functions and the very fact that they are sold in the marketplace as commodities. The debate about digital divide provokes a set of questions: What is exactly the digital divide? Is there only one? Who is excluded and by what/whom? To what extent is this divide distinctly 'digital'?

Undoubtedly, at the heart of the debate is the broader question of global inequality, not only in terms of access to new technologies and to media, but also to staggering and increasing material inequalities. Any serious debate about 'digital divides' and any attempt at 'internationalising' internet studies has to move beyond media-centric, technologically determinist arguments concerned with the technical issue of diffusion. Indeed, if anything, debates about new technologies and internet have to start by examining the ideas/theories of society, specifically the global expansion of capitalist modernity with all its implications and contradictions, and the miseries as well as the potentials that it offers in the global south.

The scale of global inequality remains one of the most scandalous aspects of global capitalism (Saul, 2004). At no time in the modern history of capitalism, despite the neo-liberal international focus on poverty and the desire to make poverty 'history', has the gap between the haves and have-nots and the north and south ever been bigger. In this period, the rich have got richer and have increased their 'share' (an interesting and co-opted term) of the wealth and resources, while the poor have seen their share of income decrease even further. Of course, there are optimistic figures indicating rather clearly that the life expectancy in developing countries has increased, that fewer children die before they reach the age of five, that people in the global south are healthier and much better educated. However, the scale of inequality remains staggering. Saul (2004) expresses this vividly: 'One-fifth of humanity live in countries where many people think nothing of spending $2 a day on a cappuccino. Another fifth of humanity survive on less than $1 a day and live in countries where children die for want of a simple anti-mosquito bednet'. As United Nations Development Reports indicate, while debates over the disparity of income and poverty continue, debates over the sheer scale of inequality remain much less open. 'The world's richest 500 individuals have a combined income greater than that of the poorest 416 million. Beyond these extremes, the 2.5 billion people living on less than $2 a day – 40 per cent of the world's population – account for 5 per cent of global income. The richest 10 per cent, almost all of whom live in high-income countries, account for 54 per cent (UNDR, 2005:4). And this continues despite the advances of global media which supposedly makes such concerns more visible. Indeed, it is a fascinating element of our global condition that rich countries were more ready to risk the 'loss' of, and indeed did lose, trillions of dollars in the so-called global credit crunch than to use this money to provide a minimum of development for the global south.

The same level of inequality is visible in terms of access to new technologies. Although we have seen a very sharp increase in the diffusion of the internet, the disparities between the haves and have-nots at national and international levels is still staggering. The early hype and the equivalent of 'making poverty history' initiatives in the case of the internet, most notably *Falling Through the Net* (which later became *A Nation Online*) policy of the US administrations in the 1990s and similar policies and announcements by the British government, managed to obscure the realities of inequality just within Anglo-capitalist countries.[2]

Table 1.1 conceals the huge disparities between nations in various geographical regions – for example that in Asia, where Japan and Hong Kong

TABLE 1.1 Distribution of Internet Users 2000–2007

World Region	Population	Population Percentage of World	Internet Usage	Population (%)	Usage (%) of World	Usage Growth (%) 2000–07
Africa	941,249,130	14.2	44,361,940	4.7	3.4	882.7
Asia	3,733,783,474	56.5	510,478,743	13.7	38.7	346.6
Europe	801,821,187	12.1	348,125,847	43.4	26.4	231.2
Middle East	192,755,045	2.9	33,510,500	17.4	2.5	920.2
North America	334,659,631	5.1	238,015,529	71.1	18.0	120.2
Latin America/ Caribbean	569,133,474	8.6	126,203,714	22.2	9.6	598.5
Oceania/ Australia	33,569,718	0.5	19,175,836	57.1	1.5	151.6
World Total	6,606,971,659	100.0	1,319,872,109	20.0	100.0	265.6

and South Korea (all with internet penetration of above 65 per cent) are lined alongside Afghanistan, Cambodia and Bangladesh (with 0.1, 0.2 and 0.3 per cent). However, it is not difficult to see where the main clusters of internet users are based, nor to see that there is a close correlation between the wealth of countries and access to internet. However, such figures also undoubtedly tell us very little about the differential access to internet within national contexts, nor how internet access varies depending on class, gender and education among other factors. Undoubtedly, much of the divide and inequality at international level remains spatially defined. That there are clear discrepancies of wealth and hence of internet access within the countries of the global south and global north, as well as between the north and south in general, is an increasingly well-known argument which urges us to move beyond what Saul has dubbed the false binaries of 'the geographical' versus 'the social' (Saul, 2004:221).

We can easily see, especially if we look at the diffusion of media technologies in historical context, that there is nothing especially 'digital' about the digital divide. Differences between rich and poor countries are as visible in internet penetration as they are for postal services, newspapers and book publication, radio and TV sets, telephony and computerisation. Diffusion of the infrastructure of the internet has a very close correlation with the wealth of a country. The optimism of the early years when advocates of the 'trickle-down' model of diffusion (Wilhelm, 2000) were predicting, or rather hoping, that with the aid, subsidy and support of governments and telecommunication firms, internet for everyone will be a 'real' option has faded.

Concerns with digital divides, as we have already argued, should not be limited to questions of physical access. As Robin Mansell (2002) has suggested, we have no reason to believe that once connected, all citizens will be empowered and will conduct and organise their social lives in meaningful ways. Borrowing the notion of 'entitlement' from Amartya Sen and applying it to media, Garnham and Mansell have called for a policy intervention to encourage citizens to acquire the capabilities necessary for a democratic dialogue (Nicholas Garnham, 1997; Mansell, 2002). 'Entitlement' to such capabilities is a fundamental human right that could finally pave the way for a truly global public sphere.

The other key concern in internet studies has revolved around issues of the public sphere and political participation (Livingstone, 2005). The early promise of the internet was based around the idea of universal access, empowerment of citizens and the potential of 'e-democracy' to provide all citizens with direct involvement in public life and policy. That the realisation of this dream and the potential of internet depends on access for all is an indisputable fact. Nevertheless, it is still significant to look at how the battle to control these new technologies is evolving and how those who have access use them to their advantage. Alternative uses of technologies are nothing new. An important aspect of all new technologies is what Williams called 'uncontrollable opportunities' and the set of interesting complications these produce. As he demonstrated with the case of literacy, 'there was no way to teach a man to read the Bible which did not also enable him to read the radical press. A controlled intention became an uncontrollable effect' (Williams, 1974:125). Furthermore, as Brian Winston (1998) reminds us, the history of technologies seems to consist of both 'accelerators' and 'breaks'. Applying Braudel's model of historical analysis, Winston suggests that in the case of technologies, the 'accelerator' is the supervening social necessity that transforms the prototype into an 'invention' and pushes the invention out into the world, causing its diffusion. But there is also a 'break'. This operates 'as a third transformation, wherein general social constraints coalesce to limit the potential of the device radically to disrupt pre-existing social formations' (Brian Winston, 1998:11). Mapping such 'interesting complications' and the contradictions and struggles for control of new technologies remain one of the most fruitful areas of media research at the national and international levels.

The case of Iran is no exception and provides us with ample evidence of precisely such contradictions and complications.

ICTS and Development in Iran

From the start, the Islamic Republic of Iran has been a developmentalist state and, since the end of the war with Iraq in 1988, even a 'liberalising' state. The development of basic communications infrastructure, including telecommunication, has been emphasised and developed rapidly. Yet the policies have been ad hoc and contradictory and therefore the development and expansion of the internet, as rapid as it has been in the last few years, is constrained by confusion in government policies, varied institutional interests and above all the dialectical tension between the imperative of the market and the 'revolutionary' claims of the state.

A brief look at the status of telecommunications in Iran demonstrates the rate of expansion and growth. In 1977, just before the revolution, the number of fixed telephone lines was less than 1 million, a little over 2 per cent of the population. Many people had been waiting 10 years or more to get a landline. Only 312 of the thousands of villages in Iran were connected, while the number of public telephone networks was only 4,294, with only 82 long-distance connect points. The decade of war with Iraq damaged a large part of Iran and its infrastructure and swallowed the resources of the country. More recently, the picture is one of rapid expansion and modernisation. By September 2009, the number of fixed line telephones had increased to 24,988,183, reaching over 34 per cent of the population. The number of mobile phones that stood at just below 60,000 in 1995 had increased to over 30 million or about 44 per cent of population. In addition, the number of cities with mobile network coverage has increased from 34 in 1995 to 1,076 in September 2009. Yet despite this rapid increase in mobile phone subscribers, Iran 'still has a long way to go to achieve satisfactory conditions since the country ranks 13th in the Middle East in this regard'.[3] All mobile subscribers are provided with SMS facility, and many are equipped with VMS, and Iranians quickly became avid texters. International roaming connection with 80 countries has also been established. The number of villages with telephone service had increased to 53,850 in September 2009. The Telecommunications Company of Iran (TCI) had launched 8,958 rural offices by September 2009 and plans to extend such offices further.

Internet access in Iran was provided for the first time in 1992 through a single line connecting the Institute for Studies in Theoretical Physics and

Mobile phone packages on sale in north Tehran bazaar

Mathematics (IPM) in Niavaran, Tehran. The link was through the BITNET network system and Iran's membership in the Trans-European Research and Educational Networking Association (Arabshahi, 1997). A year later, the private use of modems was permitted. This single line was expanded and developed with BITNET's allocation of 500 IP addresses to Iran. The main users of the internet in the early days were academicians and research institutions through their own connection to IPM. Even in 1993, Iran had no internal data networks.

In 1993, the High Council of Informatics announced that it was discussing with the TCI the possibility of establishing data communications networks over the country's telephone lines. Lack of investment by TCI as well as the absence of any clear and coherent policy meant that the market was left to itself, and private companies started to form and began to provide international links via lines leased by TCI. In 1995, fearful of losing control over its monopoly in telecommunication, the government started clamping down on private ISPs (internet service providers) and to improve its own data communication network (Grey Burkhart, 1998). Since then, the Iranian state has taken steps to expand and develop its telecommunications and informatics infrastructure, evident in Table 1.2[5].

As a result, the number of people with access to the internet has risen rapidly from the late 1990s. By 1996, 2,000 people had access – their usage mostly limited to sending and receiving emails. Since 2000, the rise in the number of internet users has been significant – from 132,000 users to 418,000 users in 2001 and to 1,326,000 in 2002 (Abili, 2002; Seyed M. Mousavi Shafaee, 2003). By the end of 2006, according to the Ministry of Communication, 11 million people had access to internet, a 50 per cent increase from previous year.[6] The TCI figures from September 2009 suggests that the number of users has reached 23 million. By September 2009, the national IT network was equipped with 3,558 data centres; 60,718 data access ports and 182,914 installed ports; 1,076 cities were under the coverage of the national IT network, and the international bandwidth had been increased to 26,154 Mbps.[7]

Internet in Iran: New Technology, Old Problems

A detailed comparison of the media markets in the Middle East allows for more critical insight into the problems, dilemmas and nature of the culture industries in Iran, which cannot be simply understood on the basis of 'Islamic exceptionalism'.

As Table 1.3 illustrates, one of the striking features in the region is the wide variation among countries in terms of population, literacy, expenditure on health and education. Another striking feature is the high expenditure of GDP on the military. While the figures have decreased from the heyday of military development and expenditure of the 1990s, the rates are among the highest in the developing world and few other countries around the world match the level of military expenditure in the region. What is distinct about the Middle East is exactly related to such figures, which stem not from the Islamic character of the region but from its peculiar colonial and political legacies. In Clement Henry's view (2003), the most important and distinctive characteristic of the region is not religion, language or culture but a colonial legacy that continues to paralyse it.

TABLE 1.2 TCIs Performance Records (1995–2009)

Title of Activity	1995	1999	2003	2004	2005	2007	2009
Fixed telephone	5,824,968	9,486,260	15,340,805	17,798,809	20,340,060	23,560,000	24,988,183
Mobile telephone	59,967	962,595	3,449,876	5,075,678	8,510,513	21,300,000	32,292,513
Connected villages	14,535	28,062	40,109	43,800	47,955	52,522	53,850
Fixed penetration factor	9,170	14/9	23/06	26/32	29/71	30.03	34.09
Data network capacity (port)	718	1,603	11,125	76,990	106,140	115,936	182,914
Transmission circuits	240,107	405,997	631,889	1,000,000	1,000,000	1,758,142	2,792,316
Local public telephone	95,807	84,971	114,433	126,154	141,912	177,753	227,456
Long-distance public telephone	7,854	11,813	30,372	44,709	64,774	113,499	175,401
Cities with mobile telephone	34	337	708	851	999	1,016	1,076
Fibre optic network (km)	—	7,205	26,800	30,000	56,000	76,500	127,000

TABLE 1.3 Human Development Indicators in Selected Middle
Eastern Countries and the USA

Country	Total Population, Millions (2001)	Adult Literacy Rate	Public Expenditure on Education (as % of GDP)	Public Expenditure on Health (as % of GDP)	Military Expenditure (as % of GDP)	GDP per capita (PPP US$)
Qatar	0.6	81.2	3.6	2.5	—	18,789
United Arab Emirates	2.9	76.3	1.9	2.5	2.5	17,935
Kuwait	2.4	82.0	4.8 (1990)	2.6	11.3	15,799
Bahrain	0.7	87.6	3.0	2.8	4.1	15,084
Saudi Arabia	22.8	76.3	9.5	4.2	11.3	11,367
Turkey	69.3	85.1	3.5	3.6	4.9	6,974
Tunisia	5.7	71.0	6.8	3.0 (1990)	1.6	6,363
Iran	67.2	76.3	4.4	2.5	4.8	5,884
Algeria	30.7	66.7	5.3 (1990)	3.0	3.5	5,308
Lebanon	3.5	86.0	3.0	—	5.5	4,308
Jordan	5.2	89.7	5.0	4.2	8.6	3,966
Egypt	69.1	55.3	3.7 (1990)	1.8	2.6	3,635
Morocco	29.6	48.9	5.5	1.3	4.1	3,546
Sudan	32.2	57.8	0.9 (1990)	1.0	3.0	1,797
The USA	288	100	4.8	5.8	3.1	34,320

Source: UNDP (2001), UNDP (2002).

Table 1.4 shows that there is a close correlation between access to 'old' and to 'new' media and demonstrates a link between the wealth of countries and their access to the means of communication. The use of media in richer countries is more common and widespread (compare Kuwait, United Arab Emirates and Qatar with the likes of Egypt, Morocco and Sudan).

In the case of Iran, it is not that basic religious and cultural values run counter to the internet, but the existing social relations hamper access. Economic crises, inflation, high levels of unemployment and escalating prices of essential goods have all squeezed the Iranian family purse. Only 26 per cent of Iran's population is employed (UNDP, 2001). This is lower than all Arab countries; in the region, only occupied Palestine (20.1) has a lower rate of employment (UNDP, 2002).

The share of cultural goods in Iranian households, despite a relative increase in the past decade, remains among the lowest. According to the

TABLE 1.4 Access to Communications in Selected Middle Eastern Countries and the USA

Country	Number of Telephone (per 1,000)	Cellular Mobile (per 100)	Estimated PC (per 100)	Internet Users (per 1,000)	Number of Radio Receivers (per 1,000)	Number of Television Receivers (per 1,000)	Number of Daily Newspapers	Circulation (per 1,000)	GDP per capita (PPP US$)
Qatar	275	43.72	18.3	65.6	450	404	4	146	18,789
United Arab Emirates	340	75.88	14.06	314.8	335	134	8	140	17,935
Kuwait	208	67.95	12.06	87.9	678	505	9	387	15,799
Bahrain	267	58.33	16.4	203.4	580	472	3	126	15,084
Saudi Arabia	145	21.72	13.02	13.4	321	262	12	58	11,367
Turkey	285	34.75	4.46	60.4	178	330	57	110	6,974
Tunisia	109	5.13	3.06	41.2	224	100	8	30	6,363
Iran	169	3.35	7.50	15.6	263	71	32	26	5,884
Algeria	61	1.28	0.77	6.5	242	105	8	51	5,308
Lebanon	187	22.70	8.05	77.6	907	375	14	110	4,308
Jordan	129	22.89	3.75	45.2	271	82	4	47	3,966
Egypt	104	6.85	1.71	9.3	317	119	15	38	3,635
Morocco	41	20.91	1.54	13.7	247	115	20	24	3,546
Sudan	14	0.59	0.61	1.8	272	86	5	24	1,797
The USA	667	451	62.44	501.5	2,116	806	1,520	212	34,320

Source: Unesco Statistical Yearbook (1999), UNDP (2001), UNDP (2002), ITU (2003).

Videogames in shop window, Tehran

Statistical Centre of Iran (2001–02) the share of recreation and entertainment (of which the media is only a tiny part) in the urban households' expenditure on non-food commodities and services is even less than the amount spent on 'personal care and effects' and 'restaurant, café and hotels'. A quick examination of the actual amount spent per year per household on 'recreation and entertainment' illustrates this point even more forcefully. According to the same source, the average annual expenditure on 'recreation and entertainment' is 328,045 rials. Divided by 365 days, the 'average' Iranian family spends 898 rials (less than 10 US cents) per day on cultural goods. This needs to be compared with the actual costs of culture and entertainment.

In Iran, as elsewhere, access to media in general and to the internet in particular is affected by many factors, but it is regulated above all by disposable income. Because of the high-tech boycott imposed by the USA and the lack of investment in importing hardware computers have been expensive to purchase. A tower computer used to cost around 45,000 toman or $450, equivalent to the average monthly wage of a bus driver or teacher. Hardware equipment sales have been a profitable part of the country's ICT market, bringing a 25 per cent annual income growth for hardware companies. Around 730 companies, yet another indication of persistence of small-scale

Hardware delivery, Tehran

production in Iran, are active in the hardware field with an estimated value of $1,200 million.

However, by 2008, Far Eastern suppliers had been sourced and a dynamic market, especially for laptops and peripherals, was flourishing in Tehran. Given Tehran's reluctance to sign any international copyright protocols, branded software is also readily available at a fraction of the suggested retail price. Computer professionals complain about the lack of state interest in developing indigenous programmes using open source software. Instead, it has turned a blind eye to, or even helped, the mass use of illegal copies of Windows and other US-generated programmes.

Furthermore, the average cost of internet access used to be about 35,000 toman ($35) per month, not including telephone line rental. For internet

Computer arcade, Tehran

access, Iranians were paying more than Americans and Europeans. The cost of internet access in general is linked to the density of a country's internet population and the distance from the main servers. The politics of bandwidth, and the fact that the USA operates as the hub of internet traffic, means countries must make payments for traffic exchanges and connectivity to international telecommunication carriers. For this reason, the cost of internet access in developed countries is lower than the rest of the world. In Iran, a computer costs two times an 'average' monthly salary in urban areas and three times in rural areas. In real terms, however, the cost is even higher. A better comparative measure of cost is PPP (purchasing power parity), which is 'a rate of exchange that accounts for price differences across countries, allowing international comparison of real output and incomes . . . PPP US$1 has the same purchasing power in the domestic economy as $1 has in the United States.[7] In 2005, the price of a computer in Iran was about 2,250PPP$, access to the internet from a netcafe cost 3.5PPP$ per hour, a dial-up connection used by many in Iran costs 1PPP$ per hour and the price of using ADSL featuring 128–512 kpbs is around 1,200 PPP$ per month. Such conditions priced the internet out of the reach of most people.

But as with that for new technology around the world, prices are coming down. The autumn 2008 price sheet from Pars Online, one of the largest ISPs in Iran looked like this:

TABLE 1.5 ADSL2+ Costs in Tehran and Karaj (Pars Online Corporation)

Code	Bandwidth	Time Limitation	Data Transfer Limitation	IP Type	Monthly Cost (Rials)	Installation Cost (Rials)
POL_HU	Up to 128 kbps download Up to 128 kbps upload	Unlimited	3 GB	Dynamic	149,500	150,000
POL_H1	Up to 128 kbps download Up to 128 kbps upload	Unlimited	8 GB	Dynamic	249,500	200,000
POL_B1	Up to 256 kbps download Up to 256 kbps upload	Unlimited	8 GB	Dynamic	299,500	200,000
POL_B2	Up to 256 kbps download Up to 256 kbps upload	Unlimited	20 GB	Dynamic	399,500	200,000
POL_B3	Up to 384 kbps download Up to 256 kbps upload	Unlimited	30 GB	Dynamic	599,500	200,000
POL_E5	Up to 512 kbps download Up to 256 kbps upload	Unlimited	Unlimited	Static	2,499,500	500,000
POL_E10	Up to 1,025 kbps download Up to 512 kbps upload	Unlimited	Unlimited	Static	4,499,500	500,000

Computer arcade, Tehran

Despite a declaration by Mohammad Khatami in 2005 that Iran was embarking on the development of a massive fibre optic network, offering faster speeds and bandwidth, this has not been rolled out, and Iranian networks remained highly constrained, not least by the speed restrictions imposed by Ahmadinejad in October 2006. The Pars price list suggests that those able to pay the equivalent of many people's monthly salary for a faster connection could do so. In 2009, the realities of the media markets in Iran indicate further polarisation of media consumers between urban and rural areas, between Tehran and smaller cities, and between those with differing levels of disposable income. The share of income/consumption of the poorest 30 per cent in Iran is just 7.1 per cent, while the share of the richest 30 per cent is 83.6 per cent (UNDP, 2005:271). In Iran, as in the rest of the world, access to communication resources is regulated through price mechanisms, and the current cost of internet access remains a primary obstacle to wider use of the internet.

Besides the harsh economic realities of Iran, a number of other factors have prevented the more rapid penetration of the internet. As mentioned, since 1979, Iran has been the subject of a number of sanctions by the US administration. The first sanction came immediately after the hostage crisis

Computer software shop, Tehran

by the order of then-President Jimmy Carter in which all assets, property and interests of Iran in the USA (estimated to be in the order of $12 billion) were frozen. US economic pressure on Iran increased after the invasion by Iraq, and in 1984, the USA approved a proposal to ban all loans to Iran by financial institutions, a ban which was extended to weapon sales or any financial assistance to Iran. In 1990, President George Bush confirmed the continuation of the embargo introduced by Carter.[8] Some limited trade between the USA and Iran emerged after the end of the war, but as Keddie (2003:265) has argued 'the Clinton administration, under pressure from Congress and the pro-Israeli lobby, announced a total embargo on dealings with Iran in April 1995. Trade with the USA, which has climbed after the war, virtually

Video stall in north Tehran bazaar

ended'. An executive order issued by a third US president, Bill Clinton, on 30 September 1997 stated: 'Because our relations with Iran have not yet returned to normal, and the process of implementing the January 19, 1981, agreement with Iran is still underway, the national emergency declared on November 14, 1979, must continue in effect beyond November 14, 1997.[9] In spring 2010, the Obama administration was heading toward even tougher sanctions. As Arabshahi (1997) suggests, 'the embargo made the acquisition and maintenance of powerful servers, workstations, and satellite communication equipment difficult, if not impossible in certain cases'. In addition, in the early stages of the development of internet in Iran, the political tension between Iran and the USA had an impact on the free flow of information between the two countries as well, despite the fact that the embargo did not include exchange of text. Thus to begin with,

> *U.S. academic sites (on NSFNET) did not even recognize Iranian IP addresses for telnet/ftp access. This problem resurfaced in 1996 only to be put swiftly to rest through the efforts of many people and organizations in the US, Europe, and Iran (including IPM, and the Electronic Frontier Foundation), who brought pressure on NSF to correct the situation (Arabshahi, 1997).*

Even access to the internet is not solely a national matter since the USA, in hosting about 80 per cent of internet sites, is the undisputed gatekeeper of the so-called super highway. Iran's internet access to the USA can be blocked. Yet, despite clear tension between the two countries and American sanctions, many Iranian companies and institutions are ready, as are many American companies, to establish ventures through an intermediary. One notable example is the Data Communication Company of Iran's (DCI) agreement with GulfSat Kuwait (a joint venture between the Kuwaiti government and Hughes Network System of the USA). In addition, two of the early ISPs in Iran, *Virayeshgar* and *Pars Supaleh,* represented the US companies 3Com and AT&T. Many of the deals with US companies are cut through their subsidiaries and joint ventures in Europe and Asia (Burkhart, 1998). However, US embargoes prohibit software companies such as Microsoft from doing legitimate business in Iran, a factor that contributes to widespread software piracy in the country, helped by the fact that Iran is not a signatory to international copyright conventions.[10] Ironically, the software that the regime uses to monitor and censor internet participation is pirated from the USA. Many Western software programmes, including Microsoft packages are remarkably cheaply available. It is worth speculating on the obverse impact of the US sanctions on Iran, which is the financial losses incurred by US firms from not trading with Iran – but few calculations are available on this.

Mediating an Islamic State

Also crucial to the development of the internet in Iran are the competing agendas and conflicting interests within Iran's state apparatus. The Islamic state that came to power after 1979 defined itself predominantly in a cultural sense. The twin aims of the cultural policy of the new state were based on destruction of an imposed western, alien culture and its replacement with a 'dignified, indigenous and authentic Islamic culture' (Alinejad, 2002), which was said to have declined under the previous monarchical regime. Because of such broad cultural aims, the state began to develop a whole range of institutions to implement and safeguard the Shi'ite Islamic culture of Iran.

Since 1979, media and communications have been key sites of contestation. As part of its programme of controlled modernisation and to maintain its religiocultural hegemony, the Islamic Republic restricted private ownership in all aspects of Iran's communication system except for the press. The

Supreme Council of the Cultural Revolution, established as early as 1980, was to oversee general cultural policy. Various other organisations were assigned the task of implementing such policies. The Ministry of Culture and Islamic Guidance was given specific tasks of managing and running the press, the Iranian News Agency (IRNA) as well as charities and religious endowments. Iranian Broadcasting – Voice and Vision of the Islamic Republic (VVIR) – which later became the Islamic Republic of Iran Broadcasting was brought under the direct control of the Supreme Leader in 1989. Two major Iranian publishing firms, Keyhan and Etelaat, which control and publish a number of newspapers and periodicals became 'public property' and were put under the control of both the Ministry of Culture and Islamic Guidance and the representatives of the Supreme Leader. Telecommunications were put firmly under the control of the state through the TCI, a branch of the Ministry of Post, Telegraph and Telephone.

The Iranian state controls the rest of the media through complex legislation and non-legal ploys, that include providing subsidies, controlling the paper supply, using the Constitution and the Press Law as well as passing new acts and setting up a variety of regulatory bodies. Newspapers have been subject to sudden closure, many editors and journalists have been imprisoned, some even executed, and censorship 'red-lines' have been the points of interpretative struggle between the press and the polity (Gholam Khiabany and Annabelle Sreberny, 2001; Gholam Khiabany, 2010). As Siavoshi (1997:513) points out, the plurality of these institutions subjected cultural developments and policies to power struggles among many factions within the state: 'Although every faction declared its commitment to Islamic cultural ideals, all consensus vanished when it came to the question of what these ideals were and which policies were required to achieve them'.

The digital environment has been similarly subject to the friction and competition between factions of the regime, the institutional interests of various agencies involved in the process and the tensions within the state as well as between the state and the private sector. The dominant conservative faction of the Islamic Republic has been quick both to try to limit the potential of the technology as well as to utilise it for its own benefit. Both sides of the divide do indeed present a highly political account of the role of communication technologies. If the private sector and advocates of civil society in Iran subscribe to the common sense view of the internet as inherently decentralising, democratic, progressive and therefore unsuitable for public ownership, the conservative state agencies and officials regard it as a threat to their interests and future. What is at the centre of the debate is the very institutional and technological structure of Iran's rapidly expanding communications and the dispute over the definition of 'public interest'.

While the Islamic Republic officially encourages the use of the internet (Farhang Rouhani, 2000; Babak Rahimi, 2003) the issues of access, control and content remain controversial and have prompted some to argue that 'the external as well as internal wariness have hindered the importation of technology tools and slowed the integration of technical tools in daily lifestyles' (Laleh Ebrahimian, 2003:98). While initial internet developments were undertaken by academic institutions, the commercial imperatives as well as the desire for effective control of the internet has meant that the government has taken the leading role in providing internet access and services. As Rahimi suggests, the tension in the early 1990s between various agencies, including the Data Communication Company of Iran (DCI), a branch of the Ministry for Post, Telegraph and Telephone; the High Council of Information and IPM, were over the quality and availability of network access (Rahimi, 2003:102).

Lack of resources, expertise and clear policies as well as the commitment to privatisation has meant that for a few years, especially after 1997 with growing public access to the internet, the private sector began to dominate the market. With more than 100 private ISPs and the increased use of low cost voice over internet protocol (VoIP), popular among those with relatives abroad, revenues of the state-owned TCI were hit severely. In early 2000, cyber cafes (*cafenet*) began to mushroom in big cities, and within a couple of years, it is estimated that 7,000 to 8,000 such establishments had mushroomed in Tehran alone (Mousavi Shafaee, 2003:194). These competed with each other and the TCI and prices began to plummet, especially when some cafes began to offer 'economy' or 'saver' packages of 10–20 hour blocks of internet access. This forced TCI to reduce the cost of international calls to avoid further losses (Ebrahimian, 2003:102). According to a report by BBCPersian.com,[11] while TCI reported $20 million profit in 1998, in 2002, despite the staggering threefold increase in the number of people with access to telephone lines in this period, TCI reported a loss of $32 million. Private internet and telephone providers were blamed for this loss. The use of VoIP service became widespread despite limited penetration of the internet, simply because of the growing number of internet cafes across the country.

The government has intervened at times, closing more than 400 internet cafes in Tehran in May 2001, in another moment of moral panic (Lebowitz, 2001). Slowly, with the evolution of such technologies, by 2008 Wi-Fi spots were becoming popular, albeit still quite scarce.

From Khatami to Ahmadinejad

The strategy of the Islamic Republic was to overcome domestic difficulties and, especially after the Iraq War, to be reinstated to its former position in the international division of labour. The contradictions in the Islamic regime's policies clearly put an end to Islamist assumptions about the existence of coherent and comprehensive Islamic thought on all contemporary matters. Many of the views and policies advocated by the Shi'a clergy in Iran before and after the revolution were prompted by immediate and often changing real circumstances. In this respect, as Ervand Abrahamian has neatly quipped, 'Khomeini was no more a political philosopher than Moliere's bourgeois gentilhomme was a literary deconstructionist' (1993:39). However, and as Abrahamian convincingly demonstrates, Khomeini – despite early promises of self-reliance, fair distribution of resources and equality of opportunity for all Iranians – shifted ground on many issues and made a number of U-turns but remained steadfast on the question of private property. From early on, he was adamant that private property was a gift from god and that the respect for private property was more important than 'respect for the dead'.

In the first decade of the Islamic Republic, per capita income of Iranians dropped by 50 per cent (Karbasian, 2000), and urban unemployment increased from 4.4 to 18.9 per cent. This was, to a large extent, due to the decline of investment of the private sector in the economy, hampered by the towering figure of the state and state-run companies, unsympathetic labour laws and a lack of political stability. Powerful constitutional constraints include Article 44 of the Constitution, that called for nationalisation of all large-scale industries, including telecommunication and broadcasting, and Article 49 that paved the way for the confiscation of thousands of private companies and transferred them to newly formed foundations, or *bonyads* (Karbasian, 2000; Khajehpour, 2000). However, privatisation including within the communications industry has been one of the key aspects of recent economic plans. This was the clear policy of 'reconstruction', which made the living conditions for the majority worse than before. Yet, despite continuing difficulties arising from liberalisation, the same set of arguments and measures were pursued even further by the reformist president, Khatami.

A national think tank *Takfa* was established in 2002 headed by Nasrollah Jahangard, who embraced the idea of launching Iran on the road towards the 'knowledge-based economy' not only through a national agenda and budget but also with provision for international private finance. Indeed, *Takfa's* vision statement was 'Powerful Iran in the 21st century through knowledge-centric

ICTs'. He boldly claimed that by the first year of the next national development plan (2005), the prerequisites of the knowledge-based economy would
be in place, including easy and inexpensive access to internet for the masses;
adequate digital literacy by the public; with e-government and e-commerce
in extensive use by 2008. Among the key obstacles to effective IT policy, he
mentioned the difficulties of effecting a 'handshake' between different government sectors and suggested the need for a new organisational architec-
ture. But he recognised that the technological challenges were comparatively
simple, whereas the processes of developing human resources, procurement
and financing were far harder to achieve, and the hardest of all was policy
development – moving out of old organisational models and disciplinary
areas, old practices of 'keeping information to ourselves' to new ones and
supporting these through legislation (interview, November 2006, Tehran).
Jahangard was a sophisticated intellectual who saw the need for public–
private partnerships and the development of a 10-year project. He participated in the Geneva phase of the World Summit on the Information Society
as President of the Supreme Council on ICTs, setting out Iran's ICT development plans.

One of the main objectives of the Third Five-Year Plan (2000–05) revolved around liberalisation, which included further privatisation, attracting
more foreign investments and the reduction of government size (Behdad,
2000; Khajepour, 2000). In tandem with the commitment to 'civil society',
the government published a list of 538 state-owned companies (out of 724)
in 1999 as the prime target for privatisation. Behdad (2000) has suggested
that such plans, as well as the commitment to the breaking of monopolies
which included telecommunication, had been halted because it would have
necessitated the IRI's unequivocal negation of its revolutionary claims and
would have implied the formal abandonment of its remaining popular base.

Nevertheless, the state did make some necessary changes to accommodate
private capital and encouraging foreign investment. In 2004, the disputed
Article 44 of the Constitution, which limited private ownership and had put
radio and television, the post, telegraph and telephone services all under the
'state sector', was finally revised. One of the greatest 'achievements' of the
reformist-dominated Parliament (2000–04) was indeed to speed up the process of privatisation. The Iranian parliament banned the establishment of any
new state-run companies and began legislating the transfer of many state-run
companies to the private sector. The revision of Article 44 coupled with the
ruling of Iran's Supreme Leader that up to 80 per cent of shares of major state-
owned companies including banks could be given to the private sector,[12]

removed the last legal barriers to privatisation of the major industries in Iran, including the post and communications. In this process, the shares of the state-run companies will be sold to the private sector, which includes foreign investors as well as rich expatriates, and the generated income will be used to further development of the 'real private sector'. Hassan Khosropour, the director of privatisation affairs, has suggested that in this process, the state wants to 'institutionalise a share-holding culture among members of the society'.[13] Despite continuing problems and limits, the recognition of private property has been on the increase and the private sector has gained increasing status in the Iranian economy. The Tehran stock market has been expanding slowly but with regular banks offering savers rates of interest of 20 per cent and higher, the market has to boom to beat such dividends.

The significance of the communication industries has not been lost to private capital.[14] Reform and construction is explicitly equated, to some extent, with marketisation and privatisation of the communication industry (Gholam Khiabany, 2007). However, in this process the contradiction between the imperatives of the market and the 'revolutionary' claims of the Iranian state is significant. The Iranian state is clearly embracing private capital, but it is also wary of losing control of major institutions of Islamic hegemony.

In a 2008 report, the TCI claimed that 'TCI privatisation is underway to provide the requirements for the national ICT sector development by selling its shares in the stock market to be a holding company'. The aim, the report claims, is to empower 'the private sector in the industry to produce mobile handsets and equipment, support the domestic telecom products by the leading council as well as granting loans, daily response to the demands for new telephone lines, Intelligent Network set up, internet band width increase up to 4.5 times, reducing the internet tariffs, planning the national Internet network'.[15] But this policy is open to dispute and serious questions are raised over the extent of privatisation. As *Iran Daily* reported, initially privatisation was initiated for engineering reasons. But issues of profit overshadowed all other matters when it came to the sale of telecoms and the revenue generated. The head of the board of directors of TCI, Vafa Ghaffarian, told *Iran Daily* that 'mobile, fixed or data networks have different layers of cores, access and services, of which only the layer of access could be privatised'. The responses of private and international capital, which TCI is keen to attract for their resources and experience, to such proposals remain to be seen. *Iran Daily* has pointedly asked: 'Why should the private sector purchase a company whose tariffs it cannot determine and enter a market that will have tough competitors such as second and third private mobile phone operators?'[16]

The End of Reform and the Coming of Ahmadinejad

There was a moment of quite considerable political transition in Iran after the unexpected victory of Ahmadinejad in the 2005 presidential elections, a process in which there was considerable lack of clarity that prompted concern about due process. The entire orientation of the political and bureaucratic infrastructure shifted from an open engagement with the world under the remit of 'Dialogue of Civilisations' promoted by Khatami, to a reassertion of the original radical Islamic roots of the revolution as defined by Ahmadinejad.

The manpower of many ministries and organisations has radically changed. Takfa was disbanded and Jahangard's position taken up by Mohammad Soleimani. The Fourth National Plan continued the rhetoric of 'knowledge-based stable economic development' and the ICT development plan is 'generating development with focus on exports' (National ICT Strategic Plan, p. 2). Yet the provision of e-governance remains weak, as few government organisations have websites and few services are provided on the internet. By 2008, passport and ID card renewal and driving licences could be done online but, for the most part, dealing with Iranian government services requires considerable face-to-face time over repeat visits. The e-economy is profoundly hampered by economic sanctions, especially the absence of international credit card facilities, as well as by a postal system that has only just started to utilise postcodes and is hardly ready to cope with the volume of parcel post that any Amazon-type or web-based buying process would create.

For a long time, Iran has faced problems of unemployment, lack of suitable employment and insufficiency of wages. Trained architects, engineers and teachers drive taxis as their sole income or to supplement income. What is needed is convincing evidence that the development of these new e-sectors would produce new jobs and increase productivity and a coherent strategy towards that goal. So far, that is noticeably lacking.

Internet Development and Institutional Confusion

Beyond economics, the organisational confusion has hampered e-development. Policies and institutional responsibilities are unclear and roles are disputed; indeed, as in many areas, the formal policy is not adhered to, while the informal practice is what is meaningful. The formal prohibition on ownership of satellite dishes and their widespread use is just one case in point. Mostafa Mohammadi, managing director of *Parnham*, a private ISP, in an interview with the daily *Hambastegi* pointed at such confusion:

> IRIB [Islamic Republic of Iran Broadcasting] believes itself to be in charge of the Internet because it believes that it is a media. But on the other hand, the Telecommunication Company, the Ministry of Culture and the Islamic Guidance as well as the Intelligence Ministry believe themselves to be responsible for the Internet, whereas none of these institutions have the power to support the Internet.[17]

The state-owned and state-controlled broadcaster Islamic Republic of Iran Broadcasting (IRIB) has tried to influence state policies on the internet. Hated by many, including reformist officials, for its constant campaign against intellectuals, student and women activists and the reformist press, IRIB's tentacles have reached out into more and more of Iran's cultural life. It now controls not only a range of radio and television channels in Persian, Arabic and English but is also involved in research, publishing, film production and festivals. It has become one of the, if not the, key political actors in Iran and wishes to extend its remit to the internet. In an interview with the now-defunct reformist daily, *Norouz*, the then Minister of Communications and Modern Technology, Ahmad Motamedi, responded to the question of whether Islamic Republic of Iran Broadcasting sponsored internet development by saying:

> We are strongly opposed to this measure of the IRIB. Their activities must be within the limits of the radio and television organization. Establishing two-way communications is among the duties of the Communications Ministry. In all bylaws (so far approved) all these duties have been entrusted to the Communications Ministry. Of course there are certain people who hold contrary views but we are fully opposed to this. Nothing has been approved to the effect that the IRIB can function like a ministry.[18]

He was proved wrong, as one of those 'certain people who [held] contrary views' was the Supreme Leader, Ayatollah Khamenei, who in a decree not only disappointed the private sector by putting the state in control of the internet, but reserved a role for IRIB in all policymaking decisions about the internet.

Thus, attempts to develop and control the internet have revealed, once again, the existence of many contradictory institutions, policies and competing interests within the Islamic Republic. As we have suggested, by providing cheaper forms of communication and much cheaper telephone connections, especially popular among those with relatives abroad, the internet has seriously threatened the state monopoly on long-distance calls. But more importantly, as broadcasting inside Iran remains a tightly controlled state monopoly and as one reformist and semi-independent newspaper after another has been banned, more and more people, including publishers, writers, journalists and ordinary readers, are turning to the internet for information, debates and as a platform to express concerns. News websites have proliferated as have sites about technology, music, sports, entertainment, women's issues and student matters. Portals that aggregate clusters of Persian language materials, including the range of diasporic radio and television channels, have also proliferated, and so too have blogs.

Weblogs ('veb be-logs'!)

Weblogs have become the most significant area of internet growth in Iran. The wave initially started in September 2001, with the development of Persian instructions by a young Iranian blogger, Hossein Derakhshan. However, by early 2009, blogging had grown into a massive collective phenomenon, sometimes estimated to include 400,000, even 700,000 blogs, making Persian one of the leading languages in the blogosphere and increasing the share of Persian material online. We develop this more fully in the next chapter.

A combination of factors paved the way for such a rapid growth of the blogosphere, including the disabling factionalism of the central Iranian state and the ongoing conflicts between Islamism and Republicanism; intense pressure from private capital in Iran that had long relied on the mediation of the state seeking a larger share in the expanding and lucrative cultural industries; and above all, the existence of an already dissatisfied young population challenging the Iranian state and actively seeking a new order. As a result, weblog service providers in Iran – blog farms – have emerged as part of the economic liberalisation in Iran's communication industries. Companies such as PersianBlog and Blogfa are recognised online brand names in the Iranian new media, and these provide a range of services. Iranian sites and blogs are new sources of information about various aspects of public life in the country, providing a strong link between activists and intellectuals in Iran and the opposition abroad. The internet has become the latest tool to offer alternative news channels to Iranian activists inside Iran and much needed international support and solidarity, including from some Iranians living in exile.

Foreign and Iranian films on sale in a north Tehran bazaar

The battle to control the internet, therefore, cannot be separated from the broader social movements and political concerns which produce the very contradictory developments and the ongoing conflict between 'accelerations' and 'breaks', between the state and the private sector, in the Islamic Republic.

2 The Politics of and in Blogging

A Brief Historical Overview

University students were the originators of blogging in Iran in 2001. The first Iranian weblog was created on September 2001 by Salman Jariri.[1] Two months later, Hossein Derakhshan launched his weblog in Persian (editormyself.com and i.hoder.com).[2] Derakhshan was a young Iranian journalist who had worked for some by-then defunct reformist newspapers such as *Asr-e Azadeghan* and *Hayat-e No* and had moved to Canada after the closure of many publications in 2000. In response to numerous queries from his readers about how to create and run a weblog, he released a weblog construction guide in Persian in the hope that the number of Iranian weblogs would reach a hundred within a year.

In less than two months, by the end of 2001, there were more than 200 Iranian weblogs, and by the beginning of 2003, their number had increased to the tens of thousands. A report by Masoud Behnood on BBC persian.com[3] estimated that there were 13,000 weblogs in Iran in 2003, while Pedram Moallemian, another Iranian blogger[4] claimed that the number of active weblogs written in Persian had reached 50,000 by May 2003. Yet another estimate suggests that even by 2002 the numbers had increased to well over 60,000.[5] Estimates later shot up to 400,000 and a 2005 report[6] estimated the number of Iranian blogs at 700,000. Undoubtedly, this is a remarkable figure, but it is not quite clear (as is the case with all remarkable figures about online media) how the numbers are calculated. This report noted that the figures referred to total blog numbers and not active blog numbers, which it estimates to be between 40,000 and 110,000. The internet is riddled with dead blogs, including in Persian. The generally accepted figure in 2009 for live blogs by Iranians seems to be around 70,000 active blogs.

In addition to the question of the actual number of 'active' blogs, there is another dispute over what constitutes an Iranian blog. If Iranian blogs are defined in terms of language, this means omission of a large number of

Iranian bloggers who write in other languages, most notably English, while including a number of bloggers from Afghanistan or Tajikistan who write in Persian. Focusing on Iranian bloggers writing *inside* the country also leads to excluding a large number of Iranian bloggers writing in Persian *outside* Iran. One important analytic issue about the Iranian blogosphere centres on the dynamic relationship between Iran and its diasporas, activity inside Iran and activity outside. There is little doubt that the internet in general and the blogosphere in particular blurs issues of distance and geographical separation, ties diasporas to their national and cultural homelands in often unexpected ways and supports the emergence of new forms of political engagement between those inside the polity and those outside identifying as Iranian and wanting to be involved. We explore this phenomenon more in Chapter Six.

To return to numbers, simply focusing on Iranian blogs that use blog providers such as PersianBlog is not useful either because many of those inside Iran use foreign service providers such as blogger.com to escape the restrictions and controls exercised by Iranian weblog farms. Also, increasingly Iran's blog service providers have international clients from countries such as China and Germany.[7] Another reason for disputing the accuracy of figures provided by many sites is the very significant fact that there are many collective (*grouhi*) weblogs, and it is not clear whether figures refer to the number of blogs or the number of bloggers. Nevertheless, even the most conservative estimates of the number of weblogs in Iran is impressive, a point highlighted

TABLE 2.1   Top 10 Weblog Farms 2003

Farm	Rank	Numbers	%Share
blogspot.com	1	60,642	21.85
persianblog.com	2	20,440	7.37
blogdrive.com	3	17,831	6.43
modblog.com	4	14,785	5.33
livejournal.com	5	10,518	3.79
20six.fr	6	6,422	2.31
myblog.de	7	4,988	1.8
nikki-k.jp	8	3,630	1.31
co.uk	9	3,434	1.24
cocolog-nifty.com	10	3,172	1.14

Source: Blogcount.com[8]

by then-president Mohammad Khatami during the WSIS summit in Geneva in 2003. In order to defend the record of his administration and brushing aside serious criticisms raised by many that Iran was actively repressing the potential of technology, he stressed that Persian weblogs were ranked only behind weblogs written in English and French.

The phenomenon of Iranian blogging was slowly being recognised within global blogging networks. For example, the aforementioned figures came as an astonishing shock to blogcount.com, which wrote: 'persianblog is second. Large surprise. Considering its alphabet, impossible for me to really know. Are the Arab language weblogs in another country also blogs of Iran?'[9] The answer, of course, is no. But the figure is even more astonishing considering the fact that not all Iranian bloggers use PersianBlog as a farm, with thousands using other weblog service providers. This staggering and unexpected growth in blogging has whetted the appetite of private service providers, and in the last few years, many more have emerged to compete for dominance and revenue. These include persianblog.com, blogfa.com, blogsky.com, mihanblog.com, parsiblog.com, jablogi.com, ariablog.com, blognegar.com and caspianblog.com. The first four above-mentioned service providers are also the biggest, and while PersianBlog remains the oldest and the biggest of all service providers with around 600,000 blogs[10], its competitors have made a huge dent in its popularity. According to the alexa.com Web traffic monitor, in April 2009, the top sites in Iran were Google; Yahoo; Blogfa; Facebook; Mihanblog; YouTube; blogger.com; MSN; Cloob.com; PersianBlog; revealing an interesting shift in online activities.

Reasons for Blogging's Rapid Growth

Weblog farms in Iran have emerged as part of the rapid changes in Iran's communication industries, economic liberalisation and the growing demand for communications channels. Many reasons have contributed to the expansion of blogs in Iran. The availability of software, expansion of internet access and usage as well as the existence of many technologically literate young Iranians are key factors but these do not in themselves explain the growth and popularity of blogs in Iran.

Economic reasons are undoubtedly significant. Unlike other media including press, broadcasting and music, blogs can be launched with very little economic resource. Undoubtedly, one needs a computer, a connection to the internet as well as some ideas for content, but the huge economic barrier to entry, as is the case for other media, is not an issue. In most cases, even collective blogs do not require much division of labour; making money or breaking even is not a key target or necessary for survival. Blogs in this sense are a good example of forms of 'small media' that can exist as long as the bloggers have the necessary commitment, time and connection. In this sense, at least in the Iranian context, blogs are like individual poems that can be produced and reproduced with little financial capital rather than a high-quality song that requires a band, producer, studio, a music label committed to promoting/distributing it and a degree of commercial success for the continued existence of the band. The irrelevance of a 'business model' for bloggers is a major advantage. Iran's environment is one where the state remains the biggest media proprietor that is actively trying to juggle various interests within its own domain; where broadcasting remains a state monopoly and a tightly controlled propaganda machine; and where the closure of newspapers (including those that support the state but are critical of certain practices and policies) are common events. Hence, blogging has emerged as a versatile, easy to launch and re-launch medium. But then again, if any of these reasons can partially explain the rapid expansion of blogs in Iran, the key question is why has this not happened in some other countries? Neither the broader financial model of blogs nor political repression in general is sufficient explanation.

All these technological, economic and political factors have contributed to the expansion that is Iranian blogs. But by this definition one might argue, with reasonable justifications, that the same thing could and should have happened in many societies, not least across the Global South and in particular other Middle Eastern countries such as Egypt and Turkey.

Attempts to count blogging around the world suggested that it reached 50 million in April 2005.[11] David Sifry claimed in April 2007 that 'Technorati is now tracking over 70 million weblogs, and we're seeing about 120,000 new weblogs being created worldwide each day. That's about 1.4 blogs created every second of every day.' However, the problems of counting are legion, not least because of language. Far from the 'blogging is so over' comments in the USA and UK, with SMS and Twitter now considered the new technologies for social and political communication, many commentators suggest that blogging is still growing:

I don't think the blogosphere is quite mature yet. Technorati currently states it is tracking over 112.8 million blogs, a number which obviously does not include all the 72.82 million Chinese blogs as counted by The China Internet Network Information Center. Blog statistics often concern the English language blogosphere but we should not forget about the millions of other blogs that are not always included in estimations.[12]

People do not automatically start a blog just because the technology is there or they feel strong anger towards the state or major corporations blocking a meaningful and democratic communications between citizens. Even if we accept the exaggerated claims of blogs as democratising, even revolutionary, then surely we need to look at the 'revolutionary situation' (context) and the 'revolutionaries' (bloggers) too. As we explain later in some detail, far from being an undifferentiated 'mass', bloggers and their 'politics' assume a range of broad orientations with different aims, content, forms of expression and connections to various networks, many of them contradictory and even hostile to one another. In this sense, while the tools and technology may be universal, the contexts and the content are not. Therefore, neither the availability of technology and its cheapness nor the desire for expression explains the activities of bloggers or the outcome of their efforts. A combination of factors has paved the way for such a rapid growth of the Iranian blogosphere.

As we have suggested, the expansion of the internet and the popularity of blogs in Iran is regarded as a lucrative business, and this has paved the way for national private capital to seek a firm foothold in this sector of Iran's culture industries. With the big state-owned companies in Iran dominating the press and broadcasting market, private companies in Iran have emerged as key players in new media. Most ISPs and Weblog Service Providers are privately owned, and their services are increasingly part of much bigger media activities. PersianBlog for example is part of Ariagostar Company,[13] which provides a variety of services based on online Persian user needs. Their holdings and activities include a number of online initiatives:

- PersianBlog (launched in 10 June 2002);
- Persian Talk, which is introduced as 'one of the biggest and most popular Iranian Online Forums' and provides discussion forums for topics such as literature, music, culture and history, theatre and cinema, and the like, and boasts of 22 public rooms and 2 private ones;
- PersianPetition.com, which provides free online petition service for 'reasonable public advocacy';
- Parsvote.com, which started its activity with the 2005 presidential election in Iran and introduces itself under the banner of 'national participation for self-determination' and aims to provide a space for marketing researches and studies;

- MyPardis.com caters to online communities that have formed interest groups and is introduced as 'a place to simply enjoy using the internet';
- FavaNews.com, another online initiative of Aria Group, is a news site or a 'news agency', which focuses on the IT and communication fields;
- FavaDargah is an ICT Portal and provides a comprehensive listings of various companies and services. The Aria Group is well connected to international partners. They have three 'technology partners' from the USA (Microsoft Corp, Cisco Systems and the Planet Data Center); two from Australia (Creative Digital Technology and Global Payment Solution) and one from the UK (Web Host Automation). Their international 'business partners' include Honafa IT Group (an Iran–UAE joint venture), Ejey Networks (Malaysia) and Baud Telecom Company (Saudi Arabia).

Other weblog service providers are also private companies. Blogfa, the second largest service provider, is privately owned and established by the Iranian search engine company parseek.com, and it is financed and maintained/sponsored by other private companies including Ouriran Network Solutions, Inc. which has head offices in Tehran and Toronto. The rise of Blogfa and other service providers and the introduction of new services by each of these have intensified the competition.[14]

Parsiblog was launched in 2005 with the aim of promoting and encouraging religious blogs and currently hosts around 4,000 blogs. In an interesting development, according to the IT News Agency,[15] parsiblog announced podcasting as a new addition to its services and had offered the possibility of internet radio, but retreated and suspended its offer after pressure from the state-owned Islamic Republic of Iran Broadcasting. As mentioned, under the Iranian constitution, broadcasting remains a state monopoly and parsiblog's new activities were regarded as the private sector's attempt to launch private radio.

Technorati's April 2007 report on the state of the blogosphere[16] reported that in terms of blog posts by language, Japanese retook the top spot with 37 per cent of the posts followed closely by English at 36 per cent, down from 39 per cent. Additionally, there was movement in the middle of the top 10 languages, highlighted by Italian overtaking Spanish for the number four spot. It also noted that 'the newcomer to the top 10 languages is Farsi, just joining the list at #10. It has been very interesting to watch the growth of the blogging world in the Middle East, especially in countries like Iran, and it is reflected in the language distribution above'.[17] Yet it is noteworthy that Arabic does not appear in the top 10 languages, while Chinese reflects only 8 per cent of all blog posts. Its April 2007 report further mentioned that Persian blogs including TodayLink.ir, Persian Blog Fans Club and Giliran.com were now making the Top 100 blogs.

What's the Focus and Content of Iranian Blogs?

A closer look at the categories of existing blogs hosted by persianblog.com and blogfa.com shows the diversity as well as the directions that blogging in Iran has taken.

Blogging is distinguished from other media by its format and the tools through which it provides readers with the expression of views and opinions but is similar to other media for the symbolic content that it delivers. In their current form, weblogs do provide a relatively free space for expression, albeit with limitations of time and resources, and without the pressure of media deadlines. There is, of course, much to be said about the attempts at control and censorship of the internet by the Islamic Republic, and we return to this in a separate chapter.

There are some recognisable categories of blogs most frequently used by Iranian blogfarms, notably literature, political, personal diaries, photo-blogs and some clear examples of creative writing. This can partly be explained by the nature of blogging and its preferred format as a diary, but also by the very fact that the press and journalism in Iran developed, as was the case in much of southern Europe (Daniel Hallin and Paolo Mancini, 2005), as part of the literary and political world. Most blogs consist of time-stamped postings with the latest items appearing first and the rest organised in reverse chronological order. The informal nature of blogs and their un-professional form liberate most bloggers from the conventional restrictions of other media: their producers are frequently untrained and always un-paid, they are predominantly the result of individual authorship and there is always the possibility of expressing opinions under a false name. Most re-main a platform for expressing opinions and ideas and polemics rather than news and information. In this sense blogs, rather than targeting a large audi-ence, are indeed written for the benefit of other bloggers and 'communities of interests', configured through politics, lifestyle, poetry, technologies and so on and manifested by links from one blog to many others. Therefore, despite their growth and popularity as a form of communication, they are

TABLE 2.2 Numbers and Categories of Blogs Hosted by Persian-Blog and Blogfa, 2007

PersianBlog			
News		*Society*	
News	1,777	Commerce and exchange	2,985
Journalism	852	History	969
		NGOs	479
		Philosophy	2,178
		Religion	3,176
Total	2,629	Total	9,796
Leisure		*World*	
Humour	4,047	Afghanistan	724
Visual games	999	Tajikistan	116
Total	5,046	Total	840
Art		*Sports*	
Literature	7,104	Football	39
Cinema	1,338	Tennis	81
Music	1,813	Climbing	130
Writing	2,364	Sport (general)	529
Art	3,086		
Total	15,705	Total	779
IT		*References*	
Software	1,584	Medical	359
Hardware	307	Nature/environment	386
Security	633	Educational/research	5,987
Computer	8,060	Quran	132
Internet	4,237		
Total	14,821	Total	6,864
Family			
Private	8,869		
Public	29,560		
Life	7,050		
Total	45,479		

(*Continued*)

TABLE 2.2 (*Continued*)

	Blogfa		
News and media	718	Computer and internet	2,397
Commerce and economy	700	Photoblog	200
Culture and history	146	Sports	509
Personal	5,113	Travel and tourism	56
Art and literature	4,378	Science and technology	1,307
Idea and religion	1,082	Blog and blogging	404
Society and politics	612	Leisure and humour	1,241
Family and life	254	Persian speakers in other countries	128

not the most popular sites or channels of communication, albeit that Technorati's monitoring of popular sites shows that, in general, blogging sites are creeping in to the top 100 sites and displacing some mainstream media. The same factors, including their informal nature, unprofessional aspects, individual orientation and forms of expression, that have contributed to the rapid growth of blogs have also contributed to their limited reach. Their huge volume undoubtedly contributes to the fragmentation of audience, and it is the well-known media brands with their massive resource that will continue to play their established roles as major providers of news and information.

Blogging, Politics and the Public Sphere

Considerable literature suggests that blogging everywhere in the world is associated with increased democracy and political participation, essentially with the extension of a public sphere. However, not all blogging content even in Iran is oriented towards rational agonistic debate, the traditional stuff of politics. However, that does not render other content apolitical; because of the particular situation of cultural and social life under Islamic Republic, much struggle over participation and 'voice' happens literally over music and singing, with its bans on pop music concerts and on single women's voices being heard. The struggles over expression, over space for enunciation, over definitions of problems is the stuff of politics in Iran, a vibrant example of what Chantal Mouffe (2005) describes as the ongoing challenge of defining the 'political' in different moments and contexts.

It is far too easy to assume that Iranian bloggers are all highly politically motivated. Actually, there has been a strong strand of criticism that bloggers are too oriented towards the popular rather than to the 'public'. Studies by Hossein Derakhshan and Ebrahim Nabavi, a well-known Iranian journalist and blogger, point to the triumph of the 'popular' over the 'public'. Using the same source of information/data available via Nedstatbasic, both have argued that the most popular sites in Iran are entertainment sites that show little or no interest in public matters. In an entry entitled *'Jeegar' vs. political freedoms* posted on 9 January 2004, Derakhshan (aka Hoder) argued:

> If you need a proof that Iranian youngsters don't have any interest in politics, you must see this stats report [Nedstatbasic] for the most popular Iranian websites. You see that a website called jeegar is on the top with over 100,000 visitors everyday. Its content: links to soft porn material on the Net.

Hoder suggests that he 'noticed the huge impact of Jeegar.com when I discovered the hugest hike in my visitors ever as a result of a link on *Jeegar* to a post in my weblog about board games; over 4,000 visitors had come to my blog by a single link from *Jeegar* in two days and they keep coming'. Nabavi raises a similar concerns in his article entitled '60,000 Editors'.[17] According to him, of the 18 Iranian sites with more than 10,000 visitors per day, 13 were about entertainment (or 'yellow sites', as he calls them in a wave to tabloid journalism), three were about internet, two were about commerce and only one was a news site. He suggests that because of the continuing pressure by the judiciary on media in Iran, many bloggers who write under their real name bypass politics and take refuge in their own private world and their individual concerns about literature, society and culture.

Of course, both these commentators define and link the 'political' rather simply to an interest in hard news and information and also assume that entertainment has no political implications. Yet, in the context of a would-be hegemonic state that has opinions about and acts in relation to most areas of social activity, including those of gender relations and sexual expression, it is important to consider that a search for entertainment, for sites of freer sexual expression and even explicitly sexual material is in part engendered by these macro-level dynamics and are often seen by Net users as small acts of defiance, even resistance, against the state. Further evidence for the 'cultural' as the site of political contestation can be found in Shahram Khosravi's excellent (2008) analysis of the defiance in Iranian youth culture, while Pardis Mahdavi (2008) describes in vivid detail the 'passionate uprising' or sexual revolution happening inside the Islamic Republic. These are not simplistic celebratory accounts but detailed analyses of how cultural expression and sexual relations become so impregnated with collective meaning. Thus, the simple dismissal of such topics as 'nonpolitical' is to write too narrow a definition of the nature of what constitutes the 'political', indeed what has become politicised, inside the Islamic Republic.

However, while the sites have not remained the same, and new ones have replaced some old favourites, more directly politically oriented sites linger in a relegation zone of the top league of Iranian sites. A close look at latest statistic by Nedstatbasic site for 18 May 2006[18] revealed that only two Iranian blogs appear in the list of top 100 Iranian sites. While nourizadeh.com is ranked 42 (up four places from previous week), behnoudonline.com is ranked 81 (up seven places from previous week). Both are well-known male journalists based outside Iran with extensive networks, exposure on Voice of America (VOA) and access to many sources. Each site has between 2 and 3,000 visitors per day. Other popular blogs include alipic.mihanblog.com (99) a blog with nothing but photographs; irjokes.blogspot.com (111); alpr.30morgh.org (131) containing political commentary; shima.blogspot.com (141) a personal diary of an Iranian girl in Tehran; parastoo.com (148) a weblog in Persian and English combining political, cultural and social commentary; and bourse.blogfa.com (149) a blog dedicated to news and information about Tehran stock exchange and linked to the company itself and its site, tse.ir. None of the Iranian journalists inside Iran with a blog makes it into the top 150. According to the same statistics, while the reformist daily *Shargh* remained the most popular site over many weeks with between 15,000 and 20,000 page views per day, the rest of the popular sites are dominated by general entertainment oriented sites, offering a mixture of music, sports news and commercial services.

A good way of assessing the accuracy of Nedstatbasic data is to look at the information that it provides on other countries. Top UK sites listed on 18 May 2006 revealed the shortcomings and the inaccuracy of its data. It included 12 adult sites in its top 50 list, 6 football sites, and a number of game, entertainment, technologies and business sites. There were only two news sites. While one – lankaweb.com, the highest ranking news site that contains news about Sri Lanka – was ranked 29, the other – mathaba.net, an alternative world news site – was ranked 44. If this is not enough of an indication of the inaccuracy of data, consider the fact that Stevenage Football Club site was ranked 50. News sites including the BBC were nowhere to be seen in the top 50, 100 or 200. Surely, it is inconceivable to imagine that

Stevenage Football Club site, a nonleague football club, had more visitors than the BBC or, if we want to remain in the category of 'infotainment', than BBC Sports, or Chelsea, Liverpool, Arsenal and Manchester United websites.

Another source, alexa.com, presents a rather different picture of the internet in Iran. This site, which measures sites and their rank on three months of aggregated historical traffic data from millions of Alexa Toolbar users, combines page views and users. The 10 most popular sites in Persian in 2006 were Blogfa, PersianBlog, BBC Persian, Mehrnews (internet news agency), IRNA (Islamic Republic News Agency), Baztab (another news site), al-shia.com (a religious site providing religious information, documents and discussion in 26 languages including Persian, English, French, Italian, Arabic, Kurdish, Turkish, Azari and Bengali), ISNA (Iran Student News Agency), Fars (another internet news site, claiming to be the first independent news agency in Iran), and p30world.com, a site dedicated to computing and the internet. Alexa computes site traffic at the domain level, and the reason why two Iranian blog service providers (Blogfa and PersianBlog) are ranked first and second, respectively, is because all blogs carrying their domain are treated as part of the same site. It is not an indication of the popularity of a blog as an individual site. The most popular entertainment site listed by Alexa.com is Niksalehi.com (ranked 18), a site created by Mohammed Niksalehi, a final-year undergraduate student of electronics in Mashhad. This site contains games, trivia, horoscope and the like. The top-ranking blog (ranked 57) is webneveshteha.com written by a mid-ranking cleric Mohammad Ali Abtahi, one of Iran's six vice presidents during Khatami's presidency. This is followed by parastoo.com (ranked 82), and kosoof.com which is a photoblog containing Arash Ashoorinia's photography (ranked 87). Undoubtedly, Alexa's method does not provide an accurate picture of the popularity of blogs as related to each individual blog. It is conceivable that blogs that are more popular have been lost under the aggregate system that counts them as part of the same domain. Nevertheless, it points out, in contrast to Nedstatbasic, that news sites in Persian, including those operated and maintained outside Iran (such as BBC Persian, the US–financed Radio Farda, VOA and a number of other news sites) are very popular sites.

However, one needs to treat all such statistics cautiously for there are serious issues regarding internet-related statistics. While such statistics might aid certain notions of the 'public' as defined by interests in news and serious journalism and enable some commentators to seek closure to the debate with some well-intended judgement, we need to open up the investigation further and check and cross-check existing data and surveys. Even if such figures were accurate, which they are not, one still needs to be able to explain why things are the way they are, how they arrived at this point, and what they tell us, or more importantly fail to tell, about Iran. These are crucial questions in the context of Iran where everything from attending football matches, dress codes, talking to the opposite sex or watching purely entertainment oriented satellite channels can become a 'public' concern and therefore political. By this, of course we do not imply that all forms of 'political' expression are the same or of equal significance. One can appreciate that the 'politics' of a world cup match between Iran and the USA is not as significant as their current international confrontation over nuclear issues. Nor would we wish to argue that watching pornography is a political act (sometimes, a cigar is a cigar and a naked woman just that) but in a context where the boundaries of public taste and morality are so heavily and literally policed, refusals to accept those definitions can take on political meanings. Our argument is that we need to move beyond the narrow sense by which the 'political/public' has been defined, explored and investigated, particularly by Iranian commentators themselves.

The growth of blogging has also shifted the attention of many young users from chat rooms towards reading and writing weblogs. Iranians have had a visible presence in major chat rooms such as Yahoo Messenger and on many Persian chat sites. Iranians also have a strong presence on social networking sites such as Orkut and Facebook.

These remain popular, and many political and social organisations organise regular meetings in Paltalk.[19] However, weblogs have created a new platform for establishing contacts, networks and public spaces. Various blogging sites with links to each other that create a chain effect have emerged, with different sponsors and spaces for product placement. E-zines such as Cappuccinomag.com are increasingly popular, attracting more than 50,000 visitors per month. *Balatarin*, with the highest traffic, is a community website launched in August 2006 based on Web 2.0 principles where users post the best links of interest to Iranian internet users around the world. Once a link gets enough positive votes, it is moved to the top of the front page, providing more visibility. It has shown how popular criteria can drive such a website, and this community site itself is popular. In 2007, it was selected as the best Iranian website of the year by Iranian internet users; *7Sang*, an Iranian media and internet magazine, chose *Balatarin* as the best website in Persian for two years in a row. It provides a space where journalists and bloggers can congregate, and its claimed 8-million page views indicate a lively audience for what it offers. *Balatarin* expanded in 2008 with Tehran Broadcast (tehranbroadcast.com), which aims to bridge the gap between English and Persian newsmakers, media, bloggers, twitters and so on. It brings firsthand news from Iran, with material written by people from Iran and translated by some 300 translators. Interestingly, while access to Facebook and YouTube had been denied, although many young people shared hacking software to gain access, in early 2009 these sites suddenly became available, part of the preparation for the presidential election (this is further developed in the last chapter).

Weblog content and functions vary and attract different readers. They have certainly increased the volume of Persian content in cyberspace and have readdressed the imbalance of content in terms of the language. Blogs provide the possibility of finding dates and jobs; many bloggers have been hired by newspapers and many journalists of closed newspapers have found the blogosphere a place to continue to write. Some have encouraged collective efforts in campaigning for various issues, including first-hand accounts and reports of student activities and protests.

Most notably, they establish a better link between Iran and Iranians living outside by providing information about the new and unofficial Iran. This new linking was vividly seen in the 2009 post-election debacle, described in the last chapter. Many Iranian bloggers have opted for bilingual blogs, and many write only in English (perhaps to appeal to a wider audience or because they lack skills in written Persian, or both), but the majority of blogs by Iranians inside and outside of Iran are written in Persian. The available data suggests that 60 per cent of the visitors to popular weblogs come from inside Iran, the rest logging-in from North America, Europe and Asia.

State and Election Politics on the Net

It is not only 'oppositional' politics of various kinds that find a presence in the Persian blogosphere. Hence, the notion that all blogs are somehow 'resistant' to the Islamic Republic (Nasrin Alavi, 2005) is wrong and ignores the fact that many religious figures were early adopters of the form and that there was an early strong and growing presence of religious individuals in the blogistan. Equally, many figures in government have established blogs, making the blogistan a far more diverse environment than is often recognised. Some parts of the regime have actively embraced e-development so that the Islamic Republic has a large presence online. Some of the formal politics of the regime has migrated to the Web, with a great many government departments, public statistics and material available on the Web. We examine this aspect of the blogosphere when discussing embedded bloggers/intellectuals in Chapter Five.

Some government officials have also started their own blog. One of the first and most celebrated of such blogs is www.webnevesht.com, written by Abtahi. Launched in September 2003, his site became an instant hit. He quickly launched an English site, which according to some reports (Bazzi, 2004) gets 15,000 visitors a day, and later added an Arabic version. He announced his arrival by posting a message: 'I am here as well!!!' His site consists of daily articles and diaries, well-kept and extensive archives, articles about him in other media, interviews and photographs. He pokes fun at himself, the government, friends and especially his conservative rivals. Proud of his latest mobile phone, he uses it to take pictures of his colleagues in informal situations and his trips abroad, including one to Venice. He writes commentary on cultural issues, including the controversial movie *The Lizard*, and regularly criticises any crackdown on weblogs and the internet. Abtahi was one of those arrested in the 2009 post-election clampdown on dissent; his thinner and weakened appearance during the 'trial' process led many to wonder what he had been administered in prison (see the last chapter).

From early on, the internet in general and weblogs in particular have been regarded as so influential that the government could not ignore their existence and actually began to endorse them. In January 2004, in response to the vetting of reformist candidates by the Guardian Council, many MPs organised a sit-in. Lacking access to state-controlled broadcasting, the protesting MPs launched their own blog. As was reported by the *World of Computer and Communication*, the aim of this blog was to publicise the event and provide up-to-date information.[20] By 2004, blogging in Iran had attracted so much attention that PersianBlog organised a three-day festival of blogging, possibly the first in the world.[21] Abtahi, then vice president, opened the festival by urging the government to encourage blogging and giving bloggers the freedom to write and express themselves. Nasrollah Jahangard, then deputy minister of information, similarly expressed government support for Persian blogging and mentioned increased efforts to expand the presence of Iran on the internet, and in the closing speech of the festival, he wished for the day that every Iranian had a blog.[22] Under the previous monarchical regime, it was often wished that one day every Iranian should have a *Paykan*, the Iran-built Hillman car.

The 2005 election was the first to reflect the growing impact of the internet. As the election approached, many other officials began to launch their own blogs. Ali Mazrooie, a key figure of the reformist Iran Participation Front, began to blog in March 2005. In his first post, he suggested that the main reason for starting a blog was the arrest of his son, Hanif, because of his connection with two reformist websites *Emrooz* and *Rouydad*. Mazrooie suggested that since his son's arrest, he had become an internet convert (*interneti*).[23] He was soon followed by presidential candidates, including the main reformist contender Mostafa Moeen.[24] Reporting the launch of Moeen's blog, Derakhshan suggested that Moeen 'is the first presidential candidate who has a weblog and if elected, would be the first Iranian president with a weblog'.[25]

Thus, weblogs played a key role already in the 2005 elections, with all candidates having their own dedicated site/blogs. Many religious institutions and agencies also deemed it necessary to establish an online presence, with even Ayatollah Khamenei – the supreme jurist – establishing a website. As Iran was getting ready for a very unpredictable presidential election, the alternative site, Alternet, in an article entitled 'Building Blogs' suggested:

> *Persian blogs represent a grassroots movement that is paving the way for Iran's political awakening. These thousands of online journals show their tyrannical government that social change is inevitable. 'If the Supreme Leader was a fan of reading blogs,' Derakhshan quipped 'then Iran would be a different country.' Moreover, these genuine Iranian voices are trying to tell the rest of the world that not only are the people of Iran ready to embrace democracy, but that they are fully capable of bringing about this change themselves. Iranian bloggers are ready to open the bridge, the café, the window with the West and start an international dialogue.*[26]

It was the surprise victor, Mahmoud Ahmadinejad, who later became the most famous blogger in the country as well as the imprisoner of many.

Blogs: Individual Space or Community Construction?

Abtahi's blog, mentioned earlier, is one of the few to contain no links to other bloggers, which raises an interesting question about whether blogs are simply individualised phenomena or part of a wider collective process. Much of the brouhaha about blogging in the West focuses on the massive desire for individual expression and global presentation of self that would have given Erving Goffman (1959) sleepless nights. Certainly, youthful insouciance about privacy is becoming a global concern as not only paedophiles but employers, educational institutions and others survey 'private' spaces such as Facebook to discover exactly what their members are up to.

Yet, even individual blogs are increasingly hosted by major weblog providers and many contain more links than material[27] to produce a more evident collective phenomenon. Undoubtedly, many Persian blogs are organised and written by an individual and express the aspirations, thoughts and sentiments of one person. Derakhshan's aptly name blog, *Editor: Myself*, indicates the importance of an individual taking control over content and finding their own voice, free of editors (although, it could be said that there are almost as many 'editors' as there are bloggers).[28] Many blogs are locations for the presentation of individual lives, with family photos, love poems, laments about failed relationships, whimsy and wit, and all the accoutrements of bourgeois individualism as to be found on British or American blogger sites. However, even the most private and anonymous blogs have become part of a wider community of interests through the addition – and the significance of – links. Increasingly, there is a clear and visible sense of connections and networks amongst Persian bloggers and there are trends towards establishing a sense of solidarity, camaraderie and belonging. Thus, while weblogs are one of the most individual and private forms of expression in public space, there are visible trends towards collective efforts in producing a weblog as well as the creation through linkages of networks of friends, professional colleagues, sympathisers and other relevant blogs and sites.

One site, tahsilat.webialist.com, was created to introduce student blogs and has compiled a list of more than 700 weblogs written and maintained by students. A feminist site, womeniniran.net, provides a rich list of more than 100 women bloggers in Iran, some of whom are producing powerful critical observations on public life in Iran. This site has added a new section, 'From Weblogs', and in addition to existing links, has announced that it will provide links to any posted materials on blogs that deal with women's issues. It aims to provide a platform for wider coverage of 'individual and independent voices' as well as contributing to diversity and richness of womeniniran.net.

Creating collective blogs has become so popular that weblog service providers have announced that, as part of their services, they will cater to bloggers who intend to work as a group. Defining 'collective' blogs, however, is as difficult as defining the blog itself. This is an evolving process and a movement that is just beginning to take shape, and it is important to watch this development. Undoubtedly, as Saidabadi,[29] one of the founders of the collective blog *hanouz.com*, has suggested, one of the key feature of collective blogs is their speed in updating the blog and presenting new materials and postings. Providing relevant information and analysis on a regular basis is a daunting task for individual bloggers, especially for those with a full-time job outside the blogosphere. Most weblog service providers terminate their service to bloggers if they fail to update and usually 'auction' the space to new clients. Because collective blogs rely on the commitment of more than one individual, they not only keep the blog running and lively, but in doing so, also maintain their visitors.

However, collective blogs are more than just a pragmatic and practical solution to avoid losing visitors and webspace. They provide a platform for more diverse sets of arguments, opinions and analysis. This, as Saidabadi suggests, creates circles, *halghe*, that can open up spaces for dialogues between bloggers and their readers. The highly individualised Iranian blogosphere has been the target of serious criticism. Daruish Ashuri, a well-known Iranian writer, has argued (somewhat ironically, it must be said, by posting on his own blog[30]) that the volume of bad, rushed and ill-conceived opinions and ideas that are posted on thousands of blogs can be regarded as nothing but a sad waste of the time, energy and intellectual abilities of many young Iranians. He argues that this is especially dangerous for a nation that needs to produce its own knowledge and develop its own ideas. Ashuri's own site is part of another circle, *halegheh malakut* (*www.malakut.org*), which describe itself as 'a collection of weblogs with diverse identities intended to produce critique, dialogue and friendship'. It also describes itself as a decentralised network where the only condition of membership is accepting the rights and freedom of individuals, respecting pluralism and freedom of speech.

The Nature of Collective Blogs

We can identify a number of different trends among collective blogs. One such trend is an effort to gather a number of blogs under the same umbrella, creating *networks* of individual bloggers with diverse views who are willing to express their commitments to certain aims and conditions. Malakut.org is a good example of this trend, where 39 individual bloggers see themselves as part of this loosely defined circle. The site itself provides no postings and the only general information is related to the conditions of membership and the required conditions and etiquette for writing. There are also no links except the list of all individual bloggers who use the *malakut* domain name.

Similarly, *debsh.com*, a homepage of 10 regular blogs, is the brainchild of a number of Iranian journalists, including some who wrote for the banned reformist daily, *Shargh*, researchers and a photographer. The site claims that it was formed on the basis of acceptance of differences of opinion. Bloggers on this site are asked to observe and uphold two principles. One is to abide by the law and the 'red lines' of the Islamic Republic, because all the managers and bloggers live in Iran, manage the site from inside and have 'no interests in creating problems for themselves or family and friends'. The second condition, not irrelevant to the first, is 'to avoid over-politicisation and marginal issues'. The site claims that all members have agreed to avoid producing constant political materials, although this doesn't prevent them from occasional engagements with political matters.[31] This seems to be an obligatory 'disclaimer' by a number of Iranian sites and one cannot take it seriously, not least in the case of debsh.com. One blog member's recent posting (Mahmud Farjami), for example, contains a note on the meaning of Khordad[32] and how it brings a bitter smile to his face. There is an item on the government's policy for removing beggars from the streets of Tehran and how the same methods have been used on intellectuals, making a direct reference to the arrest of the Iranian scholar Ramin Jahanbegloo. Two readable and satirical items are letters supposedly written by Pope Benedict and George Bush in response to Ahmadinejad's much discussed letter to the US president (for more on the latter, see Annabelle Sreberny, 2008). The first one contains some fascinating passages and as we get closer to the end of the letter, the language becomes friendlier as the Pope refers to Ahmadinejad as 'Dear Mahmud', 'My Son', and 'I'll die for you!' (*fada'at sham*). The 'letter' from Bush also raises some very important questions wrapped in humour. In one passage, the blog says that Bush was very happy to receive the letter:

> *Dear President, I think that, leaving aside the current situation and public opinion in Tehran and Washington, me and you think similarly about a number of issues. For example you are worried about us turning Iraq back 50 years, and we are worried that you might turn Iran back 50 years too! You are worried that we might take hundreds of million dollars from other countries and spend it on our unnecessary needs, and we are worried that you might spend hundreds of millions of your own country's reserves and spend it on the irrelevant needs of others! For example you have asked me why there is such a widespread objection to a referendum, and I'm asking you why there is a widespread objection to a referendum. But you ask a president of United States about a referendum in Palestine while I am asking an Iranian president about a referendum in Iran.*[33]

This blog provides links to a number of Iranian and foreign sites.

Doxdo.com is another loosely defined collective blog/site, describing itself as an 'online news reader'. It acts as a newsletter providing the latest news and information posted on a number of websites and blogs. Launched in

September 2005, it offers a search capability that allows users to search the content of all the blogs or site as well as all the information and links posted on *Doxdo.com*. There is no specific editorial policy and no overall control over the content of individual postings. Blogs and sites can join the site if they have more than 50 visitors per day, are introduced and recommended by an existing member or introduce five weblogs with 50 readers. There are currently more than 200 sites/blogs that are members of this network, which is a quick way to glance at news and information as reported in the Iranian blogosphere.

The aforementioned blogs are indeed created as an amalgamation of a number of individual blogs with no particularly defined aims and do offer a wide variety of concerns and issues as expressed by individual members, resembling a neighbourhood or a community of individual households with different looks. Such a portal creates a sense of community by housing so many diverse sites in one virtual space or electronic street.

If such collective blogs act as a network and maximise traffic to a site, there are some collective blogs that have more focused aims and objectives and are organised around a more tightly defined subject. Blogsports.net/ is a collective blog dedicated to sports and launched an special page (fifaworld-cup2006.blogsports.net/) dedicated entirely to World Cup 2006, with links to related and relevant stories and reports. Weblog.eprsoft.com is another specialist collective blog dedicated to mass communications. Of the seven regular writers who contribute to this blog, only Hossein Emami (pr.eprsoft.com/) and Ali Mazinani (mazin.eprsoft.com/) share the eprsoft.com domain name. Launched in May 2004, this blog was an attempt to offer specialised knowledge, comments and analysis of wider trends in mass communication and public relations.

Another specialist collective weblog is haftan.com, a popular 'station' dedicated to the arts, which presents postings under 14 different sections including literary criticism, film and television, visual art, translation, photography and internet and media. Membership to this site, launched in August 2005, is free. Saeidreza Shokrolahi, who has his own blog (*khabgard.com*), is the founder and a number of volunteers, again each with their own blogs, help maintain and design this site. Daruish Mohamadpour, a member of malakut.com circle, is also involved in this network.

Running a collective blog has its problems. fanus.blogspot.com, another collective blog, the brainchild of Parsa Saaebi (a pseudonym) was launched in July 2002 and gradually turned it into a collective blog as he invited friends to write and maintain it. However, there were reports of internal conflicts and difficulties within the group. A report on Gooya news site[34] wrote 'do not let *fanus* [lantern] go off', and writes that 'their yellow flame has turned blue, which is cleaner but not more natural'. It seems as if the bloggers' commitment to their studies had acted as a major obstacle to improving the quality of their writing despite the rapid increase in the number of visitors. They had failed, despite having more than 10 contributors, to update their blogs on a regular basis. Saaebi, the founder, shed a different light on the difficulties that collective blogs face. In an interview with another Iranian blogger,[35] Asad Alimohammadi, who is regarded as the 'Larry King of the blogistan',[36] Saaebi argues that working as part of a team of a collective blog is not as easy as it seems. 'The expectation of a collective blog is high. If anything happens everyone expects that the collective blog should express an opinion. If anyone is insulted, all are waiting for a reaction from collective blogs.' Saaebi suggests because of these expectations, collective blogs are in constant need of new and quality materials, individual bloggers cannot be themselves and have to be formal and have to address officials. *Fanus* is still surviving, despite losing a number of contributors, but Saaebi sees a conflict between the function of collective blogs that need sustained collective effort and teamwork with the individualised nature of blogs.

Another significant collective blog is herlandmag.com/weblog/. This blog clearly highlights the complexity, aspirations and multidimensional character of many online initiatives in Iran. The 'Association of Lively Women (*Anjoman-e Zanan-e Zendeh*) is part of a network, including NGOs, media, political activists, etc., which came about as a result of many years of campaigning by a number of Iranian feminists. It is the weblog of an Iranian NGO called Women's Cultural Centre (*Markaz-e Farhangi-e Zanan*). Launched in March 2000 and officially registered as NGO in July of the same year, it was a response to the urgent need for more organised efforts by secular feminists. The two people behind the initial effort were Noushin Ahmadi Khorasani, director of the publishing house *Nashr-e Towseh*, and Shahla Lahiji, another independent publisher behind *Roshangaran* (The Enlighteners) (see Gholam Khiabany and Annabelle Sreberny, 2004). The centre announced its arrival onto the political scene after organising an event to celebrate International Women's Day in 2000. The aim was to

> learn from our experience; become aware of the 'perceived natural' situation used and reproduced against women; spread and expand feminist knowledge among ourselves and other women; to look at our issues critically and not from an individual perspective, but as public and social issues; and strengthen ourselves via our collective efforts to transform unequal situation which grip us.[37]

Activities of the Centre in the last few years include organising a petition and campaign for Iran to join The Convention on the Elimination of All Forms of Discrimination against Women (CEDAW); regular meetings, seminars, gatherings and workshops focusing on a range of issues such as 'Afghan women in exile', 'Killing of street women', 'Violence against women', 'Impact of war on women', solidarity with Palestinian women, women workers in Iran, objection to anti-women policies of Islamic Republic of Iran Broadcasting, as well as publishing an internal bulletin *Nameh Zan* (Woman's Letter). The centre launched its site *Feminist Tribune*[38] in 2003, which after nearly two years was 'filtered' by the Iranian regime in November 2005, but after a few months resumed its work. In March 2006, the centre announced the launch of its second online publication (*Nashriah*) in its continuing effort to forge much stronger links between women activists inside and outside the country. This second site, *Zanestan* (www. herlandmag.com) which introduces itself as the first online Persian publication for women, published six issues covering a diverse range of topics with regular updates, polemics, statistics, news and analysis. The weblog of the site was launched in 6 March 2006 to provide additional space for regular and quicker interventions. Ahmadi-Khorasani[39] in the first posting jokingly blamed Farnaz (a feminist blogger)[40] for getting them into the mess of 'collective blogs'.

Collective blogs such as those mentioned as well as others including *sobhaneh.net, hanouz.com* and *cappuccinomag.com* highlight a specific trend in online media. Such blogs take different shapes and forms that cannot be separated from the broader conditions that pave the way for their emergence. Establishing collective blogs in many parts of the world has come through a surge of interest in blogging and as a way of building on the strength of an already existing commercial media 'brand', exemplified in the online initiative *commentisfree* by the *Guardian*.[41] However, in Iran collective blogs have often emerged as a 'substitute' for other kinds of activity. The Islamic Republic state dominates the press, controls broadcasting and even configures NGO/civil society activities so that running an independent media channel carries more than financial risk, and attempting to develop autonomous political organisations is a highly precarious activity. Thus, many print newspapers morphed into collective websites when titles were closed by the regime. For example, in September 2004, after the closure of the reformist newspapers *Emrooz, Rooydad* and *Baamdad,* they reappeared in weblog format (*Emrooznews.blogspot.com; Rooydadnews.blogspot.com; Baamdadnews.blogspot.com*). The virtual NGO sector might be less imbricated with state policy than the 'real' ones ('might be', because this issue needs careful analysis). So Persian collective blogs have many different functions.

Using the Net for Advocacy and Solidarity

The internet in general and weblogs in particular have provided a strong link between activists and intellectuals in Iran and the various Iranian oppositions abroad. The internet has offered alternative news channels to Iranian activists in Iran as well as much needed international support and solidarity, including from Iranians living in exile. For example, in the autumn of 2004, the government cracked down on reformist websites that had been launched to continue their work after their newspapers had been closed down. Hoder posted a message in October 2004 calling upon Iranian bloggers to publish the contents from the reformist sites and to display the title of *Emrooz* as the title of their weblog in order to express their solidarity and to highlight censorship in Iran.[42] This move generated a storm of publicity in Iran and was heavily criticised by conservative papers such as the daily *Jomhouri-e Eslami*.

Other acts of solidarity included a petition for the immediate release of Sina Motallebi, a well-known Iranian blogger[43], who was arrested on 20 April 2003. Motallebi, a film critic who had worked for reformist dailies such as *Ham-mihan* and *Hayat-e No,* launched his blog under his real name. Problems with the 'content of his site' and 'interview with foreign press' were the reasons given for his arrest. However, as Moallemian, who came up with the idea of the petition suggests, Motallebi's arrest had no clear rationale.

> *His last few posts before being summoned were (in order) about an Iranian newscaster's inability to pronounce names properly; the retirement of the 'superhuman champion' Michael Jordan; his son's teething problems, and a reprint of an already published statement by Kambiz Kaheh, another film critic arrested on bogus charges of distributing illegal videos. Hardly risky materials.*[44]

The petition[45] to free Motallebi was quickly supported by more than 4,000 signatures, attracted publicity and banners across a number of sites and blogs and even the BBC covered the story. He was released but soon moved to Holland and by 2006 was actually working for the BBC Persian Service in London. Another noticeable and more practical achievement of solidarity and collective action was bloggers' ability to raise an estimated $4 million after the tragedy of the Bam earthquake.[46]

Other example of collective action was the posting of a logo by large number of weblogs in objection to the banning of the word 'women' as a search item. Many Iranians still use prepaid cards to access the internet in Iran, but the cards are designed so that searching for the term 'women' using search engines such as Google is impossible. The campaign has been supported by large number of bloggers, using the slogan 'censorship is indecent, not women'.

Women

همچنان سانسور!

Women: still censored!

Another such collective action was the quick response of Iranian communities to the arrest in May 2006 of Ramin Jahanbegloo, a prominent Iranian political philosopher who holds the Rajni Kothari Chair in Democracy at the Centre for the Study of Developing Societies (CSDS) in Delhi, India, and is head of the department of Contemporary Thought in the Cultural Research Bureau (CRB), Tehran. In addition to a widespread campaign, activities and petitions against his arrests, two dedicated blogs emerged that focussed exclusively on his case and campaigned for his release. One of these blogs[47] was edited by Hoder, already mentioned, and Mohamad Tavakoli, a professor at the University of Toronto and editor of the journal *Contemporary Studies of South Asia, Africa and the Middle East*. Both editors of this blog were based in Toronto, where Jahanbegloo worked and lived for a number of years. Behzad Homayoonpoor Shirazy[48] also launched a blog dedicated to the campaign for Jahanbegloo's release. Jahanbegloo, arrested in April 2006, was released at the end of August 2006. Similar campaigns and blogs were launched to free Akbar Ganji, an Iranian journalist, who was arrested in 2000 and only released after an extended hunger strike and widespread international campaign in Spring 2006.[49] There is even an Association of Iranian Bloggers (penblog)[50] that has been campaigning for the freedom of blogging and against any repressive measures over internet activity. This association has its own constitution and around 200 members and is structured like a formal political party with six subcommittees, including a women's committee, communiqué committee, social committee, refugees committee, publication committee and membership committee.

Blogosphere as Politics by Other Means

There is thus a complex set of reasons for the rapid emergence of a Persian blogosphere, connected to wider communications development in Iran, to the state of the press and to the possibilities of political organisation and different forms of expression – private and public, formal and informal as well as individual and collective.

After the collapse of the Soviet Union, the lack of artistic expression was explained by the lack of things to fight against. Conversely, the emergence of a highly politicised Persian blogosphere is evidence of the wide range of issues – social, cultural and more overtly 'political' – that have been politicised within the Islamic Republic.

While a poet *might* just be a poet in England, a poet in Persian is most probably writing between the lines, evading the censor and pushing the boundaries of publicly acceptable expression. A woman blogging about fashion in the West *might* be doing just that; a woman discussing the constrictions of *hejab* under the Islamic Republic is raising questions about the reach of public politics into the private domain. There are evident dangers in pushing these differences too far – to end up denying any politics to blogging in the West and the desire sometime for mere entertainment in Iran – and a danger of reproducing rigid stereotypes. So our argument centres on the importance of contextualising blogging in Iran within the broader sociopolitical and cultural environment of the Islamic Republic. This is not just a phenomenon of access to new technologies, although it is obviously that. This is not just young people enjoying internet chat, although there is that too. This is about the construction of a public space to debate and define the 'political' that escapes and evades – however tenuously – the control of the regime. This is about the practice of and continuation of politics by other means, inside and outside the country.

Web of Control and Censorship: State and Blogosphere in Iran

3

AS WE HAVE SHOWN, in recent years the communication industry in Iran has emerged as one of the fastest growing economic sectors, and 'new media' constitute one of the most dynamic and vibrant politicocultural spaces. We have so far examined the expansion and development of the internet in Iran and have provided evidence of how market forces and the realities of the digital divide in terms of access limits the reach and the potential of the internet. The previous chapter indicated the range and nature of some of the politics on the Iranian internet and moments when the regime has reacted against individuals. In this chapter, we provide a more detailed analysis of the range and kind of controls the regime utilises, and the drawbacks and impacts of these.

Here we look at state policies that have hindered and suppressed the democratic and participatory potentials of the internet. The case of Iran demonstrates the real potential of new technologies for empowerment of citizens, but it also shows that the realisation of this dream and the potential of the internet depend on access and political entitlements for all. This chapter looks at how the battle to control weblogs/bloggers as well as citizen journalists/intellectuals has evolved in Iran. It examines different layers and methods of control and censorship, as well as significant moments of dispute. It will demonstrate how the very contradictory nature and factionalism of the Iranian state inevitably makes for an intriguing and contradictory blogosphere, and how the potentials of new media are constrained by confusion in government policies, varied institutional interests and above all the dialectical tension between the imperative of the market and the revolutionary claims of the Iranian state.

As Table 3.1 'Global Blogging Arrests, 2003–08' indicates, Iran is not keeping very salubrious company in the list of countries that do most to restrict blogging activities on the Net.

TABLE 3.1 Global Blogging Arrests, 2003–08

Blogging Activities	Total	2003	2004	2005	2006	2007	2008
Using blog to organise or cover social protest	15	China (4)			Egypt, Iran	Burma (2), China, Egypt (4), Iran	Egypt
Violating cultural norms	14			Singapore (3)	Egypt, Greece, USA	China, Egypt (2), Hong Kong, India, Philippines	Egypt, UK
Posting comments about public policy	12		France	Iran (2), Tunisia	Egypt, Iran	Fiji, Malaysia, Pakistan, Saudi Arabia, Syria, Thailand	Syria
Exposing corruption or human rights violations	9	Iran				China (3), Tunisia	Burma
Other reason, or no reason given	8				Canada, China, Syria	China, Egypt, Fiji, Malaysia, Thailand, USA (2)	
Posting comments about political figures	6		Iran	Egypt		Egypt, Iran, Kuwait, Russia	
Total number of cases	64	5	2	7	10	35	5

Source: World Information Access Project, www.wiareport.org, 2008.

Legal Context of Media

As we have argued, the Islamic state that came to power after 1979 defined itself in a 'cultural', multidimensional, sense. However, Siavoshi has perceptively noted that 'although every faction declared its commitment to Islamic cultural ideals, all consensus vanished when it came to the question of what these ideals were and which policies were required to achieve them' (1997:513). The case of internet in Iran is no exception.

The dual system and the contradictions within the Islamic polity and the Islamic Republic mean both the recognition and the negation of the right to free expression and communication. The Iranian Constitution's notions of freedom, dignity and the right to express and publish are contradicted by the idea of the mass media as a megaphone to advertise and further the cause of the ruling elite. In the introduction to the Constitution we read:

> The mass-communication media, radio and television, must serve the diffusion of Islamic culture in pursuit of the evolutionary course of the Islamic Revolution. To this end, the media should be used as a forum for the healthy encounter of different ideas.

Amendment 2 of Article 3 of the Constitution states that one of the duties of the Islamic state is to raise 'the level of public awareness in all areas, through the proper use of the press, mass media, and other means'.

A range of articles protect other 'freedoms': Article 23 states that: 'The investigation of individuals' beliefs is forbidden, and no one may be harassed or taken to task simply for holding a certain belief'; and in the case of the print media according to Article 24 of the Constitution 'the press have freedom of expression'. Article 175 also recognises the freedom of broadcasting: 'The freedom of expression and dissemination of thoughts in the Radio and Television of the Islamic Republic of Iran must be guaranteed in keeping with the Islamic criteria and the best interests of the country'. As for the press-related offences, the Constitution also is clear on legality, accountability and transparency of the judiciary. Article 168 states: 'Political and press offences will be tried openly and in the presence of a jury, in courts of justice'. Iran is also a signatory to the International Covenant on Civil and Political Rights (ICCPR).

Although there are references to freedom, dignity, debate and development of human beings, the main aim of the media seems to be the construction of Islamic society and the diffusion of Islamic culture. Although, in its introduction, the Constitution suggests that the media should be used as a forum for healthy encounters, it identifies the limits forcefully and clearly too: media 'must strictly refrain from diffusion and propagation of destructive and anti-Islamic practices'. Article 9 also contains clear warning against any 'abuses' of freedom of the press and speech:

> In the Islamic Republic of Iran, the freedom, independence, unity, and territorial integrity of the country are inseparable from one another, and their preservation is the duty of the government and all individual citizens. No individual, group, or authority, has the right to infringe in the slightest way upon the political, cultural, economic, and military independence or the territorial integrity of Iran under the pretext of exercising freedom.

Article 24 also sets the limits of the press. The press is free 'except when it is detrimental to the fundamental principles of Islam or the rights of the public'. The same section of the Constitution that deals with the 'right of people' also contains Article 40: 'No one is entitled to exercise his rights in a way injurious to others or detrimental to public interests'. And, as we have already seen, Article 175 recognises the freedom of broadcasting within a certain context: 'The freedom of expression and dissemination of thoughts in the Radio and Television of the Islamic Republic of Iran must be guaranteed in keeping with the Islamic criteria and the best interests of the country'.

Undoubtedly, the writers of the Islamic Republic Constitution recognised that there was a degree of institutional tension in the document itself as well as in the system. As we have seen, certain articles contain clear elements that grace the constitutions of many democracies. However, every one of such 'democratic principles' is negated by theocratic elements and clear limits to the 'rights of people' and the 'media'. The dual nature of the Islamic Republic and the tension between Islamism and republicanism as well as the tension over the source of legitimacy and sovereignty is evident in the case of the media too. Close reading of the film and press regulations provides further evidence. In both cases, while the significance of artistic and journalistic production is recognised, in trying to codify the Islamic values, the wording of regulations is ambiguous and vague and, as the experience of post-revolutionary Iran demonstrates, subject to varied institutional, local and expedient interpretations.

The regulation governing exhibition of films and video in Iran, approved in 1982, for example bans films and videos 'that weaken the principles of monotheism, insult the Prophet, Imams and the ruling councils of clerics, blaspheme against Islamic values and teachings, encourage wickedness and prostitution, lower the taste of the audience' and the like (Hamid Naficy,

2004). The Press Law of 1986, which was amended in controversial circumstances in 2001, (Gholam Khiabany and Annabelle Sreberny, 2001) is similarly ambiguous. Articles 3, 4 and 5 of the Press Law recognise the rights of the press. According to Article 3, 'the press have the right to publish the opinions, constructive criticisms, suggestions and explanations of individuals and government officials for public information'. Article 4 states that '[n]o government or non-government official should resort to coercive measures against the press to publish an article or essay, or attempt to censure and control the press'. Article 5 lists acquisition and dissemination of 'domestic and foreign news aimed at enhancing public awareness' as lawful. In each of these articles, the limits of these rights are also vaguely emphasised, such as those of 'constructive' criticism and how the press need to take into 'consideration the best interests of the community and by observing the provisions of the existing law'.

The Press Law is more explicit and precise when it comes to the limits of the press. Article 6 lists all those 'exceptions' that are argued in Article 24 of the Constitution. Such exceptions are as follow:

1. Publishing atheistic articles or issues that are prejudicial to Islamic codes, or promoting subjects that might damage the foundation of the Islamic Republic;

2. Propagating obscene and religiously forbidden acts and publishing indecent pictures and issues that violate public decency;

3. Propagating luxury and extravagance;

4. Creating discord between and among social walks of life specially by raising ethnic and racial issues;

5. Encouraging and instigating individuals and groups to act against the security, dignity and interests of the Islamic Republic of Iran within or outside the country;

6. Disclosing and publishing classified documents, orders and issues, or disclosing the secrets of the Armed Forces of the Islamic Republic, military maps and fortifications, publishing closed-door deliberations of the Islamic Consultative Assembly or private proceedings of courts of justice and investigations conducted by judicial authorities without legal permit;

7. Insulting Islam and its sanctities, or offending the Leader of the Revolution and recognised religious authorities (senior Islamic jurisprudents);

8. Publishing libel against officials, institutions, organisations and individuals in the country or insulting legal or real persons who are lawfully respected, even by means of pictures or caricatures; and

9. Committing plagiarism or quoting articles from the deviant press, parties and groups which oppose Islam (inside and outside the country) in such a manner as to propagate such ideas (the limits of such offences shall be defined by the executive by-law).

Further limits include a ban on activities such as 'publishing a publication without a license and a publication whose license has been cancelled', 'publishing a publication the greatest part of whose items are incongruous to subjects which the applicant has undertaken to publish', 'publishing a publication that may be mistaken in name, symbol or format for the existing publications' or 'those which have been temporarily or permanently closed down', 'publishing a publication without mentioning the name of its license holder and the legally responsible director' or 'the address of the publication and its printing house' and finally 'publishing and distributing publications which the Press Supervisory Board deems to be in violation of the principle stipulated in this by-law' (Article 7: a, b, c, d and e).

The breadth and lack of detailed definition of many of these points is evident. The competition between competing ministries and between political and religious actors is inevitable. The sometimes creative but often trying attempts by journalists, broadcasters, bloggers and others to interpret the law as it best facilitates their activities does not always end well. One of the greatest difficulties facing those who wish to debate and create, whether in film or journalism or other media, has been to determine precisely where the 'red line' is, how it can be negotiated and how hard it is being policed. The 2004 film, *Red Lines and Deadlines*, by Taghi Amirani powerfully explores such journalistic dilemmas, while Saeed Zeydabadi-Nejad (2010) explores the phenomenon for film. And, of course the threat of violence lurks behind the legalese.

Internet Policy and Control

Similarly, regulation of the internet in Iran reveals the existence of many contradictory institutions, policies and competing interests within the Islamic Republic. While the IRI officially encourages the use of the internet, the issues of access, control and content remain controversial and a certain wariness has hindered the importation of ICT technology and their integration into daily life (Laleh Ebrahimian, 2003). The conjunction of commercial imperatives and the desire for effective control of the internet means that the government has taken the leading role in providing internet access and services.

The government has devised a range of controls, which are implemented with greater or lesser degrees of efficiency, depending on the moment. As in other spheres, the regulation is best understood in its violation, and the letter of the law is rarely the detail of the practice.

ISP Licensing and Control

In a May 2001 announcement entitled 'Overall Policies on Computer-Based Information-Providing Networks', the Supreme Leader, Ali Khamenei encouraged the use and development of the internet. However, contrary to the initial plan for wider participation of the private sector and capital investment, he put the state in charge and reserved a big role for the Islamic Republic of Iran Broadcasting. He urged the government to 'make access to the global information-providing networks only through authorised entities'.[1] Following his direct instruction, the High Council of Cultural Revolution, which has no constitutional powers to issue a ruling on the internet or other matters, contradicted its own previous policy announced a year before and passed a resolution regarding the regulation of the internet.[2] In this document, published in November 2001 and announced on state-owned television, the Council ruled that notwithstanding an emphasis on the free access of people to information and facilitation of the free flow of information, internet connections would be a state monopoly and all connectivity would be provided through the Telecommunication Company of Iran (TCI). Yet, while even government organisations were required to get the permission of the High Council of Information (HCI) to connect independently from the TCI, IRIB was exempted from seeking the HCI's permission to broadcast their programmes on the internet. Applications for access provision were to be assessed by the Ministry of Post, Telephone and Telegraph and the Ministry of Intelligence. In addition, the document required all access providers to prevent access to immoral or political websites (neither defined) and to make available the databanks of their users' activity to the Ministry of Post, Telephone and Telegraph, which would be handed to the Ministry of Intelligence, on request.

As for the ISPs, permission is required from the Ministry of Post, Telephone and Telegraph to provide voice over internet protocol (VoIP). The rest of the document that deals with conditions, quality and objectives of the ISPs was very similar to the pre-existing Press Law, one of the key reasons for the six-day students' revolt in the summer of 1999. Section B of the document states that the managers of the ISP companies have to be an Iranian citizen and committed to the Islamic Republic Constitution; at least 25 years old; free of incapacity, bankruptcy by fraud or guilt; free of moral corruption and criminal conviction; a believer in one of the recognised faiths in the Constitution; and finally not a member of illegal and 'anti-revolutionary' organisations.

The ISP service providers, similar to the limits on the press in the Press Law, must desist from

- publishing any atheistic articles/issues and items which undermine the Islamic Republic, Islam and the teaching of Khomeini, and are against the unity of the country, its constitutions and its Islamic values;
- creating discord between and among social groups;
- encouraging acts against the security of the country;
- propagating luxury;
- publishing obscene and religiously forbidden articles and pictures;
- disclosing information; and
- creating any broadcasting networks without the control of the Islamic Republic of Iran Broadcasting.

Similar rules and limits are also listed in section C, which deals with internet cafes. The only major difference is that those applying for a licence to run an internet cafe are required (in addition to the conditions listed for managers of ISP companies) to have finished their military service, be at least 30 years old and married. One can only guess that the inclusion of marital commitment as a condition for internet cafe owners is yet another indication of the paranoia over the perceived immoral dangers that are associated with the internet. Yet we have spoken with cafenet owners (December 2008) who did not and do not satisfy these details (being unmarried and not having completed military service) and who, indeed, seemed rather amazed to be told that such were the precise criteria of the law. Also, the owner of blogfa.com told us (November 2008) that while he has tried personally to control access to pornographic sites through any blogs on his network, he never intervened to regulate any political content, leaving that realm to the government to control.

In each *Ostan* (province) a committee consisting of representatives of the TCI, the office of Culture and Islamic Guidance, a district attorney, internet cafe official guilds and finally a representative of IRIB control the activities of net cafes. The committee's decision regarding any violations of the internet law is final. In a separate announcement, the duty of observing all internet-related matters at a national level was given to a committee of three members: a representative from the High Council of Cultural Revolution, a minister for Post, Telephone and Telegraph and the Managing Director of IRIB.[3] In 2005 two new members were added to this committee, one from the conservative Organization for Islamic Culture and Communication, which is mostly funded by the Supreme Leader's office, and one from the Supreme Cultural Revolution Council, which is another conservative body consisting mostly of hardline conservatives appointed by the Supreme Leader.[4]

This resolution and subsequent announcement was yet another indication of the dilemma of the Islamic Republic, caught between the need for liberalisation and its 'revolutionary' claims. Both the Islamic Republic of Iran Broadcasting, challenged by foreign satellite channels and calls for the introduction of private channels, and the Telecommunication Company of Iran, challenged by the private sector, have tried to keep their grip over their respected fields but were also given further opportunity to influence the development of the internet in Iran. The Iranian ISP Association, one of the newly established institutions of 'civil society', criticised the decision requiring them to provide internet access through the TCI. Initially, the filtering seems to have required regular visits by TCI officials to each cafenet to download and set up the requisite software. By 2009, all ISPs except the largest and cafenets were being routed through Tehran and the controls were administered there.

As we have seen, state regulation requires ICPs and ISPs to use a filtering system, take notice of regulations and update themselves with the lists of banned sites provided by the authorities. Delegating censorship to ISPs and obliging them to filter sites deemed 'corrupt' and 'un-Islamic' (which ironically includes many news sites run and maintained by factions within the Iranian state) allowed the state to share the blame with companies and small businesses such as internet cafe owners. Such control is an expensive business. A Data Communication Company of Iran (DCI) official reported that in 2003 alone the company had spent more than 70 billion rials ($70 million) on censoring the internet in Iran.

Filtering and Banned Sites

A 2005 report by *Opennet Initiative*[5] argued that Iran, along with China, was among a small group of states with the most sophisticated state-mandated filtering systems in the world. Iran and many other countries use the commercial filtering package SmartFilter, which is somewhat ironically produced by the US-based company, Secure Computing, as the primary technical engine of its filtering system. DCI began to use this software in 2004.[6] Secure Computing Corporation, which produces SmartFilter, say that their customers can protect their 'organization from the risks associated with employee Internet use with SmartFilter® Web filtering. By controlling inappropriate Internet use with SmartFilter, organizations can reduce legal liability, enhance Web security, increase productivity, and preserve bandwidth for business-related activities. SmartFilter puts you in control'.[7] This as well as the cooperation of many companies and corporations in search of profit with states across the globe – like Google's early acquiescence to PRC demands – has challenged the myth of the uncontrollability of the internet.

Since 2000, the Iranian state has produced lists of sites and blogs to be censored. A report by the BBC announced that a list of 15,000 sites had already been drawn up by the government in 2003 and sent to internet service providers to be blocked[8] And in December 2003, the Iranian government finally admitted that such a 'blacklist' existed. However, the then minister of communication, Ahmad Motamedi, suggested that all major Iranian ISPs must only block those websites and nothing else. He also announced that the government had purchased new software to make the censorship more effective and precise.[9] Many private ISPs were closed down for not installing the filtering system, including five in Tabriz.[10] Under pressure while attending the World Summit on the Information Society summit in Geneva, President Mohammad Khatami insisted that the country only blocked access to 240 'pornographic and immoral websites, rather than the reported 15,000 of which many were about news and politics'.[11] He said the ban applied to only those sites 'incompatible with Islam' and a government official added that 'all political sites are free'. He added that the government would publish the blacklist.[12] The list was never published, but many organisations and sites have tracked the process of filtering and updated lists of sites that have been banned. *Open Initiatives*, for example, has provided lists of blocked websites and blogs presented by various agencies. Comparing the lists provided by StopCensoringUs[13] and Reporters sans Frontières[14] in August 2004, in a report entitled 'Internet Content Filtering in Iran: Verification of

Reported Banned Websites', *Open Initiatives* concluded that 'at the present time, Iran seems mostly concerned with filtering Iranian, and mostly Farsi, content'.[15] The same report confirmed that Iran was engaged in extensive internet content filtering that extended well beyond the authority's claim that they were only concerned about pornography – to include many political, religious and social weblogs. The sites of many oppositional groups in exile were blocked, such as *www.rezapahlavi.org* (the site of the eldest son of the last Shah), *www.jebhemelli.net* (National Front), *www.fadai.org* (Organisation of Iranian People's Fedayyan, Majority), *www.fadaian.org* (The Organization of Iranian People's Fedayee Guerrillas) and *www.tudehpartyiran.org* (Communist Party). So too were many news sites, including *emrooz*, *gooya*, *roshangari* and *peiknet*. According to the same report there were 69 filtered blogs on the list, mostly written in Persian. *Open Initiatives'* analysis showed that the majority of global sites remained unfiltered except for those focused on gay life styles[16].

According to reports published by stop.censoring.us, a site maintained by Iranian blogger Hossein Derakhshan with help from other bloggers, Iranian state actions also included the filtering of the collective news blogs, *Sobhaneh*[17] and the filtering of BlogSpot in June 2004. In 2004, there were reports the Iranian telecom was ordering ISPs to filter Orkut, the popular social networking website, as well as blog providers such as Blogger and PersianBlog. According to a report by *IT Iran* in early January 2005, Pars Online – the biggest private ISP in Iran – was filtering some of the major blogging services, including TypePad, LiveJournal, Xanga, Pitas, SkyBlog, CrimsonBlog, UBlog, Tripod and Weblogs.com.[18] This, *IT Iran* reported, was in addition to regular filtering of BlogSpot. In response to reports of clampdowns on blogs and blog service providers, the head of the Communication Department of Allameh Tabatabai University in Tehran, in an interview with Iranian Student Agency (ISNA), urged the government to stop using laws similar to the Press Law to regulate the blogosphere. He suggested that 'there are thousands of weblogs in Iran to express the personal thoughts and beliefs of their writers as a different means of communication', and argued that a new legal framework is needed that could safeguard the freedom of bloggers.[19] Despite protests by bloggers the filtering of some of the major blog services continued. Major ISPs continued to filter Blogger, BlogSpot and Flickr and – in August 2005 – Blogrolling that was owned by the Canada-based Tucows.

Trying to control content is especially difficult. The Iranian state is also trying to control the technological infrastructure itself, perhaps an easier approach.

Control of Speed

In October 2006, new regulations issued by the Radio Transmissions and Regulations Organization of the Ministry of Communications ordered all ISPs in Iran to limit their download speeds to 128 kbps for all residential clients and internet cafes.[20] The new law effectively banned the possibility of offering high-speed broadband at a time when many customers were demanding higher speed access. It was widely seen as trying to limit users' ability to download foreign cultural products, especially music and films, and to organize political opposition. According to one report,[21] the Ministry claimed that this was only a temporary measure and would be lifted once criteria and regulations for high-speed access had been designed and ratified. But Mohamad Soleimani, then Minister for Information, Communication and Technology (the new name for the Ministry for Post, Telephone and Telegraph) suggested that the new regulation was an experiment and if successful would remain in place. He said that 'reducing the speed of Internet to 128 kbps will not create a problem for domestic users since according to our analysis they don't need more than that. . . . However, there are certain users who might need a higher speed and we will find a solution for their problem'.[22] As reported by the *Guardian* the move came as part of a renewed attack on cultural freedom and the government hyperbole of 'cultural invasion' that included another round of campaigning against satellite dishes and the closing down of yet another reformist newspaper, the daily *Shargh*. Parastoo Dokoohaki, a prominent Iranian blogger, told the *Guardian* that the move was designed to foil the government's opponents. 'If you want to announce a gathering in advance, you won't see it mentioned on official websites and newspapers would announce it too late. Therefore, you upload it anonymously and put the information out. Banning high-speed links would limit that facility. Despite having the telecoms facilities, fibre-optic technology and internet infrastructure, the authorities want us to be undeveloped'.[23]

Censorship Area
Speed Limit
128kbps

This new regulation actually angered many officials and MPs including Ramazan-ali Sedeghzadeh, chairman of the Parliamentary Telecommunications Committee, who complained that the reasons for introducing the new measure were not clear and that he wanted an explanation. He suggested that modernising Iran required high-speed internet access.[24] Interestingly, at the time of introducing this ban, according to BBC Persian, Iran was reported as having around 250,000 broadband users who were receiving their services from 11 companies licensed to provide broadband without any competition from state-owned ISPs.[25] It is possible to speculate that slow speeds would also allow state ISPs to enter, if not take over, the business.

Bloggers also responded to this law with anger. Parviz Zahed[26] asked why such limitations were not introduced for water and electricity that were in short supply. He moaned that the internet in Iran has the speed of a dead tortoise and that 'perhaps in this way, "poverty" (read "poverty of information") is equally distributed. This is what "equality" really means'. Another blogger in a short and sarcastic entry[27] suggested: 'maybe the gentlemen assume by setting a speed limit they can reduce the numbers of accidents on the roads'. Saeed Razzaghi, in an entry on 12 October 2006,[28] informed his readers of this new regulation, saying that so far Iranians had faced filtering, but now they could only dream about broadband. He wondered if 'maybe this new regulation is part of the preparation for international sanctions against Iran? It's difficult for me to imagine surfing the net with speed of less than 128 kbps. I hope in sanctioning Iran they'll leave internet alone. I think my comment is a little bit political. But I had no option; if I didn't write this note I would have had a heart attack'. This blogger assumed external powers were involved in regulating the speed of the net. Others assumed the opposite, that with the increasing popularity of P2P file-sharing among Iranian users and the limits of filtering in stopping the downloading of 'immoral' (gheir-e akhlaghi) material, limiting the speed would make accessing and downloading such materials more difficult. Yet others pointed to the contradiction in Iranian internet policies. Pooya, who maintains asemannet,[29] argued that Iran was moving in the opposite direction to other countries in relation to internet speed but also, and more importantly, that this regulation contradicted the goal sets by the Fourth Economic Development Plan of the Islamic Republic in which both public and private companies were given the task of creating 1.5 million high-speed internet ports across the country. Indeed, according to the DCI website, the goals of the company in the fifth year of the Fourth Economic Development Plan included increasing the number of internet users to 23.5 million people; connecting more than 10,000 villages to the worldwide network;

strengthening the core of the network; encouraging and facilitating the participation of the private sector in country's IT industry in a healthy competitive environment; and providing the suitable infrastructure for IT activities.[30] Even some Iranian MPs set up a website under the banner of 'More Speed More Progress'[31] to campaign for better broadband access and asked concerned users and activists to display their logo on their sites and blogs.[32]

In 2009/2010, the speed restriction remains a major limitation on Iran's internet development and one of the biggest frustrations facing many internet users, something that was mentioned spontaneously many times in conversation with people about the internet in Iran. It had a huge impact on coverage of the June 2009 election and post-election aftermath, when slow speed made it very hard to upload and download video footage of demonstrations and other events (see the last chapter).

Arrests, Even Deaths

When other controls fail, then individuals are targeted. Over the years, a number of bloggers and journalists have been arrested, imprisoned and, most recently and tragically, have died in prison. Reporters sans Frontières has maintained such a list.

We do not wish to provide another such list, and simply note a few key moments:

- The detention of two bloggers accused of maintaining an 'erotic' blog in July 2004.
- The detention of two journalists/bloggers for assisting the reformist websites Rouydad and Emrooz.[33]
- The arrest of blogger/journalist Omid Memarian[34] who maintained his 'Iranian Prospect' blog in both English and Persian.

- The arrest of Hoder, November 2008, on his return to Iran; he remains imprisoned and untried after over 500 days, April 2010.
- Sadly, in April 2009 Omid Reza Misayafi become the first known Iranian blogger to die in jail.

Criminalising the Net

For 30 years the Iranian state has tried to frame all public matters and policy according to what they regard as 'Islamic'. In the case of internet, as it was for films and the press, users are set the task of promoting state-defined policies and to refrain from producing what are perceived to be anti-Islamic values. Yet, because of factionalism within the Iranian state, the expediency of the system as a whole and the continuous challenges from social movements, activists and journalists, such policies and measures have come under attack and been revised, ignored or shelved all together. In most cases the authorities have accepted that there are ambiguities and problems, as is evident in the debate about internet speed, and have promised to set up yet another committee or body to address or resolve them. Yet changes have come as a result of pressure from below, the impossibility of reinforcing such regulations – as in the case of satellite dishes, which are formally illegal but widely used – or the degree of security that the authorities have felt after trying to contain a specific crisis or threat to the system as a whole.

The increased activities of various ministries including the judiciary and the new wave of policy initiatives and attacks in 2006 and 2008 came in the context of mounting internal and external pressures. Mahmoud Ahmadinejad's government faced rising inflation, which meant a further decline of living standards, triggering a wave of strikes by workers and teachers, students and women disillusioned with the new president who had come to power on the back of promises of more equal distribution of resources. From the outside, there was growing pressure from the Bush government's rhetoric of 'exporting democracy' and concern about Iran's supposed nuclear weapons programmes, so that the spectre of war lurked.

In 2001, when the government first introduced its internet policy, access to the internet was limited and the amount of Persian language content was not great. The increased availability of internet, the rise of the Persian blogosphere and the migration of large numbers of journalist to the net after the closure of many reformists newspaper (see Chapter Seven) made the net a much more serious issue for the state, which elaborated new internet policies in 2006. Three key regulations were introduced in 2006. One dealt specifically with blogs and required that all bloggers register their blogs, a rule introduced in

August 2006 and brought into force in January 2007. The other two regulations both introduced in November 2006 aimed to make the control of the internet more manageable and systematic by specifying previous regulation as well as specifying the punishment for cyber crime (Cyber Crime Bill).

These regulations, as *Open Initiatives* reported,[35] were a response to a directive of the Supreme Cultural Revolution Council (SCRC) to manage internet activity 'while considering individual rights and safeguarding Islamic, national and cultural values'. The main bodies behind these regulations and in charge of enforcing them were the usual suspects: the Ministries of Islamic Culture and Guidance (MICG), Justice and Information. In terms of licensing, all websites and blogs that did not have a required license or obtain one from the MICG would be considered illegal.

The Cyber Crimes Bill highlighted what many ISPs in Iran had feared since 2001, that they were to be held criminally liable for the content they carried. Under this law, ISPs that did not follow existing regulations and failed to filter specified websites and pages could be suspended, lose their licence or face hefty penalties and prison sentences. Article 18 of the bill required ISPs to ensure that 'forbidden' content is not displayed on their servers, that they immediately inform law enforcement agencies of any violations, that they retain the content as evidence and that they restrict access to the prohibited content. The bill also included provisions for the protection and disclosure of confidential data and information as well as the publishing of obscene content.[36]

This law effectively reproduced the existing Press Law which had been revised in 2000 to take account of the growing criticism of many semi-independent newspapers and their online versions and required all 'publishers' to obtain a license. As was the case in the press law, insulting Islam and religious leaders and institutions, as well as fomenting national discord and disunity and promoting prostitution and immoral behaviours, all figured in the new internet regulations and ISPs and users could be punished for not abiding by these rules. Some of the articles in the Cyber Crime Law are similar to various attempts across the world to prevent invasion of privacy and control child pornography. Articles 16 and 18, for example, set the punishment of three months to three years prison sentence and fines of 2–15 million rials (US$200–1,500) for these crimes: producing/storing/distributing sexual images of minors under 18; encouraging and forcing minors to participate in sexual acts, suicide or taking drugs and, in the case of Article 18, publishing visual and audio materials of private affairs of individuals without their permission. The latter seen as a response to the circulation in 2006 of privately-made camcorder footage of Zahra Ebrahimi, an actress, having sex with her then-boyfriend that was posted on the internet and widely downloaded.

Closer analysis of the filtering and banning of sites demonstrate the contradictions, institutional interests and the ad hoc nature of some of the recent rulings. The closure of the conservative site, *Baztab*, is a good example. *Baztab* was close to the former commander of the Revolutionary Guards, Mohsen Rezai, and had been highly critical of President Ahmadinejad. On 12 February 2007, it became the first site reported to have been blocked by the November 2006 regulations. *Baztab* was accused of publishing 'false' information, 'violating the Constitution' and attacking 'personal privacy' and 'the country's unity', after it published reports on Iran's nuclear industry and on corruption which angered President Ahmadinejad.[37] The judiciary took a different view and ruled against the ban on *Baztab*. Yet *Baztab* was banned again on 19 March 2007 only to have the ban lifted again a day later, and banned again on 29 March. The president's supporters had issued 15 lawsuits against it, and the charges were always the same. According to *Open Initiatives*, this incident sparked a debate within Iranian legal and media circles over the authority of the Committee in Charge of Determining Unauthorised Sites, and whether as an executive body, it was improperly involved in making legislative or judicial decisions according to the Constitution. The *Baztab* editors protested against the ban, insisting that parliament was responsible for anything to do with control of the media and that the November decree was 'illegal' and 'unconstitutional'. This was a view shared by 136 MPs, who in a letter to Ahmadinejad, on 21 February 2007, demanded the lifting of the ban imposed on 20 February against *Baztab*.[38]

Closing Proxies, Censoring Keywords

In addition to these modes of control, there are further methods of censorship.

One method is to close all ports that have been used by savvy internet users to bypass filtering systems. In the past few years, internet users have managed to break through the existing filtering system by using proxy servers. However, since 2004 the committees set up to control and monitor the net (Committee in Charge of Determination of Unauthorised Websites) have provided ISPs with regular lists of proxy servers to be censored. According to a report by *Open Initiatives*,[39] among the sites banned in Iran were around 30 proxy servers and hacking sites. It is interesting to note that the use of such proxies burgeoned again during the summer of 2009, when many young Iranians received a crash course in how to become citizen journalists.

Another method is to censor keywords in URLs, yet another obligation that ICPs and ISPs have to meet. For example, many Iranians still use pre-paid cards to access the internet in Iran, but the cards are designed so that searching words such as 'women', 'birth' or 'sex' while using search engines such as Google is impossible. One colleague complained about not being able to look up a postal address in Middlesex. It matters not if the search is related to science, history or literature. One blogger[40] pointed out other banned words include condom, Annmarie, Chandice, chastity, bath, belly and ebony. But ironically, and as the same source suggests, while one can visit a site with the URL of 'www.gettingpregnant.co.uk' one cannot search for the term 'pregnant' on the internet! The banning of the search term 'women' generated a campaign supported by many bloggers that employed the slogan 'censorship is indecent, not women'. Under pressure from campaigners and various organisations, the Iranian judiciary announced in May 2006 that it had been reinvestigating the keywords banned in Iran and would revise the list according to their findings.[41] Some bloggers reported that the ban on 'women' had been lifted in December 2006.[42] Using filtering systems of course reduces the speed of the internet access. Most internet users still use dial-up services due to the limited availability and cost of broadband. Iran CSOs Training & Research Centre believes that this is yet another form of censorship and another method used by the government to restrict access to internet. It suggested that increased availability of broadband would jeopardise the state monopoly in broadcasting.

Closure of Cafenets

In addition to these stringent controls, there have been periodic crackdowns on internet cafes. Some of the earliest crackdowns on internet cafes, 400 closed in May 2001, were made on the grounds that they did not have permits while it was also to do with the cheaper price for VoIP international calls that these were offering customer in comparison to the standard telephony system.

In 2004, police in Tehran raided more than 430 internet cafes and other shops in a campaign against 'inappropriate and un-Islamic conduct'. The police closed down 25 internet cafes and gave warnings to 170 cafe owners for 'using immoral computer games and storing obscene photos', and for the presence of women without 'proper *hejab*' on the premises.

Once again, in December 2007, 24 internet cafes were shut down during a police operation in Tehran, and 23 people, including 11 women, were arrested for 'immoral behaviour' (RSF 2007). This was widely seen as partial reinforcement of the official campaign launched in April 2007 against women violating the Islamic dress code by wearing 'western-style' dress such as tight trousers or high boots, then regarded as 'inappropriate attire'.

Analysts often argue that the perceived stability of the regime can be measured in the amount of hair visible from under women's scarves; the more secure the regime, the more hair that is allowed to be shown. Perhaps the activity of internet cafes functions as the same kind of index. They are clearly sites where the regime can act out its repressive force and provide a show of strength when it deems necessary. These repetitive acts hardly make for a stable, accessible online environment.

As another response to the privatised, uncontrollable environments that cafenets were perceived to be, the government, in 2006, proposed to set up internet kiosks in Isfahan and other cities, creating a 'national internet'. Each kiosk was supposed to have a monitor and an industrial keyboard, and people were to use them with a prepaid calling card at a cost of 100 rials (less than $0.02) per minute. These did not really take off.

Blogistan Debates Control of Blogistan

Iranians were very quick to establish online monitoring of government predations on the Web and to note problems. In 2004, websites were noting the problems of 'access denied' and suggesting ways around this.[43]

The image below became quite familiar to Iranians trying to access new sites, blogs or external pages.

Access Denied!

As we have mentioned, the Ministry of Culture and Islamic Guidance announced that, based on a ruling introduced in the summer of 2006 (29 Mordad 1385), the owners of blogs and sites had to register their web site or blog within two months from 1 January 2007.[44] At the time of registering, private information such as name, family name, identity card and telephone numbers would be recorded as well. This ruling indicated, among other things, the state's perception and recognition of the significance of blogging. Of course, it elicited a big response from bloggers.

In a BBC interview[45] Omid Memarian[46] argued that the new law would only encourage more bloggers to go underground. He pointed out that the law was only effective in targeting those who already are known and write under their own name and therefore abide by the law. He argued that the purpose of the new law was to stifle intellectual debate in Iran and to crush the blogosphere: 'This legislation would mean that every blogger who is an intellectual, a journalist, a social activist, or who writes under his own name would have to blog in line with government taste'. Another Iranian blogger/journalist Parastoo Dokoohaki (*zan neveshet*)[47] connected control of the internet with broader political control of the media:

> *getting rid of all sorts of private media is one of the objectives of this government. Look at the newspapers. Every day you see fewer and fewer exclusive news stories. Do you know why? It's because government officials don't welcome reporters. At the moment, websites are the only outlet for those who care about freedom of information and for those who work in news. Ministers want to limit and control websites, because they want to get rid of the media. They have not given the issue any real thought, because destroying the media is tantamount to destroying the government. Is this practical? It would be too optimistic to say it's not possible to restrict websites. Just look at China. There, no stone is left unturned in the quest for media control'.*

Kamangir, another blogger, suggested[48] 'the registrant is even asked for his/her cellphone number, probably in case big news starts spreading and they need to call you to let you know that you really don't want to talk about it'. In a post dated on the day that the process was to begin, Kamangir argues with typical Iranian sarcasm:

> *When we talk about rules, in Iran, sometimes we do not really mean rules. Take the new mandatory law which literally forces all bloggers and website owners to register. The new law gives a two month period, after which the unregistered sites will be said to have an 'unknown identity'. What the consequences of having such a site will be, no one knows yet. The registration process begins with an*

email address, about which the rule has specific guidelines. According to the how-to-register, deliberately given only in Persian, sites which have a domain name (say www.kamangir.com) need to create an email address starting with 'info@' (say info@kamangir.com). They will be contacted using that email address. But send an email to info@ahmadinejad.ir to see it doesn't exist. What does that mean? It means Ahmadinejad has not registered his blog yet.'

Celebrated Iranian blogger, *Khurshid Khanum*, Lady Sun, responding to why she had not reacted to this law, employed a well-known proverb in Iran in her argument that *'Javab-e ablahan khamushi ast'*; 'the best answer to stupid people (those responsible for this law) is silence', further pointing out that 'if they want to continue to filter us as they have already done and will do, why should we bother to go register our blog?'[49] Leila Mouri, in her blog *Raha* (Free),[50] questioned the blogistan's silence. She worried about the vagueness and general wording of the new law, saying that 'it is precisely this vagueness which is always used to silence the press and now the target is websites and blogs' and suggested that the blogistan had to decide how to deal with this issue. One response to the new law was the creation of the Committee of Blogging Rights Advocates (COBRA), which explained itself saying:

> Our main and only goal is to defend the natural right of open and free thinking and sharing opinions. This committee is not related to any political group, party or wing, neither Iranian nor foreign ones. We are just trying to defend the most obvious and natural right of humans, freedom of opinions.

Influenced by previous collective actions of bloggers[51] the group designed a special logo 'for the unity of the bloggers against any kind of illegal limitation' and asked all bloggers to put it on their blogs on January 30.[52]

Another effort came from Nima Akbarpour in his weblog *Osyan* (Revolt) who designed another logo that read 'I will not register my site!' and again asked bloggers to put it on their blogs.[53] One blogger called the new law the 'military government in Blogistan' (*hokomat-e nezami dar weblog-abad*).[54] Another labelled it as *estebdad*[55], oppression. While yet another blogger in an entry entitled 'Censor Cuts the Sharp Knife of Our Critique' suggested that the new law and censorship in general would not lead to the destruction of struggle for democracy, but rather it would change the legal struggle into a clandestine one.[56]

Amin Taghikhani, a member of Cloob.com (an Iranian virtual community around the world)[57] posted a letter objecting to the new law on PersianPetition, a subsidiary of PersianBlog, the biggest weblog service provider in Iran.[58] However according to Reza Valizadeh, a journalist and writer of a blog (Station: Literature and Communications[59]) even the possibility of publishing this letter was denied to 420,000 bloggers, since *Blogfa*, the second biggest weblog provider in Iran had closed, preventing the distribution of this letter to all of its members.[60] Nikahang Kowsar[61] a well-known Iranian cartoonist captured the meaning of the new law as well as the frustration of bloggers in a new cartoon:

Where is your license? Cartoon by Nikahang Kowsar

Hacking and 'Filter-Shekan'

Control produces resistance and hackers are engaged in what is often for them rather amusing games with the regime.

Many users of the internet in Iran also use widely available 'filter-shekan', literally filter breakers, to go round government controls. Indeed, such evasive measures are seen as part and parcel of democratic politics. As the Iran Political Club posted in December 2004, 'We will not allow the Islamist regime to censor the Internet. They figure a high tech method to censor thoughts,

Jadi, Promoting filter-breakers

we figure a high tech method to fight back and free the thoughts and trade of ideas' and they provided a list of proxy servers.[62]

The widespread nature of such practices is vividly shown in the photograph of the back of a public bus seat, posted by Jadi in December 2006.[63]

By 2008, more sophisticated tools were available, produced by well-trained university graduates. There were programmes for Firefox that enabled users to circumvent the filter that blocked access to Flickr, the popular photo-sharing website. Another extension turned Firefox itself into a proxy that bypassed censorship on popular Web 2.0 websites such as YouTube, del.icio.us, Flickr, Technorati.com, Friendster.com, livejournal.com, MySpace, Hi5 and others, many of which were barred in Iran. Imagine the potential for a legitimate software industry in Iran!

Within less than one hour of the BBC World Service website being blocked in January 2006, one was being offered ways in to the site by people, and not all young, eager to be helpful. A widespread joke notes that government officials themselves use these filter-breakers.

Free filter-breaking software, Iran, July 2009

And, if such techniques had been the terrain of fairly sophisticated Net users, in the summer of 2009, they were even more widely circulated and publicised, with numerous YouTube videos and Facebook posts explaining how to circumvent Net censorship and how to become a citizen journalist.

Control of Mobile Telephony

As mobile telephony swept across Iran, people found many intriguing uses for them. Iranians are delighting in using SMS to send jokes – political, dirty and dirty political – as well as informational and organisational messages. In April 2007, Iran's telecommunications ministry announced that it would start filtering 'immoral' video and audio messages sent via mobile phones. The ministry was instructed by the Supreme Council of the Cultural Revolution to buy the equipment needed to prevent any misuse of Multimedia Messaging Service (MMS).[64] Yet in the autumn of 2008–09, one could travel the underground, open up Bluetooth and receive a welter of explicit pornography, gift of other travellers. Clearly the frontiers of Iranian cultural struggle are endlessly played out on new screens and platforms, suggesting that the game is perhaps as important as its winning.

Colonisation

But perhaps the most powerful weapon that the dominant faction has used in regard to the internet in general and blogging in particular is to colonise it. The regime has recognised the usefulness of the internet as a tool for propaganda and furthering their policies and aims. In that respect, they have embraced technology and there are many religious and conservative websites (Sreberny and Khiabany, 2007).

In 2008, religious figures began to speak out about the importance of the internet for religious viewpoints. At the end of the year, the Islamic Revolutionary Guards Corps announced a project to launch 10,000 blogs for the paramilitary *Basij* forces.[65]

The IGRC's official press organ, *Sobh Sadegh*, wrote that it considered the internet and other digital devices including SMS as a threat to be controlled. It announced that the 10,000 blogs would promote revolutionary ideas. The IRGC consider the internet an instrument for a 'velvet revolution' and warned that foreign countries have invested in this tool to topple the Islamic Regime.

Thus, it is that the maps of the Iranian blogosphere produced by John Kelly of Morningside Analytics over one year show a marked increase in religious and conservative blogs.[66]

Conclusion

The problems with the Iranian media and ICT environments are intertwined with the broader legal framework in the country. The Islamic Republic Constitution, which allows and recognises political participation and keeps alive the rhetoric of the popular revolutionary mobilisation of 1979, nonetheless keeps an ultimate veto for the ruling clergy on the basis that sovereignty belongs not to the people but to god, and in reality to his representatives and the guardians of his will. There is nothing in the holy text as to what Islamic media in general and the internet in particular should look like. What has been offered is made-up law in the interest of the Islamic Republic, and the press has been regulated and controlled as such. The control of the internet in Iran is not, as the factionalism of the Iranian state and objections by number of MPs to recent rulings demonstrate, part of the legislature. Rather it has been regarded as an integral part of the political power structure in which it is placed, not outside of the state and within civil society, as users, bloggers, activists and many officials want.

There is little doubt that this new technology offers lively forums for discussion on many political and social issues in Iran and is itself the subject of fierce debate. In response to the re-emergence of homegrown dissent and the increasing popularity of unofficial programming and content on satellite and the internet, and the threat of war and imperialist intervention on many of Iran's borders, the Iranian state is increasingly wary of losing control and does its best to suppress the potential of these new communications technologies. At the same time, regime rhetoric and actions show that it recognises the use of ICTS for national development, for propaganda and educative purposes. The paradoxes and contradictions in Iranian ICT policy, especially in relation to blogs, are evident. Such are the twists and turns of a modernising theocracy in the contemporary global environment. However, the case of Iran also shows that the claim that the world is entering into a distinctly new epoch where time, space, political authority, economies of scale and social relations will all become irrelevant is not grounded in reality. It illustrates that claims about the necessary and simply impact of the internet on prosperity and democracy in developing countries are illusory and naive.

In examining the state's responses to the emergence of the internet, we suggested that the state remains significant as the primary actor in engineering political legitimacy and the definer of the 'national' character and culture. While much of this political legitimacy rests on the state's use of force as its ultimate sanction, the struggle to claim the monopoly over the means of symbolic violence plays an increasing role, and in the current climate cannot be separated from the former. The contradictory cultural policies in Iran cannot be explained in terms of the general ideals of 'Islam', despite the 'Islamic' veneer that wraps many of the policy documents, but rather as the evolution of different periods of the post-revolutionary polity. The contradiction between development and control, privatisation and Islamization, imperatives of the market and political expediency explains the intriguing and undoubtedly confusing trends in development of the internet and blogging in Iran.

4 Gender, Sexuality and Blogging

ONE OF THE MOST remarkable features of modern Iran is women's multidimensional presence in public life, achieved through their own growing awareness and struggles for full citizenship and equal rights. The emergence of women's blogging is the contemporary form of the social struggle for women's rights of all kinds.

Even though historically the traditional, conservative *ulema* favoured keeping Iranian women invisible in the public sphere and confining them to private spaces, their remarkable participation during the revolution was such that the newly established Islamic Republic had to backtrack on their previous positions. One of the major incidents that had led to an early confrontation between Khomeini and the Shah was the regime's decision to grant voting rights to Iranian women in 1963. Notwithstanding the fact that under dictatorships, the right to vote does not count for much, Khomeini objected in principle to a woman's right to be elected or to elect, and in a telegram to the Shah, Khomeini accused him of total disregard for Islam and the *ulema*. Khomeini was exiled soon after, but with his triumphant return to Iran and some 16 years after condemning the Pahlavi dynasty for granting women's political rights, he stated that 'women have the right to intervene in politics. It is their duty . . . Islam is a political religion. In Islam, everything, even prayer, is political' (Azadeh Kian, 1997:76).

Thus, in contrast to the conservative thinking of the *Ulema*, the revolutionary rhetoric of 1978–9 and the Islamists' need to expand their support base actually paved the way for the participation of traditional women in politics. Women's access to education, political institutions and public domains that had been generally closed to them influenced them immensely and made them aware of the contradictions and the existing legal and moral limits to the wider participation of women. Once on the street as members of the revolutionary *umma*, once instrumental in the eight-year Iran–Iraq war, it was hard for the regime to persuade them to go back to their traditional roles and lives. The politicisation of traditional women raised their expectations – of themselves, their families and of the republic they helped build and consolidate. So, what was originally mobilised to undermine the secular, middle-class women's movement in Iran became in itself an important force in exposing the limits of *Sharia* in modern Iran.

Iranian women have challenged patriarchal policies and structures in a number of ways. Although the new post-revolutionary state immediately began to curb many women's rights and achievements made during the Pahlavi period, the reality of post-revolutionary society, the contradictions within the new state and the realities of 'everyday life' in Iran have produced women's challenges to the state. As Asef Bayat argues

> there are perhaps different ways in which Muslim women under authoritarian regimes may, consciously or without being aware, defy, resist, negotiate, or even circumvent gender discrimination – not necessarily by resorting to extraordinary and overarching 'movement' identified by deliberate collective protest and informed by mobilization theory and strategy, but by being involved in ordinary daily practice of life, by working, engaging in sports, jogging, singing, or running for public offices. This involves deploying the power of presence, the assertion of collective will in spite of all odds, by refusing to exit, circumventing the constraints, and discovering new spaces of freedom to make oneself heard, seen, and felt.
>
> (Bayat, 2007:161)

It is through such mechanisms that many patriarchal policies have been challenged and the state forced to retreat.

One such challenge is the development of more democratic and women-friendly interpretations of Islamic law and teachings. Some of the early framing of gender debate in Iran brushed aside women's movements and organisations. Equally significant, as Hamid Dabashi reminds us while assessing Soroush's writings and arguments, it 'actually intensified the further Islamisation of Iranian political culture by presenting the principal theoretical challenge to the Islamic Republic in a deeply cultivated Islamic language' (Dabashi, 2007:192).

Bayat suggests that in much of the discussion about the nature and characteristics of women's activities and resistance, the debate was dominated by West-centric models of social movements that framed the struggle into two clear and opposing positions '– either there was a women's movement or there was not – as if alternative forms of struggles beyond the conventional contentious politics were unthinkable' (Bayat, 2007:169).

A Brief History of Women's Struggles Before 1979

The history of debates about the rights of women cannot be separated from the broader history of struggle for democratic rights in Iran. Similarly, the emergence of blogging cannot be separated from the broader history of the press in Iran and the emergence of a women's press, which has experienced periods of great expansion as well as of fierce control.

The first ever woman's publication in Iran was launched almost a century ago. Before that there were a number of educated, middle-class women who contributed regularly – sometimes using pseudonyms or, more often, anonymously – to the general press. The Constitutional Revolution of 1906–10 and the evolving concerns for law, rights and equality all increased the visibility of women in public life and expanded their role in public culture, especially print culture. Women's specialist publications emerged as a result of the new openness during the Constitutional Revolution and in parallel with the establishment of new schools, associations and public spaces that educated and raised the awareness of Iranian women.[1] According to one study, between 1907 and 1913, more than 60 schools for girls and a number of women's organisations were established in Tehran.[2]

During this period, eight women's publications emerged. The first was an eight-page weekly called *Danesh* (Knowledge) edited by a woman activist Dr. Kahal, followed by a fortnightly pictorial entitled *Shekofeh* (Blossom) edited by Mozin Al-Saltaneh, the founder of *Mazininah* School. In 1919, the first ever publication to use the word 'women' in its title – *Zaban-e-Zanan* (Women's Tongue) – was launched under the editorship of Sedigheh Dolatabadi, with *Nameh-Banovan* (Ladies' Letter) publishing under the slogan 'Women are the first teachers of men'. The monthly *Jahan-e-Zanan* (Women's World) under the editorship of Fakhr Afagh Parsa created a storm[3] because it was designed to educate women, teach them the history of women's struggle and encourage them to develop their potential. It was denounced as antireligious and the editor and her husband were duly regarded as dangerous and were exiled to the city of Arak, thereby making Parsa the first woman editor to be punished for her journalistic activity, the first in a long line that stretches to the present day.

These publications played a major role in bringing previously 'private' matters into the public domain – an issue that contemporary blogging is pushing still further – and spreading knowledge among Iranian women, because they covered topics in the literature, history, culture and politics of

Iran as well as about Europe and the rest of the world. Many of these titles were set up with the help and aid of male activists, and the editors and contributors were usually wives, daughters or sisters of well-established political figures of the time, making these family businesses.

After the collapse of the Qajar Dynasty and the establishment of the Pahlavi Regime in 1921, there was a downturn in the liveliness of print culture in general and the women's press in particular. The 1940s brought a new wave of optimism and a renewed interest in journalism. The political conditions paved the way for a new generation and a more radical press. The three major forces then in Iran – Religious, Nationalists and Socialists – all had a strong presence in publishing. The 'second wave women's press'[4] lasted from 1941 through the popular movement for oil nationalisation led by Dr. Mosadeq that sent the British packing and led to the Shah's deposition, only to have him reinstated on the crest of a CIA-led coup in 1953. This was a golden age of the press. As many as 373 publications, albeit 70 of them anti-Mosadeq, were published during the oil nationalisation movement,[5] including many women's titles. Among these were *Alam-e-Zanan* (Universe of Women) a monthly magazine published by the Office of Publishing and Publicity of the British embassy in Tehran as part of its modernisation mission; and *Rastakhiz-e-Iran* (Resurrection of Iran) a family-run daily published in Tehran that devoted a quarter of its pages to women's issues.

Left-wing organisations played a major role in this period. Their calls for justice, equality and freedom in a society ravaged by centuries of despotic rule and poverty attracted massive support and sympathy. The women's organisation of the *Tudeh Party*, the official Communist party of Iran, published *Bidari-e-Ma* (Our Awakening) edited by Zahra Eskandari, which hit the newsstand in the summer of 1945 with the slogan 'We also have some rights in this house'. *Jahan-e-Zanan* edited by woman activist Najm el-Hajiah Hoshmand developed into a weekly publication and also became an official organ of the *Tudeh* Women's Organisation, published until the 1953 coup and reappearing after the 1979 revolution. Other titles included the weekly *Zan-e-Emrooz* (Woman of Today); a monthly magazine entitled *Banu* (Lady); *Neday-e-Zan* (Woman's Proclamation); *Nezhat* (Purity); *Hoghugh-e-Zanan* (Women's Rights) and *Jahan-e-Taban* (Shining World). It is important to note that in 1952 alone, prior to the CIA-led coup, the number of women involved in the press exceeded the number of women who were active in this field in the first 11 years of the Islamic Republic.[6]

With the overthrow of the Mosadeq government and the reinstatement of Mohammad Reza Pahlavi, all political and cultural organisations came under attack and many political parties and publications were banned. It would take another revolution to bring back those glorious days of a free press, in which the women's press also flourished. From the mid-1950s to 1979 only a handful of publications were allowed in the market. A number of women continued to work as journalists, editors, managing directors, photographers and so on. However, most were either employed in specialist/scientific publications affiliated to different ministries or attached to official women's groups linked to the ruling elite. Specialist publications had a low circulation and targeted a niche readership. The official organs of the ruling groups, despite carrying some useful materials, were the mouthpiece of the regime and had little respect.

Two big privately owned publishing firms slowly came to dominate the market during this period, with rival titles in fields such as youth, sports and children. Women's magazines were important titles in their stable. *Etelaat-e Banovan* (Ladies' Etelaat) was first published by the press firm *Etelaat* in 1957. Its pages were filled with gossip, celebrities, the royal family, cookery, health, beauty and housekeeping. This weekly magazine was published until 1979 and then publication was ceased for almost two years. It was relaunched in 1981 under the editorship of Zahra Rahnavard, one of the prominent Muslim women after 1979 and wife of Mir-Hussein Mousavi, who was prime minister between 1981 and 1988.[7] Their roles in the June 2009 election were crucial (see the last chapter).

The other big firm, *Kayhan*, launched its woman's title only in 1964 when *Zan-e Rooz* (Today's Woman) was published as a colour weekly. The licence holder was Moustafa Mesbahzadeh, and the magazine was managed by his wife Fourough, although it had a male editor. It soon overtook its main rival and became the most popular magazine in Iran. Adverts and pictures covered more than half of its pages, it avoided politics and devoted most of its pages to cooking, health and beauty, family matters, gossip and beauty contests in Iran and around the world. Its news pages were devoted to the royal family and foreign visitors, especially famous women visiting Iran, with an occasional serious article, say on changes in family law.[8] Its politics matched the policies of the Pahlavi regime. In the early 1970s, with the increased activities of left-wing groups in Iran, the regime tried to discredit Marxism and to neutralise religious groups by portraying itself as Islamic. The magazine pages started to report on the Shah and his family visiting holy cities and produced articles on changing Islamic fashions that could take the place of the *chadoor* (long veil).

In the heat of the 1979 Revolution the magazine made a u-turn, became critical of the Pahlavi regime's policies and denounced all role models that had been promoted in the previous years as inauthentic, corrupt and commercial. Only 23 issues of the new *Zan-e Rooz* were published immediately after the revolution. It ceased publication in 1979 and a fully Islamised version reappeared in the summer of 1980.

Women, Islam and Public Life under the Islamic Republic

Women were active in many ways during the revolutionary period, in demonstrations, in university debates, in Islamic reading groups. The absence of rights for women in Islamic countries is usually taken as the most solid example of Islam's incompatibility with modernity. The conventional Western image of Muslim woman needs no extensive introduction: veiled, faceless and subordinate. The superiority of men to women in Islamic *Sharia* is indisputable. Patriarchy, however, is not particular to Islam nor is it a reason to put forward arguments for 'Islamic exceptionalism'. Islam is no different from other major religious traditions that take for granted the superiority of men over women and protect the institutions of patriarchy; indeed, the similarities across the holy texts are probably greater than their differences.

The idea of gender equality, often regarded as an inherent aspect of European values, is not a god–given truth divorced from space and time. The demand for equality can only be born with the social awakening of women themselves, which is the result of certain social and material conditions and changes. It is precisely for this reason that Islam per se and other traditional religions cannot promote this idea. Yet, if in Western societies, women – and men – have managed to crack the walls of patriarchy, why can they not do it in Islamic societies? This is the question that many have been asking in Iran and has been the subject of intense debate for several years, most recently within the women's press. Indeed, under pressure from the spreading women's movement, many dogmatic Islamists have argued that Islam – unlike other religions – accepts gender equality in matters of 'spirit and intellect'. The pressures are so intense that an arch conservative such as Ayatollah Khamenei, the leader of the Islamic Republic, was forced to say that Islam rejects any differences between men and women in their 'development of the spirit and intellect, and also in the field of social activity'.[9]

For many years, the issues of women's rights and their roles in public life have been debated in Iran in such a context. Interestingly enough, both secular and Muslim activists inside and outside Iran have put Islam at the centre of the debate, and Islam has been regarded as the main, if not the sole, reason for the condition of women's lives in Islamic countries. Arguments by secular feminists about the lack of women's rights, the cultural relativism of the apologists and advocacy of the essential cultural differences between Iran and other countries in regards to women's status have all been explained in terms of ideology.[10] Such approaches, especially the focus on the exclusionary nature of the patriarchal policies of the Islamic Republic, overlook the possibilities of resistance and, more importantly, isolate ideology from social and economic developments. One of the important characteristics of any ideology is its elastic nature. Put simply, faced with the hard realities of lived experience, ideologies stretch to fit the social conditions. The case of the totalising programme for Islamisation of all aspects of public and private life in Iran is a good example.

The Islamic Republic's constitution does not recognise equality of both sexes, indeed it denies women's equal rights. The constitution itself was part of a wholehearted attack on women's rights and an important aspect of the overall policy of exclusion of women from public life. In the first few years of the Islamic Republic, many of the rights that women had gained under the Pahlavis were taken back. The segregation of sexes in public spaces, overt sexual discrimination, compulsory *hejab* (veiling), the exclusion of women from a number of professions and directing them to work mainly as teachers, nurses and secretaries; barring them from work as judges; reinforcing patriarchal policies in terms of divorce, guardianship of children and lowering the age of marriage for girls were among measures used to 'purify' women and society and bring back the 'glorious' tradition of what was perceived to be the true Islam. Women were to be accorded high respect, but only as mothers, daughters and wives. The future of the next generation as well as the future of the Islamic government was in their hands, and therefore women could not, under any circumstances, put a foot wrong. Women's rights, as in the case of other aspects of human rights, were overtly violated in the name of indigenous culture, self-reliance, individual emancipation and an end to all forms of domination of one human being or a country over another. As one activist has argued, cultural invasion is often seen from a patriarchal point of view; the talk of cultural invasion exists only where there are women.[11] This mirrors feminist theorising that suggests that the nation is often discursively gendered female and that women are used as symbolic markers of cultural purity and national honour, so that policing women protects the nation.[12]

Trying to amalgamate '*Sharia* with electricity'[13] was hazardous enough. Implementing the contradictory gender policies of the Islamic Republic has been even more complicated. The brave resistance and struggle of Iranian women has proved to be an obstacle to theocratic rule, an issue that is usually neglected in the analyses of the ideological foundations of the repressive and patriarchal rules of the Islamic Republic. Asghar Schirazi has noted three problems. First, the Islamists themselves had to encourage women to take up the professions thought to be suitable for females. Second, the measures have provoked the persistent opposition of modern women who, at great risk to themselves, refuse to conform to the moral conceptions of the conservative Islamists. The outward sign of this opposition is in the manner in which they attempt to evade the compulsory wearing of the veil so that while they do not dare to appear in public with no veil at all, they wear their scarf in such a way that their protest is obvious. But, the third point is also the most problematic:

> *Thirdly, it is important to note the contradictory effect that has come from the hierocracy's politicisation of women who otherwise held traditional attitudes. In contrast to the conservative quietist clergy who condemn the very appearance of women in public, the ruling Islamists quickly realised during the revolution that they could exploit for their own political ends the social importance of traditionalist women. But this presupposed that such women were snatched from their narrow social role and brought into the politically active social environment. Their inclusion in demonstrations, their active support in times of war, their mobilisation as the guardians of morality, their votes in elections, are regularly used by the regime to achieve its goals.*[14]

After the crushing defeat of the secular opposition in the immediate post-revolutionary period, the women's movement remained the only viable political alternative, and regained a new momentum after the end of the war with Iraq. To show that the conditions of women in Iran cannot be simply explained in terms of ideology, in particular Islam, it is important also to look at some of the major changes that facilitated the increased participation of Iranian women in the public sphere.

Education

Between 1956 and 1996 female literacy grew from 7.3 per cent to 74.2 per cent, an important development which has made its deep mark in political and social life in Iran. A parallel pattern can be observed in higher education. In the 1995–6 academic year over 38 per cent of students were women but by 2009, it was over 60 per cent. If we add to these over 200,000 female students who graduate from high school it becomes clear that the government needs to create over 250,000 new jobs for women every year, while the disjunct between male and female expectations about career and family is producing a potent social cocktail.[15] The growing demands for a free press and for a diverse range of cultural products are partly the result of a more general social transformation and growth in educational standards, especially for women.

This transformation has happened despite an early, and in some respects still continuing, attempt to impose gender segregation in education. Just four months after the collapse of the Pahlavi dynasty in February 1979, the new ministry of education banned co-education and many university courses were announced as unsuitable for women. Makeshift curtains segregated male from female students, with teachers unable to see half the class. In 1980, when the conflict between the student movements and secular opposition and the Islamic Republic first reached boiling point, all higher education institutions were closed as a result of what was dubbed the 'Cultural Revolution'. The use of Tehran University as a place to stage Friday prayers and the attempt to Islamise the universities were important parts of a general plan to rid Iran of all modern, secular and 'inauthentic' culture. After the reopening of universities in 1984, new measures were introduced, among them new criteria for female students. Not only did all students have to admit belief in one of the recognised religions in the Republic's constitution and provide sound proof of having no prior affiliation with 'anti-government' and anti-Islamic parties, they also had to accept further discrimination. Many women were excluded from scientific courses. A year after their reopening, the Iranian parliament passed a law that banned single women from studying abroad, justified by the claim that it would prevent them from the corrupting influence of Western values; again, the danger of 'cultural penetration' did not apply to men. Nevertheless, women took up all the possible opportunities and always did well and often better than their male counterparts. The opening of the all-female *Al-Zahra* University as well as the establishment of the private *Azad* (Free) University paved the way for wider participation of women and opened up new opportunities. The ban on single women studying abroad was finally lifted after more than a decade of bitter struggle when the Iranian parliament passed a law in September 2000 that allowed single women to apply for government grants to continue their studies outside Iran. It was third-time lucky, as two previous *Majles* had rejected the bill.

Employment

Employment has been another crucial site of struggle and change in Iran since 1979 and especially after the end of war with Iraq. In 1976, the entire employed female workforce was less than 14 per cent. This dropped to 8 per cent and dropped further immediately after the revolution, when many women were forced to retire, were sacked, regarded as unsuitable for the job they were doing (or, in the case of traditionalist women, took voluntary retirement). Immediately after the revolution, the Islamic regime actively pursued the Islamisation of society and the segregation of the sexes in public life was an important part of this policy. Changes in family law, especially the reversal of the Family Law of 1967, deprived women of their hard-earned rights. The Islamic Republic Constitution clearly stated that the revolution and the Islamic government would free women from 'multifaceted foreign exploitation' and that they would 'regain their true identity and human rights' within the family as the fundamental unit of society. All female judges were sacked (see Shirin Ebadi, 2006). Many nurseries in factories were closed down. Men regained their 'right' to polygamy, to being able to prohibit their wives and daughter from paid employment, as well as unconditional rights to divorce and custody of children.[16] This situation got worse as the expensive war with Iraq began to take its toll on an economy already in crisis, swallowing up already-limited resources.

However, the sexual apartheid policy of the regime met with resistance. Under Islamic rule, female students, children and patients should be attended by female doctors, teachers and carers. As the crisis began to bite harder many households could simply not survive with only one income and women needed to work. As more lives were lost in the war, many women became the head of household. For all these reasons, the government simply had to allow the continued presence of women in paid employment. Thus, despite the constitutional rhetoric of the 'Islamic Economy' that aims at the 'fulfilment of the material needs of man', Iran continued to be part of global capitalism and increasingly continued the modernisation policies of the Shah. The early rhetoric was gradually shelved as the Islamic Republic was faced with the harsh realities of economic and social crises. The end of the war with Iraq and the phase of 'reconstruction' signalled further liberalisation. The 'structural adjustment' policy and privatisation arrived together with World Bank loans in 1991 and 1994, and so too did new changes in family law. Contraception and abortion, previously denounced as un-Islamic, were now promoted to slow down one of the biggest population growth rates in the world. Such changes were made partly because of vigorous campaigns by women activists and women's media. There is no consensus as to whether the actual number of women in paid employment has declined since 1979. Studies of comparative statistical data[17] have argued that the policy of the state to abolish women's labour has not been successful and that the number of women workers employed by state ministries – especially health and education – and in private enterprise not only has not fallen, but actually shows a relative increase. Essentially, powerful Islamic ideology was counter-balanced by the exigencies of war, economic growth and demand for skilled labour, and women's mobilisation and growing political participation is a central part of these complex processes.

Gender, Politics and Media since the Revolution

In terms of women's participation in politics, the post-revolutionary period can be divided into four distinct phases:[18]

1. The revolutionary period of 1979–81 in which the visible secular opposition played a major role but was finally repressed.
2. The war period between 1981 and 1988 when the actual process of Islamisation was carried out under the guidance of Khomeini.
3. The period of construction marked by the end of the war, Khomeini's death and intensification of factional conflicts within the regime and marginalisation of the 'radical' wing.
4. The rise of a new gender-conscious movement in Iran resulting in the victory of Mohammad Khatami and the post-1997 period.

During the revolutionary upheaval of 1979, a large number of women's organisations and groups appeared all over the country. The biggest Islamic organisation to emerge in this period was the Women's Society of the Islamic Revolution, which gradually took over the previous official and legal organisation, the Women's Organisation of Iran, which was established in the 1960s and was led by the Shah's sister. The new organisation did not last long because the government refused to provide a budget, but many of its well-known members set up other organisations. Zahra Rahnavard, the wife of a future prime minister, took over the role of editing *Etelaat-e-Banovan* (Ladies' *Etelaat*) and changed its title to *Rah-ye-Zaynab* (Zaynab's Path). She played a role in the Islamisation of the *Etelaat* firm in this period.[19] Azam Taleghani, a political prisoner under the Shah and daughter of a respected cleric Ayatollah Taleghani, set up the Islamic Institute of Women and launched the monthly *Payam-e-Hajar* (Hagar's Message). She was among the first Islamist women who called for a radical reinterpretation of Islamic law. One key

concept within Shi'ite Islamic movements has been *ijtihad* (independent rea-
soning or/and interpretation), which has been used effectively by reformists
in Iran to push forward arguments for modern readings and interpretations of
Islamic principles and texts in a way that is more appropriate for contemporary Muslim societies and the realities of modern life. The battle between
different factions in Iran since 1979 and especially after 1997 has also revolved around this concept and its conflict with yet another concept, *taqlid*
(emulation).[20]

Some of the biggest women organisations, however, were part of the
secular opposition. The first women's demonstration occurred already on
8 March 1979, International Women's Day, triggered by Khomeini's revi-
sions of family law and imposition of *hejab*; already the slogan rang '*Dar tolu-e
azadi, ja-ye azadi khali*' (at the dawn of freedom, the place of freedom lies
empty). The National Union of Women was then established and produced
its own organ, *Barabari* (Equality) a biweekly publication that was replaced
after just three weeks by a monthly magazine *Zan dar Mobarezeh* (Women in
Struggle). It was affiliated to the biggest left-wing organisation of the time,
Sazeman-e Fadayan-e Khalgh (Fedayyan). Most of the existing left-wing organisations spawned their own women's section and paper. *Sepideh Sorkh* (Red
Dawn) was the organ of the women's section of the Maoist Communist Party
of Workers and Peasants; *Bidari-e-Zan* (Woman's Awakening) was the organ
of another pro-China organisation; *Rahaie-e Zan* (Emancipation of Woman)
was the product of yet another communist organisation and the women's organisation of the Union of Iranian Communists produced *Zanan-e Mobarez*
(Militant Women).

The war period, unlike the first, was marked by the clear absence of any
independent women's movement and by the passage of major anti-women
legislation. After the collapse of the early consensus of the broad anti-Shah
alliances and the growing isolation of the Islamist-nationalist groups, the state
came to rely more on grassroots support, including women. Their support,
however, was not rewarded as a call for the full participation of women in
public life was rejected and justified by reference to the circumstances and
problems created by war. This period saw a massive campaign to raise the
profile of women as mothers and wives, a campaign in which state-sponsored
television and cinema played crucial roles.[21] The few women parliamentarians
shared the same view as their male counterparts; since all were associated
with their well-known husbands or fathers, they were part of the established
elite and the occasional cry about raising 'women's issues' was not met with
enthusiasm.

TABLE 4.1 The Number of Candidates and Elected Parliamentarians in Iran

	Total Candidates	Men	Women	% Women	Elected (men)	Elected (women)	% Women
Ist Majles (1979)	3,694	3,628	66	1.79	95	4	4.4
2nd Majles (1983)	1,592	1,564	28	1.76	118	4	3.28
3rd Majles (1987)	1,999	1,962	37	1.85	176	3	1.68
4th Majles (1991)	3,223	3,152	81	2.51	133	9	6.34
5th Majles (1996)	5,366	5,046	320	5.96	131	14	10.53
6th Majles (2000)	6,853	6,340	513	7.49	262	12	4.38

Source: Extracted from www.iranwomen.org/zanan/charts/politics/majles.

The end of the bloody war with Iraq and Khomeini's death was the beginning of a new phase, the Second Republic. The gender debate, which had resurfaced and contributed to the lifting of some restrictions on women's university studies, became prominent. Family planning became official policy in 1988. The divorce law was amended, and women judges were allowed back in court, if only in advisory capacities, in 1992. In 1988, the state established the Social and Cultural Council of Women to encourage further participation of women in social and economic sphere. The Council of Women soon began to produce its own quarterly publication, *Faslnameh*. The Office of Women's Affairs, part of the new-look presidential office, was created.

Segregation remained as much as issue as the compulsory *hejab*, which has come under attack more vigorously in recent years. A new wave of Islamic reformism as well as calls for a more radical rethinking and rereading of Islam arrived in newly established cultural and political journals. Gender became a hotly contested area. The new wave of optimism as well as the necessity of changes after the war encouraged more participation in politics among certain groups. As a result, more women stood as candidates for election and more were elected. In addition to the increase in the number of women deputies, there were other distinct changes. The average age was lower, there were more women representatives from outside the capital city and more had formal education and university degrees.[22] Slowly 'gender problems' have been inserted into formal political debate, especially within parliament and governments began to pay more attention to the issues raised by women activists. After the landslide victory of Khatami in 1997, many ministries took on women advisors. Khatami himself chose Massoumeh Ebtekar, the editor of *Farzanehh*, as the vice-president in charge of environmental affairs; Azam Nouri was selected as deputy minister by the then culture minister, Mohajerani, and the interior minister, Abdollah Nouri, another well-known reformist and editor of the now-defunct *Khordad*, selected Zahra Shojai, a professor at Al-Zahra women's university, as director-general of women's affair.[23] The women's press, or at least some of them, played an important role in forcing gender to the top of the agenda.

A Women's Press and Islamic Feminism

Nowhere is the exposure of religion to modernity so evident and publicised as in the case of the press. Changes in the political process under the Islamic Republic and debates about 'native' solutions to gender issue have often been linked to the women's press in Iran. A wide range of studies on gender issues in Iran in recent years have been more or less studies of these newspapers.[24] The key debate that has created a great controversy and even rift among Iranian secular feminists is whether Islam is compatible with feminism and if the gender consciousness movement and campaigns for changes in law can be regarded as a feminist movement per se. Ziba Mir-Hosseini[25] clearly thinks so, while Shahrzad Mojab and Haideh Moghissi[26] find the whole term misleading and inaccurate and criticise those who do so of falling into the trap of cultural relativism and backing away from the ideals of feminism. Valentine Moghadam, while critical of Islamic reformists who insist that changes will only arrive as a result of the 'modernisation' of Islam and who seek a 'religious' solution, also takes issue with the secular feminists, particularly Moghissi, for offering a narrow definition of feminism. Moghadam argues:

> *Feminism is a theoretical perspective and a practice that criticises social and gender inequalities, aims at women's empowerment, and seeks to transform knowledge – and in some interpretations, to transform socio-economic structures, political power, and international relations. Women, and not religion, should be the centre of that theory and practice. It is not possible to defend as feminist the view that women can attain equal status only in the context of Islam. This is a fundamentalist view, not one compatible with feminism. And yet, around the world there will be different strategies that women will pursue toward empowerment and transformation. We are still grappling with understanding and theorising those diverse political strategies.*[27]

Most of those identified as 'Islamic feminists' are publishers, editors, journalists, university professors and activists. The term was coined outside the country and many of the activists in Iran to whom the label attaches have hesitated and sometimes, as in the case of Shahla Sherkat, refused to call themselves feminist. Nevertheless, many studies of 'Islamic feminism' in Iran and women's struggles against patriarchy focus and indeed chart its progress by critically analysing articles and arguments within the pages of the women's press.[28]

Among the most celebrated examples of the new women's press are *Zanan* (Women) and *Farzaneh* (Wise). Because *Zanan* has been by far the most influential in recent years, it is appropriate to start with it. *Zanan* was first published in January/February 1992 and was regarded as the twin sister of its more influential and now defunct brother *Kian*.[29] There are solid reasons for this assumption. The main cadres of the two monthly publications embarked on their 'modernist Islamist' project in the 1980s. Those who became involved and published these two papers had previously worked for two magazines published by the *Keyhan* firm. Sherkat, editor of *Zanan*, was the editor of *Zan-e Rooz* in the 1980s; while those who later published *Kian* used to run *Keyhan-e Farhangi* (Cultural Keyhan). Many of the early ideas and polemics of the modernist Islamists were published first in these two papers, at the time when ex-president Khatami was the managing director of the firm.[30] The early articles by the religious intellectual Abdolkarim Soroush and other influential thinkers as well as conservative responses were published there. If *Keyhan-e Farhangi* could not publish these articles, *Zan-e Rooz* provided the space, and vice versa. These intellectuals, activists and journalists were among the early circle of the reformist grouping in Iran.[31]

As managing director, Sherkat rapidly transformed *Zan-e Rooz*. Its cookery and knitting pages were replaced with hard-hitting analyses and commentary about physical punishment in schools, the problems of widows, women's domestic and unpaid work, women's employment and participation in public life and critical analyses of the portrayal of women in state-controlled television programmes. After a critical review of the renowned filmmaker Mohsen Makhmalbaf appeared in *Keyhan*, written by its managing director under a pseudonym, Sherkat published a rebuttal by Makhmalbaf that attacked the managing director. The firm gave Sherkat three options: to accept regular control of the content of the magazine by the firm, to create an editorial board or to relinquish the role of managing director. Sherkat refused, correctly seeing this as a ploy to 'cleanse' (*paksazi*) the staff in the *Keyhan* firm.[32] A large number of staff involved in the two publications as well as others were sacked or left, *Keyhan-e Farhangi* stopped publishing for a year and a half, and *Zan-e Rooz* continued under a new editor.

So *Zanan* was born in early 1992. The editorial of the first issue stated that the magazine had a clear mission to debate gender-related issues in four areas: religion, culture, law and education. *Zanan* was to target a wider readership to create a sound financial footing, and thus provide financial backing for the more intellectually oriented title, *Kian*, which was launched by those who ran *Keyhan-e Farhangi*. With a circulation of nearly 120,000 of mostly urban, educated readers,[33] *Zanan* became the most popular women's publication in Iran, offering alternative readings of the *Quran* and *Sharia* in the modern context. It contested the inequality of the sexes in Islam, family law, political participation, individual freedom, employment and civil law.[34] Men wrote many of the articles in the early stages, but what is most celebrated is the way in which *Zanan* paved the way and opened up a space for contributions by secular writers. Two of its best-known contributors were Mehrangiz Kar, a legal attorney, and Shirin Ebadi, the jurist and Nobel prize winner. In *Zanan* these writers managed to explain legal issues to a wider readership and inter alia exposed the patriarchal and hypocritical nature of the existing laws on education, marriage, divorce, custody of children and employment. They thus paved the way for more informed challenges to the ruling conservatives.

The now infamous Berlin Conference in April 2000[35] created a massive controversy. Mehrangiz Kar and the publisher Shahla Lahiji attacked the repressive policies of the Islamic Republic in their speeches and were arrested on return to Tehran. This put in doubt the cooperation between the two sets of women activists – modernising Islamic feminists and secularists – that had seemed so successful and creative. It provoked a conservative backlash, aired and supported by Iranian television and some conservative titles including *Keyhan*, and ended the collaboration between many secular and Muslim activists. Sherkat, the editor of *Zanan*, was among the participants in Berlin but avoided arrest and made no efforts to support the cause of the two women. In an interview with the Iranian feminist website, *badjense* (disreputable), Kar said, 'We always sensed there was a gap. It simply became very clear after Berlin that the reformists would never take any risks for us, pay any price for us, or defend us. They used us. Especially after our imprisonment, we felt this with our body and our soul.'[36] The publication of Lily Farhadpour's book on women's experiences in Berlin, *Zanan-e-Berlin*, has been regarded as an important step towards renewing that partnership.[37] But it seems unlikely that *Zanan* will again provide such a platform for critical engagement with these diverse views of Iranian women activists.

The desire to remain on newsstands while a large number of publications have been banned has proved to be the determining factor for Sherkat. In 2001, in interview with a foreign website and in response to why the magazine has survived for 10 years, she said:

> One reason is that Zanan is a women's magazine and is not a political magazine. The magazines and newspapers that were closed down may have had a strong political side, and in dealing with political issues of the day they ended up with problems. I prefer for Zanan magazine to remain a trade and women's magazine that can solve women's problem that are not necessarily political.[38]

But, of course, there are almost no women's problems that are not explicitly political in Iran. In a country in which even holding your partner's hand in public is regarded as un-Islamic and by definition anti-state, nothing is ever outside of politics. This represented a major retreat from the original mission statements of *Zanan*, announced more than a decade ago. Finally, after 16 years, in 2008, the magazine was closed down by the state and this historically important space of debate for women was removed.

Another celebrated women's title is *Farzaneh*. It began publishing in the autumn of 1993 as a biannual journal. The licence holder was Massoumeh Ebtekar and its editor-in-chief Mahboubeh Abbasgholizadeh, both members of the Women Studies Centre in Tehran that was headed by another influential woman, Monir Gorji. Prior to the publication of *Farzaneh*, Abbasgholizadeh had been a member of the editorial board of *Zan-e Rooz*, and later *Keyhan*. She had written articles for *Zan-e Rooz* in which she examined the impact of feminism and the possibility of Islamic feminism. The tone of the articles was openly critical of feminism, although they were far removed from the official stance that saw feminism as a disease and a corrupting Western influence and triggered considerable debate. *Farzaneh*'s editorial board was quickly invited by the president's advisor on women's affair to help them with future planning,[39] but the women clearly saw themselves more as *karshenas* (experts) than as feminists or even activists. *Farzaneh* was never a campaigning journal, but a platform to engage in theoretical/theological debate and a bridge between policymakers and experts/intellectuals, as well as between traditional thinkers and modernists. Published in both Persian and English, the journal clearly wanted to appeal to 'experts' both inside and outside Iran.

Another interesting publication was the first-ever daily paper devoted to women, *Zan* (Woman). Launched in August 1998 by Faezeh Hashemi, daughter of the previous president Rafsanjani and a member of parliament in her own right, Zan managed in its short life to create considerable controversy by raising some key issues at the height of conflict between different factions of the ruling elite. Hashemi's high profile allowed the paper to challenge the conservatives on a number of fronts. It campaigned for women to stand as candidates for the Assembly of Experts (*Majles-e Khobregan*) and resulted in 10 women putting forward their names as candidates; however, all were rejected. From early on, Zan attracted the wrath of the conservative faction. It was banned for two weeks in January 1999 for 'assaulting' security forces and was fined 250,000 tomans. The actual charge, as Shadi Sadr[40] has explained, was unlawful since the article of the Penal Code that was used by the judge to condemn Zan only applies to 'real persons' and not general categories such as 'security forces'. Zan was finally ordered to cease publication on 3 April 1999 for publishing an interview with the widow of the Shah, Farah Diba, although this had already been reprinted by conservative dailies and gone unnoticed, as well as for publishing a satirical cartoon criticising the *ghesas* (retribution) law. According to the 'eye for an eye' policy of *ghesas* law, the blood money for a murdered woman is only half of a man. The cartoon showed a gunman pointing at a couple with the man shouting 'Kill her, she is cheaper!' The short-lived Zan had developed a 40,000 circulation. Hashemi also helped to create women's committees in a number of cities to better organise women activists and to create sustained pressures on local government. But, in the 2000 parliamentary election, despite having had the second highest number of votes in Tehran in the previous election, she lost her seat. Her association with her father who had become, more than ever, a hate figure even among Islamists, cost her dearly.

The groups and publications labelled 'Islamic Feminists' are not exactly the same, do not share the same ideas and certainly do not have the same approach; the three different types that Noushin Ahmadi Khorasani[41] usefully analyses are distinguished mainly by their involvement with the state apparatus. The first are those independent writers such as Ebadi who have no links with any factions of the ruling elite. The second group are those who have a close and tight-knit link with the structure of state, part of the political elite who know only too well that repression of societal needs is impossible and who certainly do not want to disregard international pressure. Zan clearly belonged to this group and focused primarily on issues of central concern to the international community such as stoning, human rights abuses and elections. The third type is not independent, but no longer has the same level of access to the centre of power as the second type. Thus, Zanan focused more on the urgent needs of Iranian women and has been instrumental in gathering support for the reformists among Iranian women and forcing some legislative reform. Thus, despite some clear openings, establishing an independent publication is still extremely difficult, especially for women. A focus on these publications, while important, does not reflect the current diversity in the women's press.

The conservative's response to such publications also needs greater attention. Not only has the mainstream conservative press maintained attacks on the reformist press, they also established three women's publications to challenge the modernist interpretation of Islam. *Payam-e-Zan*, a monthly, is the attempt of the Qum religious seminary to engage more systematically with the gender conscious movements of the recent years. Unlike other titles, it is run, managed and edited by men, although occasionally the 'Sisters Section' of the Office of Islamic Propaganda is mentioned as helpers next to the editorial board.[42] The aims of this publication include increasing awareness of what they regard as 'Islamic knowledge' among Iranian women and awareness of moral and sociopolitical issues; consolidating family relationships; introducing the true Islamic female role models and so on. *Payam-e-Zan* is strongly against any kind of feminism and regularly publishes articles on women's place in the Quran, in Islam, women from the point of view of conservative religious thinkers and Imam Khomeini, women in families and the importance of *hejab* (veil).

Neda (Proclamation) is a quarterly journal firmly in the conservative camp as the organ of the Women's Society of the Islamic Republic of Iran, first published in the spring of 1990. Its licence holder is Zahra Mustafavi, the daughter of Khomeini, and its current editor is Fereshteh Arabi, his granddaughter, and much of the early issues were devoted to the life of Khomeini, the leader of the Islamic Revolution.[43] It is not a specifically women's journal, although since 1997, the number of articles that deal with women's issues have increased. It supported Khatami in the 1997 presidential election and certainly is in favour of debating gender issues, but it is broadly critical of the idea of the equality between men and women and has tried, perhaps because of its association with Khomeini, to remain uncontroversial and follow the letter of the Islamic Republic.

Another publication that is not often recognised by commentators is *Faslnameh* (Quarterly), a quarterly journal published by the Women's Socio-Cultural Council (WSCC). WSCC began its activities in June 1988 with two main objectives: to create a collection of information and statistics on women as well as to contribute to the study and assessment of women's sociocultural status in Iran. The organ of the council was launched in 1998 and its website[44] has a large collection of data. Managed by Mehri Sueezi and edited by Akram Hosseini, WSCC's journal is not distributed widely and not well recognised. This publication is anti-feminist and blames the 'translation movement' (translation of Western books into Persian) for introducing and spreading feminism. It condemns even 'Islamic feminism' as foreign and a ploy to find a way to realise feminist ideas and goals in Iran. Identifying the enemies of Islam, criticising their view and neutralising their impact were listed among the major duties of this publication.[45] In 2001, however, the journal changed its name to *Ketab-e-Zanan* (Women's Book), jumped on the bandwagon and turned its attention to women's demands in Iran and towards improving women's condition in society. Only 13 years after the formation of the centre, this organisation that was originally developed to play a role in policymaking and planning for women in Iran finally began to turn its attention to women.

There were other more minor secular titles as well. The most famous and influential of such limited titles was *Jens-e-Dovom* (Second Sex). By far the most informed and radical of women's press in Iran, it was launched in 1998 and edited by Noushin Ahmadi Khorasani. The director of the publishing house *Nashr-e Towseh*, she managed to bring together a wide range of articles by Iranian feminists including from those who live in exile. It had carried special reports from the Beijing Women's Conference; extensive coverage of the infamous Berlin Conference with a special focus on the two activists, Lahiji and Kar, who were neglected by *Zanan*; regular reports and articles on women workers, women writers, representation of women in Iranian literature and poetry, domestic violence as well as regional and international updates and analysis of the experience of Iranian families outside Iran. Ahmadi Khorasani's articles also appeared in a number of intellectual journals as well. *Jens-e-Dovom* had to cease publication in 2001,[46] but Ahmadi Khorasani launched a new quarterly journal, *Fasl-e-Zanan* (Women's Season) in May 2002.

Noushin Ahmadi Khorasani and Shahla Lahiji are among the most prolific and active women publishers in Iran. Lahiji founded *Roshangaran* (The Enlighteners) in 1984, which has since published over 200 books. According to Pooya[47] there are 47 women publishers in Iran, but in a recent interview with *Badjens,* Lahiji herself estimates that there are over 400 women publishers, of whom over half are currently active and support themselves.[48] These publishers have played a major role in introducing Iranian women to a range of ideas, issues and analyses and have been massively influential in rewriting women into Iranian history.[49]

The Emerging Women's Websites

It should by now be evident that the recent emergence of women's websites, Internet portals and the plethora of women bloggers follows in the long history of women's public writing and political activity in Iran. In some ways, these are merely new platforms for the same debates, albeit more accessible to more women and thus play a role in the democratisation and popularisation of women's issues in Iran.

Before the emergence of women bloggers in Iran, there were a number of websites and portals dedicated to dissemination of news and information related to gender issue and politics.

Within the last decade a large number of significant sites and portals dedicated to Iranian women have been constructed. One is IranDokht.com. Launched in 2002 outside Iran and with more than 80 contributors, the site, according to its founders, 'is an online media platform that connects the global community to Iranian women. It serves as a kaleidoscope of lifestyles, identities, art, and culture, reflecting the tensions between modernity and tradition'.[50] Irandokht produces a regular newsletter and in addition to regular news updates and interviews with activists, journalists and writers inside and outside Iran, the site showcases the products and efforts of activists, writers and artists, as well as providing advice on many issues, including health, communities, dating and jobs.

Another general site, claiming to be 'The first and biggest portal to Persian female' is persianfemale.com. The site provides information in a number of categories: News, fashion, art and culture, health, society, leisure, library, education, psychology and shopping. Much of the information in the site deal with 'feminine' issues such as cooking, beauty, keeping feet, and the most viewed items are to do with fashion, astrology, beauty, psychology of communication and the impact of exercise on decreasing pregnancy-related pains.

Blogging against Discrimination

One big issue that set the blogosphere bubbling has been attempts to alter various laws that discriminate against women. In March 2007, many women activists gathered outside the revolutionary court in Tehran in solidarity with five women on trial for organising a protest in the previous June against discriminatory family laws on polygamy and child custody. When the five women on trial left the court building, they were arrested again, together with a number of other activists who were there to express their solidarity.

Noushin Ahmadi Khorasani[51] in the first posting of the collective blog which is part of the online magazine *Zanestan* (www.herlandmag.com) announced that their blog's aim was to provide more regular and quicker interventions in debate. She also suggested that if the Iranian state wanted to have nuclear energy, then why shouldn't women?

> *For this reason, I, one of the members of* alam nesvan *(world of women) demand the establishment of an independent nuclear site for the independent women's movement; this is 'our absolute right' and one of our demands. Now even if our case goes well in various agencies and councils, and god-willing passes all different stages in good health, perhaps our slogan for next year might be: For every Iranian woman one centrifuges, for the enrichment of equal gender relations!.*

The struggle for 'the enrichment of equal gender relation' evident in various campaigns, meetings and demonstration, is supported and supplemented by a powerful presence in the online environment. *Meydaan Zanan* (Women's Field)[52] brings together various activists and campaigns. According to the site

> *Women's Field is a focal point where a group of Iranian feminists organize campaigns against gender inequality and challenge different aspects of discrimination.'* *It is open to all 'who believe that the road leading from discrimination and equality to freedom and democracy goes by way of women's liberation.*

When women were arrested for demonstrating, especially from 2007 onward, Meydaan actively petitioned for their release. 'My Mother, My Country' was another campaign for the right to nationality by children of Iranian mothers (but with non-Iranian fathers, a situation which affects many with fathers of Iraqi or Afghani origin in particular); the aim is to change the particular law that specifies that Iranian nationality can only be passed to a child through his or her father. Under pressure, the Iranian parliament passed a law in early 2006 granting the children of Iranian mothers the right to apply for Iranian citizenship after they reach 18 years of age. The bill does not, however, apply to those children who were not born in Iran, and the activists are campaigning for further changes. Another campaign 'Yes to women sports fans of Iran!' is addressed to various international and national sporting bodies and targets the contentious issue of the prevention of Iranian women from attending football matches.[53] Another campaign targets the practice of stoning women as punishment and finally there is the invitation of Iranian women to develop a 'convention for women'.

Many of women's online initiatives, however, are more than just a campaigning ground. What distinguished them from many other projects is the conscious bridging between activism and intellectual debate, between practice and theory. The website Maydaan, for example, has more than 20 articles and interviews engaging with the issue of the 1979 UN CEDAW (Convention on the Elimination of All Forms of Discrimination Against Women) which Iran has not ratified.[54] Contributions include passionate polemics about the urgency of this move to institutionalise women's rights as well as international coverage of struggles by women across the globe. Shadi Sadr, an Iranian lawyer and activist, looks at women's conventions across the world and argues that while there are universal principles, the solutions are local. Elaheh Rostami has written about the possibility of broadening the base of women's movement in Iran to all Iranian women. Rouzbeh Mircharkhian looks at the positive reasons for engaging men in the process of developing the convention for women and others have provided detailed and illuminating account of womens' struggles in various parts of the globe including in Pakistan, Nepal and Morocco. By 2009, Maydaan had emerged as one of the most powerful and effective sites for womens' activism.

Other sites such as *Iranian Feminists Tribune*,[55] *Women in Iran*,[56] *Focus of Iranian Women*[57] and *Zanestan*[58] combine news with critical analysis of women's life and experiences as well as their concerns and struggles at national and international level. The most engaging women's sites are those that are created, produced and sustained by women activists, that have become the voice of the movement and reflect the diversity, efforts, campaigns and struggles of what has been, undoubtedly, the most visible of social movements in the entire history of Iran under the Islamic Republic. Among these is the Association of Iranian Women site.[59] This online publication, like many others, is an attempt to bring together various activists and aims to cover the concerns and demands of 'intellectual women as well as ordinary Iranian women, and women in the centre as well as those in the margin, and of women's women activists as well as those in the shadow'.[60] In addition to news, the site also provides in-depth analyses and reports on various issues, including economic conditions of Iranian women, feminism and social movements, with particular focus on Iran and the global south, legal issues and discriminatory laws against women. The site also has the most comprehensive list of women organisation and has a list of 125 organisation ranging from NGOs, charitable foundations, research centre and a range of local organisation that are active in different parts of the country.[61]

Another significant site is www.womeniniran.org. Launch in June 2002, this site, has been one of the key spaces in which many activists have managed to raise a number of significant gender-related issues. The site has been the subject of regular interventions and disruptions by the authorities but has remained one of the most recognised platforms for news and information. It was one of the first campaigners to pressure the Iranian state to sign the CEDAW convention, and one of the first sites to recognise the significance of women bloggers. However, for various reasons, the site has failed to offer regular updates and been taken over by many new emerging sites/blogs.

The already-existing collective efforts in running and maintaining women's magazines and publications as well as sites have also led to formation of collective blogs. One such blog is the already-mentioned www.herlandmag .com/weblog. This blog clearly highlights the complexity, aspirations and multi-dimensional of many online initiatives in Iran. The 'Association of Lively Women, (*Anjoman-e Zanan-e Zendeh*) is part of a network including NGOs, media and political activists that came about as a result of many years of campaigning by a number of Iranian feminists. It is the weblog of an Iranian NGO called Women's Cultural Centre (*Markaz-e Farhangi-e Zanan*). Launched in March 2000 and officially registered as NGO in July of the same year, it was a response to the urgent need for more organised efforts by secular feminists. The two people behind the initial effort were Noushin Ahmadi Khorasani, director of the publishing house *Nashr-e Towseh*, and Shahla Lahiji, another independent publisher behind *Roshangaran* (The Enlighteners) mentioned earlier. The centre began by organising an event to celebrate International Women's day in 2000. The aim was to

> learn from our experience; become aware of the 'perceived natural' situation used and reproduced against women; spread and expand feminist knowledge among ourselves and other women; to look at our issues critically and not from an individual perspective, but as public and social issues; and strengthen ourselves via our collective efforts to transform unequal situation which grip us.[62]

The activities of the centre have included organising a petition and campaign for Iran to join CEDAW; regular meetings, seminars, gatherings and workshops focusing on a range of issues such as 'Afghan Women in Exile', 'Killing of Street Women', 'Violence against Women', 'Impact of War on Women', solidarity with Palestinian women, women workers in Iran, objection to Islamic Republic of Iran Broadcasting's anti-women policies, as well as publishing an internal bulletin *Nameh Zan* (Woman's Letter). The centre launched its site Feminist Tribune (www.iftribune.com)[63] in 2003, which, after nearly two years, was 'filtered' by the Iranian regime in November 2005; however, after a few months, it resumed work. In March 2006, the centre announced the launch of its second online publication (*Nashrieh*) in its continuing effort to forge stronger links between women activists inside and outside the country. This second site, *Zanestan* (www.herlandmag.com) which introduces itself as the first online Persian publication for women covers a diverse range of issues with regular updates, polemics, statistics, news and analysis. The weblog of the site was launched in 6 March 2006 to provide additional space for regular and quicker interventions.

The significance of women movement in Iran is as such that many of the popular and influential Iranian sites also have their own dedicated women section. One such news site is www.asre-nou.net.[64] Stories on this dedicated section cover a wide range of subjects from domestic violence and abuse to the role of Iranian women in the national economy, to poverty, to assessment of Iranian women MPs work in the parliament, to women NGOs in Iran, to interviews with prominent women in the region, including Nawal Al-Sadaawi and Shirin Ebadi, to assessment of women's and students publications, to representation of women in Islamic Republic of Iran Broadcasting, to prostitution, AIDS and art. Another site outside Iran, www.iranian.com, also has a dedicated section containing commentaries on various gender-related issues in Iran; as do other popular news sites such as www.akhbar-rooz.com that contain regular commentaries by women activists outside Iran examining the women movement in Iran and providing a platform for regular engagement between activists outside and inside.[65]

The significance of gender is such that even the international broadcasters have either dedicated sections or regular updates. For example, *Deutsche Welle* published a serious of articles on the Iranian women's movement as part of its commemoration of March 8, 2009.[66] VOA also has a section dedicated to women issues, as does BBC's Persian blog.[67]

Blurring the Boundary between Public and Private

Blogs bring into the public domain issues that have often been considered 'private'. A routinised physical separation between men and women happens at many social gatherings. Women amongst themselves practise very intimate *hamdeli* (shared feeling) about their husbands, children and other problems of everyday life. Iranians make much of having *darde-del*, heartache, which also becomes a social practice. However, Iranian women have shown clear elements of resistance in their everyday practices. It is perhaps true that their jogging, mountain climbing, skiing, camping and partying may not have been direct acts of confrontation and defiance but, whatever the intention, such public acts were highly visible claims to a positive expression of contemporary womanhood and meant that they have not given up on trying to make change. Thus, Bayat, developing an argument about the politics of everyday life, labelled Iranian women activism as a 'movement by implication' which 'operated through an incremental and structural process of claim-making intimately attached to the imperative of women's persistent public presence. In this structural encroachment every claim justified the next, creating a cycle of opportunities for further claims, ultimately leading to more gender equality and individual entitlements' (Bayat, 2007:171).

Beyond such politics of resistance from within the private sphere, women have also been active in formal organisations within the public sphere, including organising demonstrations, lobbying, campaigns, publishing, setting up NGOs and so on. Clear elements of such practices are visible in the cases of some of the websites that we introduced earlier. Such tendencies and variations, the ordinary, the irresistible 'politics of nagging', the dispersed and the organised, the collective and the individual, the Islamic and the secular aspects of public visibilities of Iranian women is also reflected in the blogosphere. Yet the combination of public and private, the linkage between the two and the complexity of gendered Iranian identity is obvious even from the most cursory of glances. The poetic, political, emotional, personal and in most cases courageous voices clearly defy the clichés of Iranian women as repressed, voiceless, shapeless figures covered by *hejab* or as the exotic Shaharzad of *1001 Arabian Nights*. As the great Iranian poet, Ahmad Shamlu, once wrote 'only the tempest bears peerless children', and undoubtedly the tempest of 1979 gave birth a new generation demanding their pride of place and the rights that they deemed as theirs. With very little or no recollection of the previous order, deprived for so long of the experience of previous generation of activists, the new generation of women activists have began to remember the shared history of generations after generations of activists for women's right and emancipations.

Engendering Blogs

It must be evident by now that the Iranian 'digital divide' is not heavily gendered. That is to say, considerable numbers of women are online, are blogging and are expressing themselves. As we have mentioned, there are other areas of relative gender equality: for example, there are high numbers of women in universities in general and in engineering and other fields that are often deemed 'male' in the West. The most recent international comparative analysis of gender gaps has Iran as 118 of 130 countries, that is limping among the most gender-unequal countries in the world. Yet the report clearly shows that there is little gender divide in health and life expectancy or in education or higher education. There is however a strong divide in economic matters – with women earning far less than men – while the core of the poor score is centred upon the almost total invisibility of women in the formal political environment.

There are clear obstacles to women's full participation in public life. According to the Islamic Republic's constitution being a man is one of the conditions for the post of Supreme Jurisprudent. In the case of the presidency, the label '*rojal*' has been tabled as one of the conditions and there is intense debate as to whether this means 'male' or merely indicates a 'political figure' and is gender neutral. So far, there has been only one woman in the Assembly of Experts. There are no women in two of the most powerful state institutions, the Guardian Council and the Expediency Council.[68] No woman has ever been elected speaker of the Islamic Assembly (*Majles*) or as the head of the judiciary. So far, the Guardian Council[69] has rejected all women candidates for presidency. There have been no female ministers and women have only been appointed to different ministries as 'advisors' not as decision- or policymakers.

Yet, as we have shown through the optic of the women's press and the emergence of women blogs and websites, feminists and feminism have a long and complex pedigree in Iran and the contemporary women's movement is one of the most potent sites of cultural resistance to the predations of the Islamic Republic. Blogs provide a fascinating insight into the dynamism of Iranian society with its contradictory trends and institutions. They bring together 'public' and 'private' concerns, and name socially and culturally sensitive issues and make them political concerns, in just the way that Chantal Mouffe describes. That the name of many of such bloggers are well known and that many of the most fascinating insights are coming from women should be of no surprise to those familiar with a dynamic women's movement, which, despite all odds, refuses to go away.

The patriarchal Islamic state extends a broad remit of control over 'private' matters, making issues of appropriate dress. *hefz-e hejab*, including modesty for men too, familial relations and sexuality into matters of state. Instructions are issued about the appropriate relations between children with their parents. Women's desire needs to be controlled; sexual relations must be confined within marriage; *sigheh* (temporary marriage) is promoted as a solution for sexual relations before and beyond marriage; and motherhood is promoted as the true destiny of all women, although the national breeding campaigns during the war have given way to family planning and population control. To these ends, both state and religious institutions produce materials teaching young people about proper sexual behaviour including celibacy, and improper ones including masturbation and homosexuality (see Khosravi, 2008: 38–41) although there is little information about sexual health, with HIV-AIDs on the rise because of risky sexual practices as well as through drug-related activities (Pardis Mahdavi, 2008). Young people and women are regarded as objects to be moulded by the state, which thinks that women need protection, often through the construction of separate spaces, including the construction of women-only parks in 2008.

It is hardly necessary to invoke a motivated politics of resistance that prompts reaction to such patriarchal control. A population structure skewed towards the young and energetic, a healthy disregard for authority, a well-developed culture of social deviancy, an individualistic psychology, all work to explain the massive rise of blogs by young people and by women, especially those that challenge and rearticulate familial and sexual relations in their own voices. Thus, it is not necessary to claim these voices are intentionally political, but sufficient to say that in their large numbers, they reveal the limits of state and religious articulations and a libidinal energy that refuses to be quashed.

The balance of these forces is continually shifting. The extent of controls over women is an indication of the stability of the state; these matters are continually available for mobilisation and women can also be made an example of regime strength. But as the movement of people in and out of Iran increases, the variety in patterns of familial and sexual life is likely to increase. All writing on such topics runs the risk of aging rapidly and needs to be read with care. In late 2008 in north Tehran, it was well known which shopping malls were policed to enforce appropriate dress codes (*bad hejabi*). Young Iranians, many with great interest in style and fashion, even it might be said consumed by great status anxieties, manifest colourful and fashionable wear and numerous fashionable shops that probe the limits of acceptable 'Islamic' fashion have sprung up.

In addition to direct state interventions, the authority of the traditional hierarchical order within the family is weakening and the emergence of child centeredness is one of the significant changes in Iranian families according to Kian-Thiébaut (2005). As she succinctly points out, one of the fascinating paradoxes of Iran is that the Iranian state, despite emphasising family values and propagating authority and family, actually contributed to the weakening of parental authority by its intervention in private and family sphere by asking children to inform authorities of their parents' activities and so on. As she suggests:

> *The post-Revolutionary power elite, although elderly and traditionalist, did not openly oppose the youths' new value system. On the contrary they actively partici-pated in the weakening of parental authority that could have hindered the youths' ideologization. Moreover, with the beginning of the Iran-Iraq war (1980–1988), the authorities needed volunteers and mobilized all the ideological state apparatus, media, Friday prayers, or mosques to encourage the youths to go to the war. Because many parents were against their son's mobilization for war efforts, the weakening of parental authority served the regime. (2005:62)*

Economic factors such as the expense of housing as a proportion of wages coupled with low wages and salaries in the public sector are also creating a delay in the age of marriage, as young people cannot see a way to marry and survive independently. Such paradoxes in terms of youth, family, women and the contradictions between the ideological and material imperatives produce an interrogation of both Islam and patriarchy. As we have argued, at least in the Iranian context the 'political' is always contentious and contingent. Yet we also want to argue that an important designation of something as 'political' is precisely the 'making public' of previously inarticulate, unnoticed social is-sues. There are many issues at work here – between private matters and public matters; between the 'sphere of the private' and the 'sphere of the public'; and the processes whereby issues 'are made public' and which issues those are. The 'personal' can indeed be 'political' and that there can be all sorts of po-litical messages encoded within popular culture and entertainment formats, and indeed the Iranian blogosphere is replete with evidence of both. It is no surprise that with the defeat of the reformist political movement in the 2005 election of Ahmadinejad, that personal politics has begun to take centrestage in the blogosphere. That these issues burst on to the scene again during and after the June 2009 election, in which women were massively present and in which Zahra Rahnavard campaigned with her husband, was – in hindsight – only to be expected.

Embodied and Virtual Spaces

The other dynamic that must not be overlooked in a focus mainly on ICTs, websites and blogging is that these are partly a response to the heavy incur-sions of the state into other forms of politics. Especially from 2005 under Ahmadinejad, all forms of independent face-to-face discussions, whatever their purpose, had become harder and harder to organise and maintain. The state defined all such activities as not only 'political' but also 'oppositional'. In the autumn of 2008, the difficulties of organising even a discussion group on a regular basis had become difficult. It was hard to find a public space to hold such activities; universities would not provide rooms, and repeated group activity in a private space attracted too much unwanted attention, people worrying about what the neighbours would think and whether they would be reported. An on-going refrain by ordinary people in the autumn of 2008 was that the regime had managed to break social trust and to create a profound sense of surveillance of social activity, whether true or not. Even cafes were not felt to be safe public spaces and were certainly monitored by the morality police; a well-known cafe above a bookshop was closed down. Thus, by severe controlling of public space, the regime has pushed a lot of activity out of sight, into private spaces that are in some ways far harder to control, not least for the sheer multiplicity of locations. Thus the internet become the space for political debate when other fora such as the press and face-to-face embodied politics became suppressed. Indeed, by keeping people indoors, with little to do but fiddle with computers, the regime helped to induce a generation of digital adepts, the consequences of which it was to rue in the summer of 2009.

But the Net also allowed for the articulation of a more abstract 'body politics', about issues of identity, sexuality and sociability that have rarely been expressed before other than by a few poets and literary figures. As in most countries, bloggers – and especially women bloggers – began to explore and critique their everyday lives, relationships with parents, with friends and lovers in a novel manner.

Given the travails of the female body in the public space of the Islamic Republic, the absence of the body in virtual space can have a liberating and democratic impact. As Amir-Ebrahimi argues that

> 'virtual space in Iran is a space for shaping repressed identities in all their simple and complicated forms. Through the continuous practice of writing, individuals can assert layers of their personality that they were hitherto unable to in real life. It is a new public space, which has more qualitative than quantitative importance for Iranians. In this new space, youth, women and intellectuals (and other educated groups who have been excluded from the real public sphere) are making their voices heard, especially through weblogs'.

Yet this open space for expression is equally shaped by the gendered realities of sociocultural life; for example, women bloggers who use their real name soon face the same limitations as in real life and are required to exercise more self-censorship than young men.

Iranian blogger Parastoo who has been writing a blog since June 2002 sees her blog as a way of sharing her thoughts, ideas and emotions. She starts her Persian blog with a simple 'salaam' and explains the title of her blog (*zan-nevesht*) by saying 'why not? In my view women see the world differently from men. Women never had the opportunity to register and record their view, and those who did mostly looked at the world from men's perspectives'.[70] Her first few entries clearly demonstrate the range of concerns and issues of many of activists of her generation. For example, she recalls a visit to a restaurant with a group of friends and how the waiters seemed concerned about the level of noise and the lack of interest by this group of young women in 'observing the Islamic ethic'. She asked precisely what this is supposed to mean and why the same concern was not raised to a much smaller but noisier group of men in the restaurant. She goes on to ask whether this incident was among those contributing to the dissatisfaction of Iranian girls with their own gender?

In another entry, she describes a radio story about the installation of the first sculpture of a Native American in United States after 200 years, which she views as an indication of racial discrimination in a country that claims to be free. But she also argues that the existence of racial discrimination despite passionate opposition to it around the world is painful, but not as painful as gender discrimination which exists all over the world and goes unchallenged: 'When will we hear about the abolition (or decrease) of gender discrimination in our country? Two centuries? No.' She reports the closure of the Women's Cultural Centre by the authorities for printing a picture of the celebrated Iranian poet, Forough Farrokhzad (1935–67) in the centre's calendar without *hejab*. Parastoo sarcastically suggests that Forugh should have known that there would be a revolution and she should have taken some photos with *hejab* before she died.

While Parastoo remains an activist and writes passionately about public politics, her blog also contains personal comments and laments about university, work, family, relationship, daily life, cinema and literature. In one entry (16 December 2002) she bemoans the difficulty of juggling work, studies and leisure activities. In another (12 May 2004) entitled 'goodbye' written after another celebrated blogger, Lady Sun[71] declared she was ending her blog, Parastoo writes that 'my crying wasn't over you leaving. No, My heart aches for us being wronged (repressed) as such that in order to experience civility we have to leave and leave behind all these wonderful people. I will miss every second of our moments of naughtiness. My heart . . . ' On 7 June 2004, in a short entry labelled as 'confession' she writes of her relationship with 'one of the dearest people I know' has become foggy. She writes that she is immensely sad and this entry is accompanied by a picture of a bunch of red roses and a poem.

Parastoo is fully aware of the dilemmas of blogging as a woman. Because she writes with her own name (as she says, she wants to be honest and true to herself) she is aware of the possibility of hurting herself and others. The concerns are not just political, although that plays on her mind as she engages with sensitive political or public issues. Another significant concern is to do with her family. Her personal life is another area that needs to be self-censored. She keeps a second, anonymous blog for *darde-del-kardan* and confiding with people who do not know her. She is not the only one who finds fewer and less familiar readers can be a source of a comfort. And, she is also not the only one who has a second blog, in her case anonymous.

The case of the already-mentioned celebrated women blogger, Lady Sun, is also interesting. Lady Sun (Sanam Dolatshahi) was one of the first women bloggers in Iran and one of the best recognised, since she started in 2001.[72] She began blogging in English in 2003 with a simple 'Hi' posted on 28 April. A day later and in a post entitled 'Why an English Weblog?', she wrote:

> It was quite a fascinating idea to have an English weblog. I am fed up with all the worries I have had about my Persian weblog. People are getting arrested. Sina, our lovely friend is in jail, mostly because of what he has written in his weblog. Rumors are increasing about a new trend to close down internet sites and weblogs in Iran. My Persian weblog's name or logo is in many weblogs, around 1000 to 1300 people visit it everyday, and thanks to internet sites I work for, I am not anonymous anymore. It gets sometimes terrifying to think about the strangers who read you everyday. There maybe some government-related visitors, there may be some guys from the intelligence service; some form other places you may never know. I'm positive I'm not in danger, since I have never written anything radical or political. I have been quite conservative in the last few months, completely aware of the eyes watching every single move of us. But you can't stop the trains of thought moving around your head, scaring you as hell. I guess this English weblog will be read by much less dangerous people and I hope it will remain infamous so that I'll be able to write about my naked observations of this crazy world honestly, uncensored and real.[73]

The paradox of writing about the world 'honestly, uncensored and real' and yet hoping the blog will remain infamous, the desire for recognition and yet worry over its consequences, the joy of having large number of visitors and yet looking for less readership, or less dangerous readers, are very intriguing and opens a whole set of questions about blogging in Iran. The 'low profile' of her English blog has its own advantages, she admits.

Lady Sun considered herself 'a member of the women's movement in Iran' and has been actively participating in various activities. She worked with the 'One Million Signatures Demanding Changes to Discriminatory Laws,'[74] and since 2001 has been editing, contributing, managing and maintaining sites such as www.womeniniran.net, StopCensoringUs, the official website of human rights lawyer Mehrangiz Kar[75], as well as the first online magazine in Iran *Cappuccino*.[76] In this sense her profile is not dissimilar to many other women bloggers who are part of a much broader network of activists, including Parastoo, who build networks of contacts, or *halge*, by linking to other bloggers and websites with which they have sympathy. In this way, even an 'individual' blogger is often connected to a broader circle of collective opinion.

Lady Sun famously left Iran with her husband in 2004. The marriage lasted for about three years and her blogs informed readers of the agonies of her separation and loneliness. In one entry entitled 'low profile confessions', posted on 5 August 2007, she wrote:

> *It's good that this blog is low profile. I feel much more comfortable to write here. I know, it seems strange why I blog about something, when I don't feel comfortable writing it for the public. I guess that's part of the blogging disease I got when I first started blogging. When I write, and think that somebody, specially a stranger, will read it, I feel somehow relieved. I know then that I'm not alone; at least somebody knows what goes on my mind. It sometimes is even like making a confession. I'll probably make my confessions more on this blog, than on the other one. Low profile is always good, much better than a high profile and no profile!*[77]

Lady Sun now lives in London and works for the new BBC Persian television channel.

The use of blogging to talk to strangers as a kind of therapy and 'to get everything out' is not new in the West, but a major social shift within Iranian culture where personal and sexual issues receive no public articulation. Women making public their private pain and talking of such personal matters is a revolution in social relations in Iran. She ends the story of her divorce in 2007 on her English blog, reads:

> '*I went to Gipsy King's concert tonight, with my soon-to-be ex, in Wolftrap. It was a nice way to end our relationship, with dancing, tears, kisses, and drinks. We will remain good friends, I'm sure.*' Her Persian blog only hints at her trauma, whie under the title '*I did it my way*' she posts the same Gipsy King's song on Youtube,

as the one on her English blog, with a short note saying: 'Today in Gipsy King's concert I remembered many memories. It was a beautiful ending to a period of my life. . . .'[78]

Perhaps personal declarations in public are easier to write in English than Persian, or that is at least an option for the many bi-lingual Iranians in the blogosphere.

Against the regular and usually well-intended complaints against the lack of 'politics' in blogs, we contend that there is a huge volume of 'personal' material that raises serious political concerns. Lady Sun's blog is indeed is full of 'disclaimers' about not wanting to write anything political, yet she congratulates a well-known Iranian activist and lawyer for the launch of her own site (now defunct) and for an article mapping the progress and retreat of women's movement in Iran. Numerous stories posted in 2004 also clearly deal with public concerns: one is a campaign to raise funds for an operation on a poor Iranian women who cannot afford the surgery; one informs her readers that after long discussions and serious thinking she has decided that she will not vote in parliamentary election because it means sending representatives to parliament that do not represent women; one short entry reports the closure of popular daily *Shargh* and that the closure of *Yas* would follow. On February 2004, she laments that she doesn't want to write about politics but so desperate to do so with all things happening in Iran, the victory of conservatives in parliamentary election and that in two years time the post of president will also go to conservatives. A day later another short comment reads: 'It will be a very silly and rubbish *majles* (parliament). Fucker has been elected as representative of Mashhad again'.[79]

With two-thirds of the Iranian population under 30 and half under 20, with few public spaces to meet and living under the ever-watchful eyes of the state and their own families, it is little surprise that issues about the opposite sex, dating and emotions are being expressed in blogs. Women's blogs are full of personal stories, dealing with personal issues, sometimes in very explicit terms. *Dokhtar boodan* (being a girl) is concerned with what it means to be a girl, in terms of relationship, sex, family and body. The personal in this blog deals with the most personal inner feelings. That makes this blog no less controversial than others. She starts her blog in July 2006 with a post under the title of 'Family':

For a few weeks in a row I didn't want to come home at night. 'Where are you staying? Your friend's house? Male or female? Name? Address? Contact number?' . . . . Hey! Such questions make me sick. I would like to know whether you, who is probably boy passing through this blog, have to answer similar questions or not? I would like to ask: why do mothers only ask such questions of their daughters? What are they worried about? What if it goes with the wind? The word 'family' raies such stinking feeling.[80]

Another post titled 'Lover', in July 2006, tells readers that 'I won't see him. At least for few months. A deep sadness overwhelms me.' The reader is left to wonder whether this is a physical lover, an emotional projection onto a friend or an imagined lover. Various short entries deal with her periods, how most people she likes are no longer in the country and that her circle of friends is decreasing, the physical experiences after a long kiss and so. Her latest entry on 30 March 2008 is devoted to the issue of body. She describes how only recently she has started loving her own body consciously, and that in her blog she doesn't want to write about external pressures (religion, tradition, norms) but about the internal ones (habit, thoughts, ideas) that are preventing her enjoying her body.[81] Another blogger, Sara Mohammadi, in her blog, *Pagard* (*Darde-delhaye Sara Mohammadi*) presents her thoughts and ideas in a series of poem and prose, and letters, by herself and by Iranian poets and writers including Nima, Forough Farrokhzad as well as international writers such as Octavio Paz, the Iraqi poet Amal Al-Jubouri and the Russian poet Yevgeny Yentushenko. Her posts are accompanied by images and soft music.[82]

A critique of patriarchy and gender relations in Iran is evident in Gistela's blog *Golden Hair*.[83] She announced her entry into the blogsphere on 21 July 2004 in a short item entitled 'I've come', saying that after reading blogs for years she has decided to write her own blog, at a time that blogs have been multiplying like rabbits. Her title deliberately indicates that she is female, because she was told that she would have more readers. Her first blog, posted a day later and entitled 'Loyal Husband', is a 'nightmare' about the husband of a friend of hers trying to enter her bedroom. Another post, on July 28, is a jumble of references, to a speech by Soroush at the university; an article by Ghouchani in the daily *Shargh*, a now defunct reformist paper; and that she wants to go to driving school but she is afraid because she dreamt last night she had turned into a fish. The main focus of this posting, however, is the inner anxiety of women in Iran. She describes the caretaker of her building going on a trip and coming to say goodbye to her but how happy she felt after he had left. Why? Because she had a male friend visiting her.

The thought that the caretaker knows I have a male visitor always makes me feel guilty... Even though I know I don't have sex with him I think others think that I have, and we have been brought-up so well that we are even wary of what our

Film stall, north Tehran bazaar

caretakers think of us, let alone our family members and society. How things have become internal. When will we be free? Feminists should pay attention to this sense of inequality which comes from inside rather than from external obstacles.[84]

The title of this entry is 'where are you Simone de Beauvoir?'

The innocence in such explicit writing of fantasies and projections speaks of women's frustrations but also of the over-sexualisation of an environment in which honest sexual encounters are rendered impossible. Recent writing (by Mahdavi, 2008 and Afary, 2009) describe and analyse a 'sexual revolution' beginning to occur in Iran. Such personal blogs are yet another space where the changing sexual ethos and peculiar sexual relations produced by the Islamic republic find expression. And, where a shift from more formal politics to more personal politics is readily observed.

Individual Bloggers, Collective Actions and Protests

While broad reformist politics have taken a beating, the networking, collective efforts and campaigning on women's issues has grown to such an extent that many have suggested that the women's movement is the key agent of future social change in Iran. Cyberspaces are creatively built and developed for concientisation and mobilisation, extending the individual blogosphere into embryonic circles of action and networks of politicisation.

The Closure of Zanan

As mentioned earlier, in 2008, the Press Supervisory Council finally closed down *Zanan*. The magazine had challenged the official or conservative views on the place of women in Islam and the Iranian constitution, offering a critique and alternative readings of religious texts[85] and managed to pave the way for the collaboration of secular and religious commentators (Khiabany and Sreberny, 2004). The 2008 closure came prior to parliamentary elections in March 2008, as part of extensive restrictions which included the filtering of a number of influential women's sites. The excuse for the closure of *Zanan* was that it harboured 'an extreme feminist stance', and was disturbing public law and weakening military and revolutionary organisations including the Basij Resistance Force. *Zanan* had recently discussed the news of the rape of a woman by two members of Basij.[86]

The closure prompted a big response and a number of campaigns inside and outside Iran.[87] The bloggers' response to closure of the magazine was as swift as an uncompromising as possible. Asieh Amini, one of the contributors to the magazine, called the closure of the magazine an 'execution of the word'. She accepts the charge that Zanan was disturbing the 'psychological security' of the country but argues the problem was that the places of the accused were swapped. It is 'women' (*Zanan*) who are threatening the 'psychological security' of the country not *Zanan*, the magazine. If *Zanan* is accused of threatening this security, it is because it reflected women's voices.[88] In her post she provided readers with a link to photographs of the gathering of the Association in Tehran, published in another blog attacking the closure of the magazine. In his blog, Siamak Ghasemi, also provided readers with editorials, from the *New York Times* and *Boston Globe*, as well as further reports from AFP, Radio Zamaneh, and the statement by the Association of Iranian Journalists.[89]

Another blogger, Shirin Ahmadnia, in a short posting entitled 'no surprise', informs readers that 'Zanan's licence was cancelled'.[90] Her post has a link to the news published by Fars News Agency. Masoome Naseri called the banning of *Zanan* 'endless stupidity', writing that Iranian women could see aspects of their own images in the magazine, and the editor should take credit for encouraging debates and talking about feminism when it is regarded as an insult.[91] Leila Moori, in her blog called *Raha* (Free), wrote that *Zanan* was one of the most influential publications in her life. Leila expressed her sorrow for a generation of young Iranian women for whom *Zanan* could have acted as a window to a new world when everything reeks of hopelessness, and also for those who could not tolerate a magazine that in the past 16 years had tried to move forward slowly.[92] Another blogger/journalist, Fahimeh Khazr Haydari, in an item entitled 'gentlemen forgive us', reported the closure and wrote that we are beginning to get used to 'end of the year surprises' (Iran celebrates the new year at the Spring solstice). The closure didn't have anything to do with the content the magazine but with the threshold of tolerance of 'gentlemen':

> *'All women are well in this land, and we sincerely apologise, gentlemen. Please forgive us that we walked so softly and slowly in fear of making a crack in the delicate tolerance of yours. We had forgotten that when you stone us, when you order our execution, when you marginalise us, we have to be grateful and modest and thank you for it. What can we say, we are women. Our brain is not complete. Is it our fault that we are made of your left rib? Believe us that the problem is with your own left rib'.*[93]

She finishes by saying 'thank you for tolerating us for 16 years'. Nilofar Rostami posted a personal story, entitled 'No one will send SMS on Monday morning, again', tells her readers that no longer she will receive texts from editors of the magazine asking where she was, and no longer is it necessary for her to think of hundreds of excuses why her report is not ready. She writes how she was always bad at meeting deadlines, but that she also reported best when writing for *Zanan*, and how she also read the best material in the magazine. The report finishes by saying that this is the worst news of the day, and that on a cold afternoon of January, Shahlah Sherkat, the editor of *Zanan*, 'lost a dear one aged sixteen'.[94] Two weeks after the closure of *Zanan*, the editorial board of magazine launched a weblog to fight the closure.[95] The blog is called 'Editorial board of *Zanan*'.

Hot Issues: Debating Temporary Marriage

At the end of May 2007, the Iranian interior minister suggested that the tradition of temporary marriage should be propagated. His suggestion led to yet another controversial and heated debate. Previously Rafsanjani had made a similar suggestion during his presidency in the 1990s when he offered temporary marriage as a pragmatic solution to the sexual needs of Iranian youth, and as a way of getting over the legal restrictions that exist against physical intimacy between the two sexes. In recent years, the authorities have faced a major difficulties dealing with 'non-related' couples in public spaces. For Rafsanjani, temporary marriage was a way of legitimising sexual relations via a short contract of marriage that could be terminated whenever the couple wanted. Temporary marriage is a contract entered into for a definite period, and as Nikki Keddie argues is another Shia practice that

> 'goes back to pre-Islamic Arabia and seems to have been condoned by the Prophet, though it was outlawed for Sunnis by the Caliph Omar. As in all marriages there is a payment to the woman and children are legitimate. It flourishes especially in pilgrimage centers where men may come alone. It is wrong to consider it prostitution, and it has uses besides satisfying men's sexual desires'. (1991:8)

In recent years even the practice of *Namzadi Sharei* (Legal Engagement) has been allowed and practiced which allows engaged couples to be together.[96] The idea of temporary marriage in the Iranian context, however, is not just a religious debate and has very little to do with either pilgrims or lonely men on holiday and away from their family. The idea was floated as a religiously legitimate solution to what was already an increasingly common practice among young people of having a sexual partner. Rafsanjani's suggestion was met with a loud outcry from various institutions and individuals, and it was shelved. The resurfacing of the topic after 15 years in comments by the Iranian interior minister clearly shows the dilemma that the Iranian government faced. By spring 2007, even a blog dedicated to propagating temporary marriage had been set up by Hamid Tavakoli.[97] This blog listed 25 blogs and site that are dedicated to debating temporary marriage, its history and its meanings in religious texts, the philosophy of temporary marriage and its advantages, as well as a number of links to religious scholars who had engaged with the topic and provided advice to those who had sought guidance from various high-ranking ayatollahs and sources of emulations.[98] Tavakoli later set up a site, *Movaghati*.[99] The interior minister's suggestion for propagating temporary marriage as a solution to sexual anxieties of youth, and the topic itself became the subject of intense debate in the blogosphere.

Panahandegi (Refugee) blog in a post entitled 'temporary satisfaction', sarcastically remarked that temporary marriage has a number of advantages, including: it would get rid of AIDS in Iran forever; it would solve the problem of drug addiction and homelessness; it would result in the decline of unemployment, not to mention that it would allow mullahs who have not managed, despite political and social changes, to have the best cars and villas, to look forward to a more prosperous time and life.[100] Other bloggers, similarly critical of the announcement and seeing it as an attempt to divert debates about the nature of modern Iran, responded with a more serious tone. Omid Memarian,[101] in an article written for *Rooz Online* suggested that the announcement by the interior ministry, the most political ministry in Iran, at the time of arrests of many activists and increased political pressure, was intriguing and required a pause for thought. He argued that the issue was not new, but showed how the authorities were avoiding the formulation of proper policies in consultation with experts, NGOs, and the like, instead opting and for the easiest solutions. The regime was proposing temporary marriage at the time when even the rights of women in 'permanent marriage' were violated, and where the non-violent and reasonable demands against discrimination were met with arrests, threat and repression. Memarian argued that the worsening economic conditions, the rise in unemployment and the shortage of housing had rapidly eroded the possibility of marriage for large number of Iranian youth. This left millions of young Iranians living in a society which suspects relationships between the sexes. In this situation, the proposal of propagating temporary marriage would solve nothing.[102] Another blogger, *Bad Hijab*, in a post entitled 'Temporary marriage and its reward', also engages with the subject. She quoted officials who were dismissive of the critique by women activists that this was simply a solution to address the sexual needs of young men that would work against women. One expert, Hojatoeslam Hadi, argued that dealing with sexual needs was important and that 'western countries have tried to solve this by opening official places (presumably a reference to brothels), but Islam by making such legislation attempts to deal with human needs without spreading corruption'. *Bad Hijab* suggested that temporary marriage not only avoided addressing unemployment, addiction and so on but was also used by many men as '*Zang-e tafrih*' (a coffee break), that it remained a secret and shameful practice and that women on the other side of the contract end up with nothing. Khadijeh Safari pointed at the contradiction that people looking for a good home for their daughter through marriage could not achieve their aims with temporary marriage, so the proposal was baseless and the majority of Iranian youth were against it.[103]

Ali, the writer of *Yar-e-Dabestani* (Classmate), started his post on this item with a reminder that the next day was 'the anniversary of Ayatollah Khomeini's death, the founder of the Islamic revolution of Iran, a revolution that was supposed to provide for the material as well as spiritual lives of all

Iranians'. According to him, 28 years after the revolution, not only had no progress been made in advancing the economic situation of Iranian families, but by feeding confusing definitions and interpretations of Islam to people, they were now more distrustful. Ali pointed at the huge youthful population who were now at the age of marriage, and how Ahmadinejad's promises, to distribute oil money and to provide financial help for marriage had done nothing, so that two years after the formation of the ninth government of the Islamic Republic, the issue of temporary marriage had been raised, which not only solved nothing but was an insult to Iranian women and men.

> *'Certainly, and beside the fact that atomic energy is our absolute right, humane life is also our absolute right. And to achieve this freedom of which the right to live is its most significant foundation, we have to try harder.'*[104]

A devastating critique is offered by a woman student who writes the *Inroozha* (These Days) blog discusses how even her fellow male students were asking what is the importance of women's rights and she had come to the conclusion that all men were the same and that all considered temporary marriage a good idea.

> *Who cares what the consequences of such an infantile decision are? This government is an expert in prescribing pain killers for everything. Quick pain killers, at least until the next election … The idea of Mr Minister is a new pain killer that has just come to mind. Because the age of marriage has increased, and youth have no means to marry, the poor youths (if you see youth here and elsewhere read: boys!) are facing thousands of physical and emotional pains and illnesses. Those who are not religious couldn't care less and will seek pleasures in different ways. That leaves a bunch of moral youths (= boys) whose hands are short of women and have no way of satisfying their needs … Have you read the story? Now see what's our friends suggest for the ending: In order to prevent youths wasting themselves lets 'propagate' temporary marriage, so no one no longer will regarded as ugly, bad and shameful. Then any youth (boy) who cannot afford marriage will go for temporary marriage and this will not lead to corruption in society and its stinking smell will not contaminate! As simple as that!*

For her, the suggestion coming from a top official was astonishing. She continued:

> *Now let's substitute youths with girls! And let's see that if this plan has thought about girls as much as boys? 'Which family will give her daughter away in temporary marriage? You who promote such things will you give your own daughter and sister in temporary marriage?'*

She had attended a family court, listening to women's stories, and so the next time she sees her male classmate she will answer him by saying 'Go to family court once and you will understand why one should talk about women's rights.'[105]

By 2008, the main public activities of the women's movement had distilled into two parallel campaigns, which shared the same ideological orientation but chose different tactics of organisation.

Meydaan (Women's Field)[106] already briefly described, organised focused campaigns on specific topics such as stoning and women's access to football grounds. It made a number of short videos with handheld cameras, taken without permission, which were shown to small groups to trigger discussions and participation. Amongst its best-known figures are Shadi Sadr, Mahboubeh Abbasgholizadeh and Nahid Sotudeh.

The other main campaign was the umbrella One Million Signatures[107] campaign established in 2006 to demand changes to discriminatory laws against women, that was picked up and internationalised by Amnesty in 2008. Its founding members include Parvin Ardalan, Zhila Baniyaghoub, Noushin Ahmadi Khorasani and Mansoureh Shojaee. Among its early supporters were well-known national and international figures, including film directors such as Jafar Panahi and Tahmineh Milani; Nobel Laureate Shirin Ebadi and poet and writers such as Simin Behbahani and Moniro Ravanipour.

Many activists of these two groups have been arrested and imprisoned, some many times over and including during the post election unrest in 2009. Both campaigns have won considerable international recognition and many of their leading figures have been the recipients of international prizes.

Conclusion

The attempts to islamicise Iranian society after the 1979 revolution met with many obstacles. The rapid modernisation of Iran, the increase in urbanisation, literacy and access to education as well as the inherent contradictions in the Iranian state policies led to the wider participation of women in the public sphere and new forms of politics. The women's movement has remained the most visible and consistent throughout the entire history of the Islamic Republic. What's more, the very 'traditionalist' women who were assigned to implement and safeguard the state policies in Iran, have also began to challenge the patriarchal discriminatory policies of the state and conservative readings of Islam. Publications, later websites and blogs, became the sites where critiques and strategies to resist and change state policies were debated and formulated. Not all the sites nor blogs are radical, not all engage with formal politics, but as we have tried to indicate, even the most mundane of issues in the Islamic Republic comes to have a gendered and political twist.

These voices from the blogosphere reveal the dynamic, multidimensional, repressed yet active, public presence of many women, especially the younger generation, who find the straightjacket of the Iranian regime suffocating. In cyberspace, a wide range of organisations and individuals have been actively debating the most significant and the most mundane of topics that are related to gendered relations and state policies that affect Iranian women. No wonder they felt frustrated in the election of 2009 and produced such an instant social movement. It had been brewing for years.

Becoming Intellectual: The Blogistan and Public Political Space in the Islamic Republic

all men (sic) are intellectuals but not all men have in society the function of intellectuals

Antonio Gramsci, Prison Notebooks, 1971

Analysis of intellectual life in Iran has a long pedigree. Since the 1979 revolution, interesting work has been conducted on key individual thinkers and the origins and trajectories of their political philosophies as well as the Iranian intellectual encounter with 'modernity'.[1] Considerable attention has been paid to the 'religious/secular' divide which is often seen as a key demarcation between thinkers, although almost as often this is taken to be blurred and a false dichotomy. Perhaps the most recent trend is towards serious analysis of the emergence of a new 'Islamic modernity' as the intellectual voice of the Islamic Republic and beyond.[2]

Yet the focus of such analyses has tended to privilege select individual voices and their political philosophies at the expense of a broader sociological and communications-inflected analysis of who actually gets to speak inside the Islamic Republic of Iran, who gets noticed and how individuals are recognised as intellectuals, by definition a public process. Especially in the period since the revolution, most attention has been paid to emergent Islamic voices[3] including individuals such as Abdolkarim Soroush and Hassan Yousefi Eshkevari, which begs the question of why analysis of intellectual debate and activities should be narrowed to only Islamic intellectuals. This work pays scant attention to the social processes whereby some people become labelled as 'intellectual' so glossing over the terrain of debate, taking the 'political' as an evident and bounded sphere of focus rather than itself a contested space as well as a space of contestation.

We wanted to open up the debate about intellectuals in contemporary Iran, to try to problematise who counts as an intellectual, what constitutes intellectual work, where and what are the spaces for intellectual debate and what the implications of such an approach might be for an understanding of Iranian society. We argue that intellectual work requires a number of elements, including labour, forms of content and social space in which to perform that labour, and that the rapidly changing communications environment in Iran provokes a wider framework of analysis and a more inclusive examination of emergent public voices. Here we examine the massive growth of Persian-language websites and bloggers that have contributed to a realignment of public debate in Iran. Sociological, political and communicative questions have to be posed and tentative answers offered. Our aim is not to proffer an alternative or definitive list of Iranian intellectuals, indeed that is far from our goal. Rather, we would claim that this terrain needs to be better thought through and theorised, and that the voices and practices evident in the blogosphere are just some evidence of a shifting cultural terrain inside Iran.

Thus, our argument centres on three interconnected and mutually reinforcing issues that we wish to explore: the new range of voices who find ways of speaking, so who counts as 'intellectual'; the spaces available to do these things which is perhaps a model of resource mobilisation; and the range of topics they introduce into public debate, which we take to require more nuanced thinking about what constitutes the 'political'.

What Is Intellectual Labour and Who Does It?

The epigraph from Antonio Gramsci that opens the chapter firmly locates the debate about intellectuals within a broader set of social relations. That is central to Gramsci's argument about intellectual work, in which he stresses that everyone has an intellect and uses it but not all are intellectuals *by their social function*. Gramsci thus holds a very open notion of intellectual labour, in which 'there is no human activity from which every form of intellectual participation can be excluded' so that everyone 'carries on some form of intellectual activity ..., participates in a particular conception of the world, has a conscious line of moral conduct, and therefore contributes to sustain a conception of the world or to modify it, that is, to bring into being new modes of thought'.[4]

However, he classically identifies two types of intellectuals – traditional and organic. Traditional intellectuals are those who think of themselves as autonomous and independent of the dominant social group and are so regarded by the general population. The clergy, the professoriat and the philosophers all seem to enjoy historical continuity and seem autonomous from the Italian state although that is more of a social illusion since – despite individuals adopting more critical positions – the social location and institutionalisation of such groups is as essentially conservative and supportive of the ruling group in society.

Organic intellectuals develop together with the dominant social group, the ruling class, and constitute their thinking and organising element. Such people are created by the educational system to perform a function for the dominant social group, and it is through this group that the ruling class maintains its hegemony over the rest of society.

Gramsci's class analysis thus required that, in order for any kind of counter-hegemonic position to grow and challenge the taken-for-granted common sense that prevailed, both 'traditional' intellectuals needed to 'change sides' while the working class movement had to produce its own 'organic intellectuals'. Any ideological struggle for social change required not only consciousness raising but also consciousness transformation, while the creation of a socialist consciousness would develop out of actual working lives. Theory and practice are not separate phenomena, but critical social theory emerges out of conscious struggle in and with the real world. So the intellectual sphere is not confined to a small elite but should be grounded in everyday life, and indeed should 'speak' to and about that life in language that all could understand. As he wrote, 'the mode of being of the new intellectual can no longer consist in eloquence ... but in active participation in practical life, as constructor, organiser, "permanent persuader" and not just a simple orator.'[5]

Nicholas Garnham, in his analysis of contemporary intellectual work in the West that reworks Gramsci's model, offers three broad definitions. He writes that intellectuals

> maybe defined as a class whose power, sometimes called symbolic power, derives from monopoly control over the production of knowledge and cultural legitimation through the possession of socially accredited power to define what counts as either true, right and beautiful. Second, they maybe defined functionally as information workers, those whose specialized position within the division of labour is the manipulation of symbolic forms. Third, they maybe defined normatively as a vocation, as representatives of critical, emancipatory tradition appealing to universal values'.[6]

The first group we call 'embedded intellectuals', and it includes all those who currently work within the framework of the ideology of the Islamic Republic. Later we will look at the religious voices available in the blogosphere and suggest a rebuttal both to the simplistic argument to be found in Alavi's[7] book that all activity in the blogosphere is necessarily anti-statist and emancipatory and to the stark divide that consigns religious figures and practices simply to the space of 'tradition'. The second is an interesting category of everyday workers in the information economy, an emergent group in Iran for reasons we sketch out below, but we shall pay them little detailed attention here. The third group are of most interest to us, and a subsequent section focuses on the contemporary arguments about the role of the Left and the voices of students and union activists in the blogosphere as possible exemplars of this emancipatory potential.

But if Gramsci and Garnham help us theorise the sociopolitical locus of intellectuals, we still need to grapple with the spaces for intellectual work and better define what kinds of content might be worthy of such a designation.

The Changing Locale of Intellectual Work?

The broad shifts in the nature of and conceptualisation of intellectual work in contemporary modernity is not specific to Iran. In many countries, there is currently debate about the changing face of education and the dislocation of intellectuals from their traditional ivory towers. One vigorous voice is Russell Jacoby[8] who lambasts US academe as bureaucratised and corporatised, leading him to a mournful diatribe about living 'after the last intellectuals'. Clearly, there is a general drift of knowledge workers away from educational institutions to new bases in thinktanks, government-supported research and development activities and to the mass media where information workers produce and disseminate information about matters of public life. A further shift in the nature of intellectual work has been triggered by the massive rolling-out of information and communication technologies across the world[9] and the emergence of arguments about the so-called 'knowledge society' and its range of new knowledge workers. World leaders met over five years of summitry from 2000 to 2005 to discuss the 'information society' even as others were arguing this was no new phenomenon but merely the latest phase of global capitalism.

Throughout modern history, the democratic potential of communication technologies, variously 'new' in different historical epochs, for the expansion of the public sphere has been trumpeted.[10] The printing press revolutionised European intellectual within 50 years of its development, and remains an epoch-defining technology.[11] Walter Benjamin[12] clearly saw the revolutionary potential of film and the mechanical reproduction of works of art. Bertolt Brecht argued for the possibility of making radio into something really democratic, arguing radio was more than an 'acoustical department store' but could be turned into a two-way communication that was 'capable not only of transmitting but of receiving, of making the listeners not only hear but also speak, not of isolating him but connecting him'.[13]

Clearly, there are many large leaps from a Gramscian model derived from the practices of factory workers in the neighbourhoods of Turin to the practices of Iranian workers/bloggers in face-to-face and cyberspatial contact. Iran, like most oil-rent economies, suffers from a very peculiar and specific division of labour, and one that is not the most conducive to the spontaneous development of class-based demands.[14] However, it is true that the most significant class in the broad alliance that put an end to Pahlavi dynasty was the working class. Under the Shah's plan for the modernisation of Iran, the working class had grown significantly, reaching well over 4 million, and well over 50 per cent of the economically active population.[15] Workers arrived at the scene rather late, but it was their presence and their general strikes that clearly indicated the end for the monarchy. Lacking any pre-existing unions, workers began to organise *shora*, councils, and demand control of factories and industrial areas.[16] Almost three decades later, a wave of strikes in Iran in 2006, including the ongoing challenge posed by the bus workers' union for rights of association and better working conditions, made their leaders into national heroes and showed how many essential political-economic issues have still not been resolved by the Islamic Republic. Indeed, already in spring 2007, many external commentators started to argue that the internal economic and political problems would be more likely to bring down Ahmadinejad than the US military threat.

But one of the central points of Gramsci's argument is that the invitation to ordinary people to join in political discussion, that is their hailing or interpellation as intellectuals, is part of the social process of actually producing intellectuals. In one sense, Iranian society has been highly politicised, not to say radically divided, since the 1979 revolution – including the kinds of interactions with its extensive diaspora – and while often felt by individuals to be a huge drain of energy, this actually has the potential to lift the level of public debate.[17] It is in this context that the debate about an emergent public sphere is inevitably linked with intellectuals. Garnham suggests that the 'bourgeois public sphere was classically the creation of and ground for intellectuals. The project of the democratic generalisation of the public sphere is a project to make everyone an intellectual'.[18] Within such a narrative, the role of communication is central for it was not only in saloons and coffee houses but also through growing numbers of journals and periodicals that the aspirations for social change and collective activities were expressed.

Yet without getting bogged down in another muddy terrain of debate, we wonder whether the ever-chimeric Habermasian 'public sphere' of European origin is an appropriate concept to utilise in non-Western societies? Mouffe's notion of 'public space' seems at once less Eurocentric, more flexible and simpler:

> *The frontier between the social and the political is essentially unstable and requires constant displacements and negotiations between social agents. Things could always be otherwise and therefore every order is predicated on the exclusion of other possibilities. It is in this sense that it can be called 'political' since it is the expression of a particular structure of power relations. Power is constitutive of the social because the social could not exist without the power relations through which it is given shape.*[19]

We would argue that the social production of intellectuals and, more importantly, intellectual debate, requires sufficient public space for such debate to emerge and develop and that the diffusion of new technologies and thus the greater access of ordinary people to express themselves publicly on issues that concern them mean that around the world there is a far greater range of voices speaking 'intellectually' than ever before. Thus, Gramsci's much-cited understanding of intellectual labour in the 1920s may be challenged by the different information environment of the twenty-first century.

The Blogistan Debates Intellectual Work

Despite this rapid expansion, the internet in Iran is far from universally accessible and hardly indicates general democratic access, the provision being heavily skewed towards urban areas and access often being too expensive for ordinary users.[20] Additionally, the internet and blogging also suffer from constant pressure from the state, which has resulted in the closure of internet cafes, a crackdown on many blogs and sites and the arrest and imprisonment of bloggers.

The technologistic drift of policy ran parallel to other processes that reinforced the growing significance of the internet. These include the devastation of Iranian universities by a massive academic brain drain abroad and the post-war support to veterans that gave them privileged access to university places above higher-scoring students. These also include the state's tightly held jurisdiction over the contents of national broadcasting so that radio and television remain closed to critical and oppositional voices. Furthermore, there have been bitter incursions against many semi-independent dailies and periodicals, with over 20 titles closed down in the year 2001 alone.[21] Over

180 publications were banned or had lost their licence in the first term of Ahmadinejad's presidency, while the range of organisations, including so-called NGOs, allowed to function openly is constrained and political groups are strictly vetted. That an active blogosphere was built up very quickly is thus hardly surprising, given the control over most other social spaces of articulation.

Iran, as Lerner pointed out a long time ago, has never suffered from a shortage of intellectuals; if anything, it has suffered 'from the over production of intellectuals'.[22] And this issue is now debated in the blogosphere itself. For example, Nilgoon blog[23] recently published a number of articles engaging with the question of intellectuals. One article by Aramesh Dost-dar entitled 'Periphery Intellectuals and Problems of Language'[24] argues that intellectual works in Iran are heavily influenced by the West, and that not only are the intellectual works in Iran 'peripheral' but so too is the language in which such works are written and expressed, (that is, Persian). The limit of intellectual work is therefore the limit of Persian too. Abdi Kalantary, an-other contributor to the Nilgoon debate, lists what he regards as the essential characteristics of public intellectuals and makes a useful distinction between knowledge workers and academics who produce specialist knowledge, us-ing specialist languages and targeting specialist audiences. In his view, public intellectuals are those who make their findings and arguments available to a much larger audience and generate public debate. His two examples are Noam Chomsky and Edward Said who successfully made the transition from academics to public intellectuals. Therefore, for him there is a difference be-tween intellectuals/academics who use specialist language and public intel-lectuals who avoid academic jargon. Other contributors including Daryush Ashuri and Mohamadreza Nikfar have suggested that Persian is not a mod-ern 'public' language, and therefore Iranians find it hard to play the role of public intellectual, since Persian with all its limits also limits intellectual work. Ashuri's critique, however, moves beyond language. As we suggested earlier, much of the recent writing is about Iranian intellectuals coming to term with modernity. The problem for Ashuri as he has suggested in his contribution[25] entitled 'Intellectuals in the Public Sphere in Non-Western Worlds', the very idea of intellectuals outside a certain European geogra-phy (Britain, France, Germany) is an alien and imported idea. For the same reason, Ashuri argues that there is no point in comparing Iranian intellec-tuals with their European counterparts. He argues that intellectuals in those three European countries were the vanguards of the Western Enlightenment and the articulate voices that conceptualised modernity. In a non-Western context, Iran included, intellectuals suffer from a fundamental tension between inhabiting a modern rationalism and dealing with the emotions underpinning his/her native world. 'Eastern' intellectuals, Ashuri suggests, are also carriers of progressive, modern and vanguard ideas, but these derive from the ruins and emotional and material concerns of the shantytowns in the 'East'. The world of Eastern intellectuals, including Iran and even India and China, is the periphery – the shantytown – to the intellectuals of the rich core.

That some 'Eastern' intellectuals are concerned about 'emotional and material concerns' is beyond dispute. However, the intellectual 'aristocracy' that Ashuri is rather rightly so fond of were also immediately concerned with the modernity that was emerging out of the rabble of feudalism. If their arguments seem universally applicable it is precisely because capitalist modernity with all its contradictions is now universalised across, as well as within, societies.[26] Undoubtedly there do exist differences in practices and the question of whether intellectuals and their practices are culturally specific remains a significant and urgent research topic. However, the binary of Eastern and Western geography is unhelpful and paves the way for some unsavoury 'cultural relativism' and reactionary conservatism. Ali Mirsepassi,[27] in his reply to the aforementioned writers, rightly suggests that what is lacking in Iran is not the absence of intellectuals, because there are many Iranian writers and journalists who engage with social and cultural issues and even many state and military officials who, by obtaining PhDs, have joined the rank of intellectuals! However, the lack of exchange and dialogue among intellectuals, including between religious and secular intellectuals, and the absence of a genuinely open space for debate are major obstacles. Mirsepasi asks whether Iranian intellectuals play their democratic role, or whether the scientific and university institutions are truly democratic institutions. In response to arguments raised by Ashuri and others who see the Persian language as a major obstacle, he argues that in its simplest Habermasian definition, the public sphere derives its democratic quality through its independence from the state and encouraging citizens to engage in a rational debate about matter of public concerns. Intellectual practices, therefore, have no direct relation with the limits of Persian as a language, and it is not as if an intellectual constrained by Persian could present significant and progressive ideas in another language. The 'non-analytical' nature of Iranian language is not simply a linguistic problem and the formation of genuinely democratic institutions cannot be postponed until a period in which the limits of Persian are addressed and rectified. For Mirsepasi, there are a number of issues to be sorted out. First is the poverty of university institutions. New social thought and modern social sciences including sociology, anthropology, philosophy grow in academic environments, yet in Iran, academics (*daneshgahian*) have not played a significant role in producing new ideas and establishing critical–intellectual institutions. This role has been played by Western educated and independent and self-taught individuals, especially translators. The current post-election challenge to the teaching of the social sciences in Iran is a further handicap to the development of critical thought. Second, is the 'nationalistic' development of language. According to Mirsepasi, the introduction of modernity to Iran is mixed with the projects of establishing a central state and the consolidation of 'national identity'. The dominance of Persian (and Persian literature) was consolidated by undemocratic institutions that had no interest in the growth of critical and analytical enlightenment. This is not unique to Iran. Turkish and Arab intellectuals too regard their language as the base of their national identity and have engaged in 'cleansing' their language of 'alien' influence. Mirsepasi argues that it is not clear how in a country where there is no boundary between the private and public sphere, where the judiciary is not independent, where the freedoms of press and political associations have not been recognised and educational institutions are under the control of the state, the language can be made secular. Thirdly, establishing such a secular discourse cannot take place in a language that cannot be comprehended by the public. Therefore, it is necessary to avoid 'specialist' language, academic jargon and words invented by a translator because these only increase the gap between intellectuals and the public at large. And finally, in the struggle for a genuinely democratic public sphere the issue of agency is crucial. In relation to what causes democratic change, social philosophy or social institutions, it is crucial to emphasise the second, since the danger from illiberal philosophies and tendencies is much less in democratic institutions.

While Mirsepasi's emphasis on the broader social context, as opposed to the limits of language, is important, the issue of the poverty of Iranian educational institutions, especially universities, is more complex. As the number of students enrolling for higher education has increased, the exclusive and elite nature of higher education has been to some extent challenged. The modern history of social movements in Iran is unimaginable without the student movement outside and especially inside Iran. The 'poverty of universities' thesis is only true if this poverty is defined in terms of specialised scientific product and research. Iranian students have been a major progressive force and many independent intellectuals (as mentioned by Miresepasi) have emerged from a large dissatisfied student body that was not absorbed into academia. On the other hand, it is also true that academia in its modern shape not only encourages fragmented knowledge (sociology, political science, philosophy.) under the banner of original research; it also encourages academics to write for their colleagues rather than for the public at large. Such a narrow definition of intellectuals (such as those obtaining a doctorate, and Mirsepasi acknowledges even state and army officials are at it) presents and regards intellectuals as a 'profession' and a 'status'. Therefore, we have to acknowledge that while capitalist modernity has made education more accessible, by requiring special knowledge and expertise it has increased the divide between the public and intellectuals. This is why the idea of 'public intellectuals' remains significant as is their role in social change and movements.

What Constitutes 'Intellectual' Content?

Another significant issue, and not entirely separate from the previous point, is that while the project of the public sphere is ultimately about making everyone an intellectual, it doesn't follow that all bloggers are and can be considered as intellectuals. In a chaotic cyberspace, there are many voices, not all critical, not all about matters of public life, and not all about challenging the authority of either the state or capital. If the issue of access is significant, so is the issue of content. Equally important is the idea of 'intervention' by intellectuals, which by definition requires specific commitment and discursive strategy.

We have already argued in this book that in the Iranian context the 'political' is always contentious and contingent, not least in an environment where even simple 'private' acts such as holding hands with a member of the opposite sex, or one's clothing can become a 'public' concern. Yet we also want to argue that an important designation of something as intellectual is precisely the 'making public' of previously inarticulate, unnoticed social issues.

The issues at work here – that between private matters and public matters; that between the 'sphere of the private' and the 'sphere of the public'; and that of the processes whereby things 'are made public' – are nowhere better explored than in feminist theory, which has taken this fickle blurry binary as one of its key foci.

For our purposes, the most important two lines of argument are that the 'personal is political', and that there can be all sorts of political messages in popular culture and entertainment formats, indeed the Iranian blogosphere is replete with evidence of both.

Embedded Intellectuals and Religious Blogs

Undoubtedly, there are many badly written and ill-conceived ideas in the Iranian blogosphere but, as we present in some detail, there are also many good, articulate, intelligent voices. It is as wrong to regard the Iranian blogosphere as a 'sad waste of time' as it is wrong to present it as necessarily and universally a critical, anti-establishment and anti-regime singular space.[28] Apart from anything else, there are many 'embedded intellectuals' and members of the regime who blog.

Focusing on Islam has been a central feature of much of academic debate about Iran, and as we have suggested earlier, the debate about intellectuals is not immune from such a narrow focus. Islam is certainly an aspect of Iranian culture. It has been so for over twelve centuries. But it is only one aspect and Islamists have by no means a monopoly on Iranian culture nor are they the only influential agents in societal development; indeed, they themselves have been affected by social transformation. Contemporary Iran is also strongly influenced by nationalist sentiment as well as by a strong secular culture. Throughout the entire history of the Iranian media, the clerical establishment has remained a key player. They were among the early adopters of technologies, saw the clear advantage of the printing press and even allied themselves with various organisations and intellectuals to further expansion of the press. The Iranian state and clerical establishment quickly recognised the usefulness of the internet as a tool for propaganda and furthering their policies. Indeed, from early on, the internet in general and weblogs in particular have been regarded as so influential that not only did the government find it hard to ignore them, but they also actually began to endorse them to some extent. The internet played a key role in the 2005 elections, with all candidates having their own dedicated site/blogs, and many religious institutions and agencies have deemed it necessary to establish an online presence. A report by Mehdi Khalaji in August 2005[29] went as far as calling the holy city of Qom the 'IT Capital of Iran'.[30] In that respect, the Islamic Republic has embraced technology, and there are conservative websites that challenge the more critical websites. The most fascinating examples of such attempts come from religious centres in the holy cities of Qom and Mashhad, where websites are designed and launched to promote Islam and the teachings and values of the Islamic Republic. In one computer centre in Qom, more than 2,000 Islamic texts were transferred on to CD-ROM and later on to the internet. Sheikh Ali Korani, director of the centre, argued that the internet is a reality and Iran must learn to live with it: 'Take a knife, for example. You can use it in the kitchen or you can use it to commit crimes'.[31] This new technology, as Rahimi [32] has suggested, allows the clergy to spread Islam and provide their own *tafsir*, interpretation. Official internet cafes have been launched to tackle 'alien' and 'decadent' Western culture and provide a 'safer' environment for religious internet users.[33]

Religious blogs of various kinds are expanding too. There are more than 3,000 blogs registered on PersianBlog as religious. The second biggest weblog provider in Iran also lists over 3,000 blogs as dealing with ideas and religion. MihanBlog, another weblog service provider, even offers the domain name of muslimblog.ir. ParsiBlog was launched in 2005 with the aim of promoting and encouraging religious blogs and hosts over 6,000 blogs. Counting religious blogs is not an exact science, and undoubtedly there are religious blogs that have more to do with philosophy and ethics, as there are news blogs that have more to do with religion. Yet available sources of funding through state institutions and religious networks – not to mention the absence of filtering and censorship – makes launching and maintaining religious blogs much easier. There is even an Office for Development of Religious Blogs,[34] launched with the support of a Qom seminary to promote and finance religious blogs. An important part of this project is to encourage students of *hozeh elmieh*, religious schools, to blog. An emerging sub-group of religious blogs is Qu'ranic blogs, including *Ask Quran*,[35] *Menbar*, pulpit,[36] *Quran Blog*,[37] *Islamic Government*,[38] *Shia Superior Religion*[39] and a blog by Hamid Talebi entitled *A Muslim Journalist*.[40] There is even an Association of Muslim Bloggers[41] claiming to have more than 900 members. The association claims that 'at the time of Satan's rapid information bombardment', it is necessary to mobilise Muslim bloggers to defend and spread the message of pure Islam.

In addition to the blogging activities of the 'inner circle' of the state closely associated with *velayat-e faghih*, there are many religious intellectuals who, while still committed to the Iranian state, have in recent years distanced themselves from this theocratic structure. Many of these were part of the reformist camp that came to the fore during Khatami's two terms as president (1997–2001 and 2001–05). The most celebrated and well known of such figures, Mohammad Ali Abtahi, one of Iran's six vice presidents during Khatami's presidency[42] launched his blog/site in September 2003, which became an instant hit. He quickly launched an English site, which received 15,000 visitors a day, and later added an Arabic version. He announced his arrival by posting a message 'I am here as well!!!' Shortlisted by Deutsche Welle International Weblog Award in 2006,[43] his blogs consisted of daily articles and diaries, well-kept and extensive archives, articles about him in other media, interviews and photographs. He wrote commentary in Persian and English on cultural issues, including the controversial movie *The Lizard*, and regularly criticised any crackdown on weblogs and the internet. It is one of the very few blogs without a link to other blogs. Mohammad Ali Abtahi was arrested on 16 June 2009 during the aftermath of the presidential election, appeared in a show trial and was sentenced to six years in prison.

Other known figures with blogs include Attaollah Mohajerani[44], Khatami's deputy until he was forced out of office, and his wife, Jamila Kadivar, an activist in her own right.[45] These two blogs are hosted by the same domain, have the same design and format, and the only link which appears on their blogs is their other half's blog. One of the key figures of reformist camp and the best-known religious intellectuals, Abdolkarim Soroush, has no blog but there is an official site[46] in both Persian and English that contains works by him and on him as well as news archives and events. Listed in *Time* magazine's annual (2006) list of the world's most influential people, Soroush has been at the centre of much of the debate about the past, present and future of the Islamic Republic. Much of his reputation as an influential intellectual has something to do with the structure of access to the public sphere that has allowed him to express secular arguments that others have been prevented from doing freely.[47] Toward the end of 2008 the Islamic Revolutionary Guards Corps announced a plan to recruit 10,000 Basij bloggers to further the ethos of the Islamic Revolution and to protect the internet from subversive external voices. The longitudinal monitoring of the shape of the Iranian blogosphere by John Kelly clearly shows the growth in religious blogs by 2009.[48] Not only are religious voices increasing in the blogsphere, but the range of debate about religious matters is expanding also, with implications for intellectual discourse and state political control that is not necessarily to the liking of conservatives.

Blogging Left

As we argued at the start of this chapter, to frame the intellectual debates in the country in relation only to Islam is to explore a narrow furrow that ignores the complexity of modern Iran. Specifically, the focus on religious intellectuals has also meant ignoring the powerful contribution of the Iranian left in modern Iranian history. Any serious discussion of Iran and Iranian intellectuals has to pay serious attention to the impact of Marxism and Marxian thought in Iran. The blogosphere is no exception, a space where the contemporary presence of many with leftist tendencies and their arguments and concerns can be found. Farid Pouya, an Iranian researcher reporting for *Global Voices* has recorded some of the left-wing bloggers responses to the relationship between Hugo Chavez, the leftist Venezuelan President and Iranian president Mahmoud Ahmadinejad.[49] For example, one blogger in *New Left: 21th Century Socialism*[50] published an open letter written by 'Students of Iranian Universities', in which they address Chavez by writing 'with your trip to Iran, we as supporters of the Venezuelan Revolution, want to raise a number of issues about your relationship with the Iranian regime'. Chavez was given a history lesson on Iranian labour:

> *Iranian workers toppled the Shah's regime in 1979 but unfortunately they did not get any share in the Islamic Republic. In 1980's all unions, workers and syndicates were closed down and worker activists and left-wing parties, without exception, were repressed and thousands of activists were executed. . . . In 2003, the regime was engaged in the privatization of the universities. Students protested in massive demonstrations all over country . . . the government used all its repressive force to repress the student movement . . . that Iranian regime has already executed thousands of left-wing militants.*

The letter continues by saying that it is impossible to defend the interests of Venezuelan workers while making faces at Iranian workers.

Another blogger *Nasl-e-Farda*, The Future Generation,[51] in an item entitled 'Comradely Criticism of a South American Comrade' (posted on 4 August 2006) after expressing his fascination with South American culture, music, literature and revolutions, argues that the Iranian left should criticise left-wing government in Latin America while remembering that there are several differences between those and the Iranian state:

> *The leftwing governments in Latin America never restricted the basic rights of women. That is not the case in Iran. Not only they have never restricted the rights of ethnic minorities in Latin America, they have always been supportive of their cause. However, in Iran the rights of Kurds, Turks, Turkemen, etc., are violated by the government. Nowhere in Latin America where the left rule are there as many political prisoners as there are in Iran. If that was the case we would have never heard the end of it from US governments. Nowhere in South America where the left rule are there as many executions and deaths as there is in Iran.*

Another blogger, Havari[52] notes that many governments in South America, including Cuba and Venezuela, are supporting the Iranian government and consider the Iranian state as anti-imperialist. For him this is very confusing and it matters because, since the 1960s, the Iranian left has always been influenced by popular struggles in South America. For him, it is a tragedy that radical South American governments reach out their hands towards a regime that has a terrible record of killing leftists. It is the duty of the Iranian left, he suggest, to breakdown this shameful alliance. One blogger, *Alaihe Vazeiat Moujod*, Against The Current Condition,[53] posted the Tehran Bus Drivers Union letter to the Federation of Venezuelan Workers during Ahmadinejad's visit to Venezuela. A suggestion for 'New lyrics for the fascistic anthem, *Ay Iran*' (a very popular anthem) posted on Kaveh Abasian blog[54] generated an extensive debate about nationalism.

The emergence of many blogs[55] campaigning on class-based struggles and issues and for closer links between students, women and workers in Iran is re-flective of a new wave of unrest in Iran. Photoblogs such as *Kosoof*[56] provided vivid photoessays and visual images of recent struggles by students, women and workers in Iran. *Kosoof* was the recipient of a special prize by Reporters Sans Frontiéres in the Deutsche Welle International Weblog Award in 2006 for his tireless defence of human rights.[57]

Union Blogs

Part of this growth, and a significant aspects of blogging in Iran, has to do with the renewed struggles for democracy and a strong emergence of class-based struggles. Many have focused on recent workers' activities in Iran and their efforts for better working conditions, wages and union rights. One blog, *Kargar*, Worker,[58] provides news and analysis of labour movement in Iran and produces a newsletter. Its analysis ranges from critiques of the capitalist system of production[59], the recent attempt by the Iranian government to change the labour law in order to accommodate private interest, to in-depth interviews with sacked workers, regular updates on arrested and imprisoned workers and campaigns and messages of solidarity with striking and sacked work-ers in factories, schools and so on. *Kargar* also lists relevant articles focusing on workers' struggle, privatisations, as well as discussions about the activi-ties and the ways forward for workers' organisations that are posted on other sites.

One of the most significant and widely publicised events in recent years has been the formation of the Iranian Bus Workers Union. The union and, in particular, its leader Mansour Osanloo have been relentlessly persecuted for their efforts to secure and remain an independent trade union and for fighting for better wages and working conditions. Their effort is part of a collective movement to establish the right to democratic and free associations and unions. The bus workers began in 2001 to form the union, and after the election of Ahmadinejad, the wave of attacks, redundancies and imprisonment of activists intensified. As Osanloo told *Transport International Online*, an organ of International Transport Workers' Federation:

> *The minimum wage for bus workers in Tehran is close to US$100 and with all the subsidies we receive it comes to about US$150. The poverty line is US$400 per month. But even government statistics show that the minimum wage should be US$300 per month. At the same time, working conditions are very difficult. The air pollution is very bad. Some bus services have been privatised, which means the workers have to ensure they compete with these buses. Another problem is that they are not doing just one job, they have many different jobs: they are the driver, the helper, the ticket collector. Yet more problems are that there are two sections on the bus: the women have to be in one section and the men in another. This is a very difficult working situation for us.*[60]

The union has its blog and because of international coverage and solidarity, English and French sections have been added, providing up-to-date news and information about union activities.[61] Since 2006, various campaigns against the suppression of the union and day of actions in solidarity with arrested members have highlighted the significant rise of workers' activity in Iran. The union blogs and others have played a major role in bridging the union with other activists and fellow unionists across the world. Osanloo was adopted as a prisoner of conscience by Amnesty in 2007, but continues be a political prisoner even in April 2010.

Other blogs that have emerged include Workers Action Committee, with a slogan reading: 'In preparation for united action against capitalism'.[62] This blog, like many others, provides news, information and analyses of workers' struggle. Items posted recently include news of the arrest of six fire fighters who had refused to pour hot water on Alborz Plastics's striking workers; Iran Khodro workers' message of solidarity with Alborz Plastics's workers; news of continuing gathering of workers of Sadra factory and news of the release of Mahmoud Salehi, the former leader of the Saghez Bakers' Union. Another blog is dedicated to the Associations of Iranian teachers.[63] The slogan of the blog reads: 'The rights of teacher and student are the rights of the Iranian nation'. In April 2008, the blog moved to a new site with extensive coverage of activities of Iranian teachers, other Iranian workers, as well as international news and features. It also provides links to local branches of the association and other related blogs. The aim of the blog is to be a 'small media for expression of a big pain, a pain which threatens the future of a nation'. It continues by saying that the foundation of a people is based on educating its children, that everyone knows the source of all sins and errors is poverty, that a poor person cannot be complete and aid others, that teachers are a major source of inspiration, and that the 'main problem is this: poverty, poverty, poverty. Poverty is the source of discrimination and injustice'. The blog says that its aim is, therefore, to fight against injustice and poverty; to enhance the collective efforts of teachers for their rights; closer unity between teachers; participation of teachers in policymaking and fighting against discrimination in education including those of permanent and hourly paid teachers.[64]

With the increasing waves of strikes, demonstrations and activities in Iran, the debate has begun about how to enhance such activities, and how to bring disparate activities/unions and associations together. One blog reflecting the tendency towards coordinating workers, students and women movement in Iran is shorayehamkari.com. In addition to providing regular updates, news, analyses and interviews with key actors, it is also the blog of *Shoraye Hamkari Tashakolha va Fa'aleen Kargari* (Council for Coordinating Workers' Organizations and Activists). The council consists of six different organisations that started cooperating in February 2007, and while it recognises and indeed encourages diverse point of views among Iranian activists, it also aims to co-ordinate the efforts and unite various organisations. The aim is not to agree on any specific plans or ideas, but to find common ground for more united and concerted efforts. Their slogan is: 'Our unity is the guarantor of our victory'.[65] Radical students are a significant part of this campaign. Since July 1999, when the Iranian regime attacked a demonstration, which was sparked by news of the closure of daily *Saalam*, Iranian students have become radicalised. The reformists' cabinet of Khatami's two terms presidency, and the increased pressure since the election of Ahmadinejad, have radicalised the student movement. Undoubtedly, this is not, as is the case with other movement, a homogenous movement, but a significant part of it is unmistakably influenced by leftist ideas. Although part of the broader workers' movement, their blogs need to be considered in more detail.

Student Blogs: The New Political Vanguard?

One clear sign of the crisis of the Iranian state, undoubtedly, has been the rise of the student movement. Historically, Iranian students have been a major part of the struggle for democracy and many of the cadres of various organisations had, and have, emerged from activities on campuses. They played a crucial role during the previous regime, and participated in the revolution of 1979. The siege of the US embassy by a number of students, and the manipulation of the hostage crisis by the new state which was already under pressure, divided the left as well as the student movement into 'pro-democracy' and 'anti-imperialism' segments, and allowed the new state to consolidate its position. The subsequent closure of the universities in 1980 as part of a 'cultural revolution', the arrest of many students and lecturers, and the purging of state and educational institutions of 'undesirable' characters (secular, religious and nationalists who didn't agree with the new proposed order) (Ali Akbar Mahdi, 1999) further undermined the student movement in the country.

It is worth remembering that more than 40 million Iranians, about 70 per cent of the population, are under the age of 30, while nearly 50 per cent are under 20. None has a personal recollection of the 1979 uprising. Also worth remembering is that the total number of university students has rapidly increased, especially since 1979. In 1948, the number of university students at Iranian universities was estimated to be 6,525. In addition, 2,000 more students were studying at universities outside Iran (Daniel Lerner, 1958). At the time of the Iranian Revolution, in 1979–80, the number of university students, studying in 541 fields, had reached a record 175,675. In 1995–6 this figure had increased more than threefold to 526,621 studying in 966 different fields. If we add the 521,472 students who were studying at the Islamic Azad University a (private university that runs on tuition fees received from students) and the thousands of Iranians who study abroad, in 1995–6, there were well over 1 million Iranian students studying at different levels and fields. In the same academic year, the ratio of university students per 1,000 people stood at 1.78. Only around 6 per cent of Iranians have higher education degrees, but the importance of this group, as the student uprising in the summer of 1999 and the subsequent spate of student activities has shown, should not be overlooked. It is the desires and aspirations of the 'grandchildren' of the revolution which have become the focus of recent political debates. The 'problems' of the younger generation cannot be simply regarded as a sectional issue but as a national one. The power of the so-called 'future of Iran' comes from the anxiety of this generation who see no bright future ahead of them.

The factionalism of the Iranian state, and the contradictions between the 'Islamic' and republican elements of its constitution, caught between the imperatives of the market and its ideology, and simultaneously calling for students to be politically active and vigilant yet seeking de-politisation, has created a very intriguing social and political environment. The same is true in the case of the student movements, which are diverse, not coherent and not always well-organised. Mahdi has provided a detailed analysis of student participations in politics before and after the 1979 revolution and has rightly suggested that the optimistic tone of many commentaries about the July 1999 demonstrations were ignoring a number of key issues (Mahdi, 1996: 6):

> *Aside from the optimistic and sympathetic features of these accounts, they characterize the student movement in Iran as an organised, independent, democratic and secular movement bent on replacing the Islamic government with a democratic one. Many of the writings about the student movement in Iran are based on a romantic view of student activism and a desire to overthrow the Islamic Republic. The current student movement in Iran is quite different from the movement that developed during the Pahlavi regime.*

Mahdi suggested that there was nothing new about the student demands and the absence of anti-imperialism and anti-American sentiment was matched by the absence of references to socialism, Marxism and capitalism. However, in recent years the students, or sections of them, have been radicalised. The failure of the reform movement to achieve key aims such as the rule of law, accountability and more openness, the election of Ahmadinejad and the changing environment in the region (the invasions of Afghanistan and Iraq and the real threat of attacks on Iran), have produced a different kind of response. Some of the leading student figures are actively seeking closer relations with the USA and have an ambivalent position on US threats against Iran, while a number of students, clearly seeing themselves in a Marxist camp, have begun campaigning against the threat of war while asking for a new political order in the country. For these activists there is no opposition between anti-imperialism and democracy. Again, as Mahdi has rightly argued, the temptation to romanticise or generalise the student movement should be resisted. We have already argued that contrary to general assumptions, the blogosphere is not radical and progressive in its totality, and we have pointed out the diversity of intellectual responses including conservative elements. Here we do want to look at the example of the emerging secular and, in some cases, visibly Marxist student blogs.

Abed Tavancheh, who runs the aforementioned *Alaihe Vazeiat Moujod*, Against the Current Condition, is one such student.[66] His blog is openly Marxist, and quotes from Marx and Lenin appear on the left side of the screen. Among the recent entries on his blog are photographs of arrested left-wing students, a reply to a reformist/left student who had attacked the radical students, a poem dedicated to celebrated Iranian song writer and poet Iraj Janati Ataie, translated article by Seymour Hersh suggesting that the US excuse for attacking Iran is changing from nuclear weapons to terrorism, an anti-war announcement by Iranian intellectual Naser Zarafshan with a link to his site dedicated to campaigning against war against Iran.[67] Judging by the number of entries engaging with such topics, the future direction of struggle and the relationship between students and workers and women activists is crucial to this and many other bloggers. Tavancheh's blog provides links to many left-wing groups and sites outside Iran, including *Monthly Review*, *Marxist Archives* (English and Persian), as well as his friends, colleagues and fellow activists, many of whom are openly Marxist and are referred to as comrades.

Among these is comrade Elnaz Ansari. Her blog, *Zananeh*, Womanly,[68] in turn links readers to a number of women sites and blogs as well as to many friends. One item posted on 21 April 2008 entitled 'On Sex and Body' tell readers how bored she is of reading bloggers who write about their own experiences of sex and the body. She argues that these blogs are even more boring that those who write about their relations with friends or their brother catching cold and so on. Badly written stories written by boys about their conquests and sex with various people blur the boundaries between pleasure and repulsion, eroticism and porn. One view (erotic) of the world is beautiful, delicate and artistic, while the other (porn) is rough and sickening. For her the love poems of Neruda are extremely erotic and sensual while these blogs are sexy but also reminiscent of the dirty hands of fellow passengers in taxis. Elnaz argues that in a society that is marked by the absence of sexual education even at the university level, where everything is extremely sexual while everything is a bat used to suppress sexual knowledge and where any discussion that hints of sexuality becomes political, thinking and writing about sex is thousands times harder. Previously she had written about why she was not in a celebratory mood, nor hopeful for the new year that was approaching. The reason for her gloom was the news that apparently the prison guards in Evin's notorious prison had organised a birthday party for one of the students in jail in order to humiliate the newly arrested prisoners. Once all the students gathered, the guards brought out two of the leading figures of the students' movement, Behrooz Kariminejad and Payman Peeran. Their physical appearance and condition was so bad that some of the students burst into tears.[69]

She also writes about the Voice of America (VOA) which is busy tapping on the drum of war and propagating the economic policies of USA. However, she suggests that progressive thinkers need a new angle of critique and asks why 'we' cannot launch a news radio and wonders:

> *Don't we have enough trained personnel? Don't we have enough comrades that can financially support a left-leaning and independent radio or television?*

A number of other blogs, clearly with left leanings, also engage with the newly revived social movements in Iran, part of the diverse networks of activists inside Iran with increasingly closer connections with unions, groups and individuals outside the country. Among such sites is *Salam Democrat*: *A view from the left*[71] that provides regular news as well as analysis and commentaries by a number of commentators inside and outside Iran. Structured like a newspaper, it has editorials, articles, reports and news of recent political events. Its editorials focus on Islam and politics; 'actually existing socialism', and rethinking the legacies of Mao and Mossadeq. In addition, there are student 'publications' such as *Militant*,[72] which claims that it doesn't belong to any political organisation, but is produced mainly to defend the position of radical socialists against the reformist and centrist tendencies in the student movement and to overcome the disparity among socialist students. *Militant* also has an English site.[73] Another blog is the Socialist Youth Blog[74] supporting *Militant* and publicising solidarity acts outside Iran, workers news, as well as critiquing some left-wing organisations. It has also made certain Marxist text available to its readers, including a translation of Leon Trotsky's *The History of the Russian Revolution*. Another publication is *Be-pish* (Forward), which is managed by Arash Safar and run by an editorial board. The *Freedom- and Equality-Seeking Students*, which began in 2006, was formed as a result of radicalisation of certain sections of student movements, with the two key slogans of No to War! and Free Universities from Invading Military Forces!, in response to both the threat of war against Iran by the USA and the invasion of campuses by security forces in Tehran. They have organised various events including celebration of 8 March, May Day and Student Day in Iran. This tendency produces a number of blogs/publications including *Khak*[75] (Earth) run by Kaveh Abasian, *Armane No* (New Ideal),[76] *Gavaznha Deer* magazine,[77] *Shorah* (Council) magazine[78] in Mazandaran University in northern Iran, *Toloo* (Dawn)[79] and others.

Conclusion

It is of course nothing but a huge tragedy that the products of Iranian intellectuals, and of countless others in many countries in the Global South, are often 'reviewed' and 'assessed' not in scholarly and literary journals but in front of firing squads, torture chambers and prison, or in bitter cold exile. Such physical and emotional tests that many 'symbolic producers' have to endure is as old as intellectual history. Benjamin committed suicide waiting to escape the Nazification of Europe; Trotsky was felled by a pickaxe; Rosa

Luxembourg was shot on the street and Gramsci wrote much of his best work in prison, to cite just a few examples. There has also been a less violent Western demonisation of public intellectuals such as Chomsky and Said in recent years. Political instability and repression and the absence of any sustained period of political openness necessary for the formation of a genuinely democratic society, has meant that there has always been a high degree of political parallelism between political/economic interests and the media in Iran. And without doubt, the strong institutions of the *ancient regime*, most notably the monarchy and conservative religious institutions, made the transition to 'modernity' a long, difficult and conflictual process that continues under the Islamic Republic.

There are immense difficulties facing intellectual activity in Iran and that is why a large part of it now appears in the blogosphere. We've explored how the debate about what constitutes intellectual life and practice is itself staged in the blogosphere; we've highlighted the debate about rights for women and the new virtual life of the forgotten Iranian left that – for us – constitute important examples of the re-establishment of critical public engagement with the issues of the day. Conservative and religious bloggers are out in force, and thus a naive celebration of the entire Persian blogosphere as a site of resistance is simplistic in the extreme.

There are dangers in this argument. We would not wish to argue that every voice in the blogosphere constitutes intellectual activity. Yet we would also say that in conditions of severe cultural surveillance, even the emergence of popular culture is overlayed with more political freight than its equivalent form in the West. We would also like to acknowledge and highlight the power of writing as a central tool of intellectuals. It is of course unclear how all these writerly voices will develop, but the blogosphere sets a powerful base for an intellectual culture to come. Not everyone is an intellectual nor does everyone need to perform intellectual tasks, but many more people in Iran than might be expected are involved in the recreation of a public space of debate that remains vibrant and emancipatory in aim, even while under threat.

English Language/
Diasporic Blogs:
Articulating the
Inside and the
Outside

AT VARIOUS POINTS in this volume, we have invoked the distinction between internal and external pressures and the relationships between Iranians inside Iran and those outside. Let us develop that further.

Since the 1979 revolution, Iran has experienced an emigration of around 4 million people. It also experienced an inward movement of millions of Afghani refugees from the wars in that country so that during the late 1990–2000s, Iran had one of the largest refugee populations in the world. There are sizeable Iranian populations in many countries. The largest clusters of Iranians outside Iran are in not only Los Angeles (Tehrangeles), Toronto (Tehranto) and northern European cities (London, Paris, Hamburg) but also in Costa Rica, Malaysia, Japan and Australia. In some ways, it is important to ask not only what is Iran but also 'where' is Iran? Westwood Drive in Los Angeles offers a complete Iranian experience, almost from cradle to grave, in the services provided by Iranians for other Iranians.

There have, of course, been varied waves of emigration. Pro-Shah supporters left before and during the revolution, often carrying out considerable wealth. Leftists, democrats and secularists discovered to their great sadness that there was no role for them inside the Islamic Republic and leached away from 1980. Many young men escaped illegally from the draft and the war with Iraq. Economic migrants have tried to flee escalating inflation and unemployment. Countless thousands of women and their families have escaped the repressive culture of an Islamic theocracy.

Many in this outward movement have been middle-class in terms of educational background and financial well-being, with higher degrees and money in banks, making the Iranian diaspora a very different configuration from other migrant groups. Indeed, the IMF has regularly reported (2004, 2007) that Iran experiences one of the world's worst brain drains. The contradictions in such an outward movement are vast, not least in the ceding to others of one's place at the political table. (See Annabelle Sreberny-Mohammadi and Ali Mohammadi, 1987.)

To begin with, relations between the diaspora and home population were quite strained. The diaspora has continued to expect new political change to be imminent, whereas those at home felt abandoned with all the problems as their families and friends enjoyed the nice lifestyles of the West; the tensions were captured well in Esmail Fassih's 1985 novel *Soraya in a Coma*.

Over the years, the difficulties in getting a passport and being allowed to travel have eased. Although not easy, more in diaspora are ready for a visit home; so there is much more movement of Iranians in and out of the country. It is noteworthy, however, that some people are banned from leaving the country (*mamnoo-ul-khorooj*), sometimes only discovering this at the airport itself. Others are banned from entering Iran (*mamnoo-ul-vorood*). Which is worse probably depends on many diverse calculations. Of course, the process of getting a visa to arrive at the other end also has to be negotiated, with many Iranians travelling to Turkey and Dubai for holidays and as middle spaces to meet family when unable to gain entry to the preferred destinations of Europe or North America.

It is obvious that new technologies provide wonderful ways for this extensive diaspora to keep in touch across many international boundaries including back in Iran. VoIP provisions such as Skype are popular. The expansion of mobile telephony has brought most Iranians unprecedented and increasingly affordable connectivity; the wait for a landline in the last years of the Shah was well over 10 years. Iranians have flocked to mobile telephony and the latest 3G phone designs comprise large sectors of local bazaars.

Iranians have always been strong out-marryers and can be seen as a transnational diaspora, which means many new cultural practices and languages are pulled into the web of 'Iran'. The diaspora also means that the use of Persian is attenuated. In research conducted amongst Iranians in London in the mid-1990s, over half the families – event those with two Iranians as parents – spoke English at home (Sreberny, 2000). Pinglish, a hybrid that varies in its mix of the two languages depending on situational factors, is widely acknowledged as a new vernacular. As already discussed, the web is full of Persian material: news portals; social networking; chat; dating and marriage; online shopping for music, DVDs, and such (but hard to purchase inside Iran). Often on such sites, people write in the new transliterated orthography of Pinglish: Persian sentences written in English.

Although the majority of blogs by Iranians inside and outside of Iran are written in Persian, many Iranian bloggers have opted for bilingual blogs and many write only in English, perhaps to appeal to a wider audience or because they lack skills in written Persian, or both. Some make a point about the language they use and the reasons. For example, one blogger writes:

> I am (own name) 27 years old from Tehran / Iran. I blogged for years at my farsi weblog (www.jadi.net) but these days I'm FILTERED in my own country so I have to write here in English. It's shame but it is the situation ! I am keeping an eye on freedom of expression, censorship, internet filtering and ... (he provides an email address) Note: English IS NOT my native language. I'm not good at it. But I think writing in poor English is much more BETTER THAN not writing at all. But I'll be glad receiving friendly editorial, spelling, grammer, ... comments and I'll fix and learn.

A list of blogs in English – some by bloggers inside Iran and some by those outside – was being maintained by Hoder (blogsbyiranians.com/), but since his arrest, it is no longer available on his frozen website, and links from his own website to other blogs do not function. The list has been taken over by Fariborz Shamshiri and is maintained at www.iraniansblogs.com.

Many blogs in English by Iranians have romantic, evocative names: *Persian Garden* (written by Rouzbeh, frozen in August 2003); *Iransara* (frozen in May 2005); *The Dreamer* (stopped May 2006); *Turquoise peacock* who maintains a site from Tucson, Arizona.

Some are punning and self-deprecating: *Hooman's Scribbles* (April 2009, Kaspersky virus protection doesn't allow access because it contains a Trojan) and *The Eyeranian,* described as 'random opinions and observations written by Pedram Moallemian'.

Yet others are didactic, such as *Iran Zamin,* which claimed to provide 'personal views on the history of Iran in comparison with other ancient countries and information on Persia for those interested to learn about our heritage', but became exhausted in August 2006. And *Parvandeh* (File) which was 'dedicated to providing readers with accurate news regarding the ongoing struggle of Iranians for the acquisition of democracy along with intriguing comments worth consideration' but was stopped in March 2004. *View from Iran* has become *View from (outside) Iran.*

However, *Eteraz Online* still offers

> A Bewildered Conscience Blindly Groping for Clarity: Dissent is the Only Response to Manufactured Realities. 'Eteraz' means 'protest' in Farsi and Arabic, and the aim of this blog is to both analyze and question received dogma and the obfuscations which so often blight and warp media coverage and discussion of Middle Eastern politics and culture.[1]

That so many of the blogs in English by Iranians outside Iran had stopped by 2008 is an interesting phenomenon about which we can only speculate here. Clearly ongoing blogging takes time, effort and application. It requires an investment in one's Iranianess and in a political struggle to educate the world about it. There is a lot more research that could be done on where these individuals were located, how they worked and why they stopped, but our guess would be that the lack of a critical mass in face-to-face reality and the difficulties of seeing any real change in the Iranian polity from a distance make English-language blogging a very uphill activity. The difference from those living inside Iran who confront a range of problems as part of daily life is marked.

Again, we discover a fascinating paradox: a context that tries to control political activity produces more, while contexts in which political activity is potentially much easier to engage in often invite less. The obvious points of comparison are the widely expressed concerns about the demise of political engagement by young people in the USA – before Obama – and the UK.

There are blogs in English from inside Iran, articulating Iran to the world in more ways than one. *Tehran Post* is 'Cautiously Speaking from Inside Iran', muses about writing shorter blogs but posts a lengthy blog about the emerging faultlines of the Iranian presidential election. There are also many English versions of popular Persian websites, including roozonline.com/english/, offering interesting materials from the reformist block of Iranian politics.

Bloggers on the Move

Given the difficult circumstances for bloggers inside Iran, many who were popular inside Iran have had to continue their activities outside, in Europe, the USA and elsewhere. Sima Motallebi, mentioned earlier, resumed his blog once he left Iran. Omid Memarian continued to blog from Canada. Lady Sun blogged from California, later from London. Yet others – like Parastoo Dokouhaki, Masih Alinejad – move in and out of Iran and write about all the locations in which they find themselves. So the very phenomenon of 'Iranian blogging' has a mobile dislocated element within it.

Halfies and Returnees

But there is yet another category of blogs worth examining. Thirty years after the revolution and its massive emigration, there is an interesting process happening of return migration to Iran. The regime has often and loudly invited back its diasporic people. But the returnees are not so much the generation that left before, during and after the revolution but their children. The 'next' generation are returning, sometimes with keys to property not opened for decades and finding themselves the legatees to large houses with swimming pools or extensive apartments. Some of these 'returnees', for want of a better term, are fully Iranian. Others are 'halfies' (Sreberny-Mohammadi, 2009), with one Iranian parent and one American, or British, or French, or German, or Japanese or any other. For this generation, Iran appears a little like the Wild West, open for business, uncluttered by bureaucracy and law although heavily surveilled, available for living fantasy lives. As are many of this 'next' generation in the West, these young people are unfettered by old ideologies and know little about the 1979 revolution; indeed, many were born after it. And, while not necessarily very religious, very Islamic or very keen on the prevailing regime in Tehran, they find enough activity, possibility, dynamism and difference in Iran to stay. It is not clear for how long they will stay; indeed, many could not articulate that themselves. Simply, at the moment they are living in Iran. Moreover, many of these young people are blogging.[2]

As we have mentioned before and as have so many commentators about Iranian blogging noted, many individual blogs are forms of personal exploration conducted in a public space. Thus many of the young Iranians writing in Persian are posting very intimate musings about their personal lives, relationships with their family, issues around dating and sometimes explicit posts about their sexual lives. These could be seen as the classic Eriksonian explorations of adolescent identity, especially poignant in a context where public space for discussion about such matters has been limited and made even smaller by the rhetorics of the regime that extend deep into the realms of erstwhile 'private' life. As Mahdavi's (2008) recent book evidences clearly, many young Iranians know little about the body, about sex or about sexually transmitted diseases, yet they are caught up in rather extreme sexually explorative practices, living dangerously in many ways. It is not surprising that young people explore their problems openly on the Net, find readers who empathise with their plight, perhaps share it or perhaps offer information and resource to deal with it.

The posts by 'returnees' address a different kind of 'identity crisis' that is more cultural in definition and frequently expressed as 'what does it mean to be half-Iranian?' Or 'what does 'Iranianess' mean to me?' That such a theme also runs through many blogs by Iranians in Iran, many posts on Facebook, many videos on YouTube is food for thought. The unresolved tension between Iranian nationalism and Islam, the growing sense of collective resistance in the face of hostile rhetoric towards Iran from foreign powers, the much-vaunted sense of national pride all need more analysis and elaboration than we have time for here. Suffice it to say that the issue of 'Iranianess' is by no means resolved for Iranians and remains an radically open project for 'returnees'.

The posts on kebabandtwoveg are strongly personal, or at least start from personal experience. She says 'I don't know "Iran" but I know a little bit of Iran. I feel I have to start with what I see and feel. I can't comment about the big picture.'

Some of the posts directly address the experience of fit/non-fit in Iranian society, the desire for many Iranians to gain visas to leave and the reasons for her friends to remain:

> It fascinates me in contrast to so many people wanting to leave, we have all arrived- many for Farsi, many for business, many to be big fish in small ponds. Interesting that we have chosen to live here, with all its immense problems. But all of us enjoy the luxury of 2 passports and having a foreign currency in our bank accounts. Some talk of staying here permanently, others definitely have an expiration date. As expats opportunity is at our feet. As one reminds me 'I've had diplomats round for dinner, and the woman's national basketball team playing at the courts behind my house, do you think this would ever happen in California?'. The same can be said for my recent presence at a variety of embassy parties ... did I ever find myself being served Ferrero Rochers at the French Ambassadors in Kensington? No, never. I haven't been served ferrero rocher here either, but I have drunk champagne and danced salsa behind heavy doors and the diplomatic guard.

But there's also a sense of an ethnographic project, of immersion in a different cultural environment, with detailed comments on the production of *samanoo* for Norouz and on which women veil in which company. Hence the voice seems to address a foreign, non-Iranian audience, enculturating them into this very different environment.

Linked to this blog in English is another: deconstructinghairy. blogspot.com.[3] This is part a travelogue ('this is where I've been') and part outsider trying to become insider ('I'm eligible to vote but how do I understand the process and the politics?'). This blog seems also to interpellate Western friends and to try to explain Iran and the writer's experiences to them. She makes a rather funny comparison in a neat photo essay between Texas and Tehran as the Wild West versus the Wild East, listing shopping, cosmetic surgery, big cars, pollution, as things the two places have in common and developing the well-known love-hate relationship that the Americans and Iranians have had for a long time.

And later she writes rather movingly that:

When I went (when I started this page) I think I was going to try to discover, or figure something out about, my being Iranian. I'm still not sure I can describe my feelings about those experiences adequately with words. I didn't really reach any huge epiphany about my identity. But I guess I decided that it's nice, that I am Iranian, but really not such a big deal. I decided that from one perspective, it is all just chance. Identity is more about the decisions I make.

Iran was beautiful, and full of wonderful things, and more a part of me now. I experienced things there that I never felt anywhere else, discovered how things there were interwoven in my life and my past. The personal factor I felt there never really figured in anywhere else. The same exact thing might offend me in Tehran, and make me smile in Belgrade. At the same time, this is way too simplified – it was personal, but foreign at the same time. At times very awkward indeed. I also saw a lot of things I didn't like. And, although I am eager to go back to Iran, and it holds a special place in my heart, I am also eager to visit other places and people.

So I choose to keep some things about 'Iran' in my identity (of course some parts of that I couldn't escape anyway), but only as one of the many facets that equally define who I am, and that confusingly grow everyday.

This rather neatly also makes the important point that blogs, like lives, are dynamic. The reasons for starting them are not the same reasons for continuing them. Or for letting them die.

Some blogs provide an introduction that frames the background of the writer and a way of reading the blog. Ddmmyyyy (www.ddmmyyyy.org) describes (himself/her?) as a 'Freshly thirty dual national Brit with a shameful lack of exposure to my paternal homeland of Iran'. Worried that 'my view of the world would be forever channelled through a thick pair of National Health blinkers, I sought to correct my vision, through exposing myself completely to Islamic Republic, that is Iran'. S/He writes about ordinary encounters in Iran, about getting things wrong and misunderstanding people, again addressing an external readership, mainly friends and family.

Yeki bood, yeki nabood is the way most Iranian fairy stories start. This blog offers modestly 'one opinion of one iranian who grew up abroad. as with anything i post on this blog, it is my personal perspective and in no way intended to represent the views of iranians at large, or even other iranians in my own situation'. She begins 'kicking it off with controversy: *hejab*' and provides a fascinating discussion about men telling her that her scarf had fallen down. She protests that men should 'NEVER tell a woman, "fix your *hejab*". it's really insulting to be told what to do by somebody who never has to do what they're telling you to do.' And that it takes any autonomy away from women who might wish to push such boundaries.

Life goes on in Tehran is developed by an Iranian returned from Los Angeles who describes its mission as 'to show that regardless of what any president would have you imagine, despite what any media outlet would have you believe, life goes on in Tehran and elsewhere in Iran' and is totally image based, all photos taken from a camera phone.

Will Yong (willyong.wordpress.com/images/) exemplifies some of the real complexity of cultural heritage: 'Born in Tehran to an Iranian mother and Malaysian-Chinese father. Brought up in the suburbs of North London'. He offers 'thoughts, experiences and images from Tehran, Iran' but this multi-cultural background is stated but not engaged. Again, interestingly, the image seems to take over from the text. A number of recent books of photography (Mark Edward Harris and Ahmad Kiarostami, 2008; Tori Egherman and Kamran Ahstary, 2007) offer an eclectic range of images of Iran 'as it really is' to counter received wisdom and the avalanche of images of black-chadoored women that comprises the mainstream media's representations of Iran. Of all these image takers, Yong reflects most on the difficulties and delights of taking photographs in Tehran, slinging his camera over the far shoulder when a police car goes past, catching shots on the sly, asking people if he can photograph them and being surprised at their assent. He reveals how hard it is to capture good images of Tehran and even asks of what those would consist.

Blogging as an activity plays powerfully on the cusp of the public–private: private matters are made public; public affairs are translated and coded for private, known readers. Circles are built up of other bloggers, commentary upon commentary, because bloggers are amongst each others' most faithful readers and so new friendships are formed. But those inside Iran, writing in English, provide a fascinating set of vistas in to everyday life in Iran, albeit mainly in Tehran, and the comparisons, explicitly written or drawn by inference, with life outside. They raise important questions about who gets to articulate what 'Iran' is and for whom, and open up the space of 'Iranianess' very wide indeed. These 'returnees' have come to a place they never knew directly and are altering the relationship between Iranians in diaspora and those 'at home', refamiliarising them with each other and representing different faces of Iran to the rest of the world. Some would come to play a very significant role during and after the June 2009 election as the social mobilisation drew the diaspora and home Iranians even closer together. A few young people found themselves playing crucial and unexpected roles in articulating the inside and the outside, connecting the movement to global media and diffusing images of the popular uprising to the world.

Journalism, Blogging and Citizen Journalism

7

IN MANY WAYS, blogging is a form of commentary par excellence – on daily life, on politics, on art. Commenting on blogging is simply a continuation of the same practice, an extended essay in intermedia commentary which is the stuff of more and more of media content, perhaps of contemporary life altogether. But in Iran, the closure of newspapers – an historic phenomenon in Iranian media history but reinforced most recently under Khatami's presidency and continued under Ahmadinejad – meant the construction of websites carrying news and editorials and blogs containing new material not available within the regime-controlled channels.

The idea of 'citizen journalism' has spread rapidly in many contemporary media systems, especially in the USA and Europe, over the past few years. It seems to challenge central aspects of the classic paradigm of journalistic activity, including professional training and recognition, paid work, unionised labour, and behaviour that is often politically neutral and unaffiliated, at least in the claim if not in the actuality. Citizen journalists are, by contrast, often untrained, unpaid, non-unionised and highly politicised. However, even in Western mediacracies, the boundaries and practices are blurring and fine lines are harder to draw.

Is such a neologism of any use for understanding processes inside the Islamic Republic? Both elements in the term have significance and each is very differently configured in contemporary Iran in comparison, say, with contemporary Britain, where the authors are both based.

Citizenship and Journalism in Iran

The concept of citizenship is creeping into Iranian public discourse, with a new weekly magazine operating under that name. Until the 1979 revolution, the simplest analysis would have put all Iranians as subjects of a centralised monarchical system. The last shah dissolved all political parties in favour of his own single party, Rastakhiz, disallowed independent unions and any gathering over three people was subject to investigation by SAVAK, the secret police. One of the many strands that mobilised Iranians in revolution was the lack of political freedom to organise and to articulate concerns. But the system that emerged after the revolution is hardly more democratic.

Reform and the Media under Khatami

In a profound sense, the history of the Islamic Republic has been a politics for internal reform and opening from the beginning, and we have referred to many such moments already. Here, we focus particularly on the hopes for democratisation invested in the 'reformist' president from 1997.

The new movement for democratisation in Iran, defining itself under the banners of 'civil society' and the press as a 'fourth estate', resulted in the two landslide victories for Khatami in 1997 and 2001. The press, in the absence of an independent system of political parties, became a key space wherein the debates about political participation and the contours of the public sphere could be articulated. Khatami was elected on the promise of greater press freedom and more diversity. He was also aware that since conservatives controlled the national broadcasting organisation, Islamic Republic of Iran Broadcasting, he would need a sympathetic press to gather support for his policies.

Newspaper titles reflected the changed milieu. Instead of conservative dailies such as *Resalat* (Prophetic Mission) and *Jomhouri-e Eslami* (Islamic Republic), new colourful titles emerged such as *Jameh* (Society), *Neshat* (Joy), *Mellat* (Nation), *Azad* (Free), *Mosharekat* (Participation), *Fath* (Victory), *Hughugh-e Zanan* (Women's Rights), *Rah-e No* (New Path), *Hayat-e No* (New Life), *Bahar* (Spring) and *Goonagun* (Variety). Many were regional and local titles ensuring that the political movements were not limited to Tehran and major cities (Adam Tarock, 2001:590). They offered little space for religious and 'official' stories, instead publishing hard-hitting investigative reports on corruption, inefficiencies and abuses of power by significant institutions in the Islamic Republic, including the Ministry of Intelligence and the Islamic Republic Revolutionary Guards.

Yet the Khatami period was contradictory, many new titles flourishing immediately after his victory only to be followed by a vehement campaign against the press. The censoring and closing of newspapers and harassment and arrest of journalists marked his last few years. Advocacy of 'civil society' by the pro-Khatami press forced the proponents of conservative policy to retaliate. A new press law passed just before the parliamentary election of 2000 was used to censor publications, raid premises, take equipment and to harass, fine and even imprison journalists. By the end of 2002, more than 80 publications in Iran had been banned by the judiciary and many re-emerged in online forms (Gholam Khiabany and Annabelle Sreberny, 2001). Furthermore, by labelling the reformist and independent press as an enemy of Islam and the Islamic republic, the regime continued the tradition of mobilising supporters of the dominant faction to intimidate dissident voices and journalists. Certain elements of the 'fourth estate', namely Islamic Republic of Iran Broadcasting and the daily newspaper *Keyhan*, were used to discredit and humiliate those not considered 'sympathetic' to the Islamic Republic and its Supreme Leader.

The Iranian press market reflects the broader picture of the Iranian political economy, marked by the presence of massive and large-scale state-owned corporations on the one hand and petty production and small enterprises on the other. Large-scale media enterprises include the firm of *Keyhan* (13 titles, including three dailies in Persian, Arabic and English); *Etelaat* (eight titles, including two dailies catering for national and international readers); and Islamic Republic of Iran Broadcasting and its publishing arm, *Soroush* (seven titles including the daily *Jame-Jam*). Other major firms with direct links to the state are Iranian News Agency (seven titles, including the daily *Iran*), *Hamshahri* (a best-selling daily published by the Tehran mayor's office) and *Quds* (published by the estate of Imam Reza in the holy city of Mashhad). With massive financial resources and generous subsidies by the state, these all have state-of-the-art printing presses and facilities (Khiabany, 2007).

The other model of ownership, often perceived as simply *private*, is the *individual* ownership of newspapers. But many of these are former ministers, MPs and officials who have turned to the press market to promote themselves and their policies through some of the best known dailies. *Salam* was owned by Mohammad Mousavi Khoeini'ha, a former district attorney; *Khordad* owned by Abdollah Nouri, former interior minister; *Jameh* was owned by Hamidreza Jalaipour, former commander of the Islamic regime army in Kurdistan, and so on. And while petty production has provided a platform for the emergence of many titles and contributed to diversity in the press market, it also made the survival of such publications difficult. In addition, *Salam*, *Khordad*, and many others ran into difficulties as soon as their owners found themselves on the wrong side of the judiciary.

But was, and is, the Iranian press professional? First of all, at various times politics has impacted deeply upon the development of the press. Other elements of a professional press are also weak. Professional training, one criterion of professionalism, arrived quite late in Iran. Most of those involved in journalism came from the worlds of politics and literature and learned and practiced on the job. The first ever journalism training short course was launched in 1939 by the Law College of Tehran University, ending abruptly with the Allied invasion in September 1941 (Shahidi, 2007; Ghandi, 1998). After the 1953 CIA coup, Mostafa Mesbahzadeh – the publisher of the daily *Kayhan* – recommended that the University of Tehran establish a College of Journalism. US scholars came to teach journalism and some Iranians went abroad for training (Ghandi, 1998) and in 1964 a two-year training course in journalism was established. After the revolution, the programme re-emerged in the 1990s as part of Allameh Tabatabai University, with MA courses and a PhD programme. IRIB, the broadcasting monolith, runs specialised training programmes as does the Centre for Media Studies Research of the Ministry of Culture and Islamic Guidance while IRNA, the national news agency, offers degrees in reporting and translation. More recently, international broadcasters have also started to offer training. In 2006, the BBC World Service Trust started to provide training for aspiring journalists and has launched a Persian online magazine called Zig Zag,[1] where trainees write stories and practice their skills.

However, the lack of job security, poor pay and working conditions and the state's control of broadcasting and the press affect journalism training. The emergence of the semi-independent press and the internet and above all the renewed struggles for a more open and democratic society by workers, students, women and minority ethnic groups, all searching for spaces to communicate their, ideas and aspirations, have created a renewed interest in media training.

Professional bodies and associations for journalists have also had a chequered history. Media workers have always been at the forefront of struggle for democracy, including the right to form independent associations and unions. Prior to the revolution the only organisation 'representing' media workers was The Syndicate of Newspaper Writers and Reporters established in 1962 and backed by the government. Journalists played a major role during the revolution (see Sreberny-Mohammadi and Mohammadi, 1994) but the new regime announced there was no need for syndicates while allowing the formation of associations. Only in 1997 after the landslide victory of Khatami was the Association of Iranian Journalists established,[2] which had over 2,000 print journalist members by 2005 (Shahidi, 2007:111–12).

As already described, censorship and control drove many people, including publishers, writers, journalists and ordinary readers, to the internet to find and to provide information, to debate and make space for expression.

Some created web-based publications, or collectives of writers who behaved much like a press room, and yet other clustered in *halghe*, circles, of individual bloggers. Unpaid, sometimes anonymised, and self-organising, these forms of writing rapidly replaced the banned titles of formal journalism. But it does seem as if state repression is a galvanising force for political communication in Iran.

Journalists were never highly professionalised in the strict Weberian sense. Journalism training remains weak and non-standardised. The embryonic journalists' union came under severe attack in June 2008 when, as part of the general incursion on civil liberties and social movement activities, the Iranian government threatened to dissolve the journalist association and tried to remove the association's executive committee to replace them with conservative journalists.

If, in this dynamic, many journalists became bloggers, other bloggers have become journalists, especially outside Iran. In January 2009, BBC Persian television was launched, which employed the once radical female blogger Lady Sun and Sina Motallebi who had been jailed a few years before. Omid Memarian writes for a range of English-language websites.

If journalism is a form of writing, then the number of often young Iranian writers practising hard is a positive sign for the future. If journalism is a form of economic activity, then times are probably hard for any but the big firms that remain in the good books of the regime. If journalism is about articulating social and political issues, about investigation and analysis, the Iranian blogosphere functions as a powerful alternative, free at the point of consumption and relatively free at the point of production – if the mighty hand of the state can be avoided. Both citizenship and journalism are working hard in Iran, in innovative forms that are responses to the political context.

Given this background, the explosion of journalism and photo-journalism during the election process of June 2009 and after should have come as no surprise. Here was a cadre of talented, frustrated professionals and non-professionals prevented from doing their job and having a voice. Little wonder that so many people had so much to say in 2009 and enjoyed making their voices heard.

8 The Summer of 2009

THE JOURNEY of this book has been long and somewhat convoluted in trying to do justice to the range of issues involved when one starts exploring a topic such as blogging in as complex an environment as the Islamic Republic of Iran.

Our journey's end has a degree of arbitrariness also. We wanted to draw a close around the thirtieth anniversary of the revolution, 22 Bahman (10 February 2009). Yet the world, Iran and blogging would not stand still. So we thought we would wait for the presidential election in June 2009 and close the book there. But, of course, the post-election aftermath demanded our attention. This final chapter reviews the dramatic events of the summer of 2009, maintaining our focus on forms of alternative media and the emergence of citizen media.

2008

The year 2008 was particularly bad for free expression, with the state making noises about further extending media and cultural controls and with the number of bloggers and journalists in jail rising.

Yet bloggers used their spaces to report and comment on new issues. During 2008, considerable information about corruption emerged on websites and blogs. In the summer, a member of Iran's Judicial Inquiry and Review Commission, Abbas Palizdar, created a scandal in a speech at Booali University in Hamadan when he accused several top clerics and influential members of the Islamic Republic of corruption.[1] He offered details of many illegal business deals and criminal offences and pointed the finger at several of Iran's leading political figures, including influential Ayatollahs. Video footage of the speech spread through blogs and the internet. Palizdar was arrested, but for the first time high-ranking clerics had been named and shamed.

In another event in summer 2008, students at Zanjan University in north-west Iran recorded and uploaded a video of their school's vice president,

Hassan Madadi, with his shirt unbuttoned. He was allegedly preparing to have sex with a female student. Several websites and blogs reported that the female student had alerted her university's Islamic Student Association that Madadi was pressuring her to have sex with him.[2] Charges of corruption and of immorality within the regime had rarely surfaced with such vigour.

Perhaps as a counter, debates about 'foreign interference' were being ratcheted up. The Bush administration's investment in 'bringing democracy' to the 'axis of evil' had rendered every returning Iranian visiting from the USA as a potential spy. In 2007, for example, Ali Shakeri, Haleh Esfandiari, Nazi Azimeh and Kian Tajbakhsh were all arrested and imprisoned and international campaigns were organised to free them.

Radio Farda and VOA were condemned as fomenting a 'velvet revolution' (*enghelab makhmali*). Even before it went on air, the regime had circulated injunctions to journalists not to cooperate with the proposed BBC Persian Television channel, which was denied the right to open an office in Tehran (although domestic BBC does maintain a presence in Tehran). In January 2009, somewhat delayed, the BBC did launch its new Persian Television, BBC PTV.

2009

In February 2009, the thirtieth anniversary of the revolution that brought the Islamic Republic into being, was celebrated in a somewhat low-key fashion. The launch of a missile created some international interest, but the domestic crowds were thin and indifferent. Young Iranians seemed to be more interested in such domestic cultural 'deviancy' as listening to underground music and watching foreign films and satellite television channels than paying much attention to the revolutionary rhetoric of Ahmadinejad.

Obama and the Norouz Message

Iranians had broadly welcomed the election of President Obama and hoped that the political stalemate between the 'great satan' and the 'axis of evil' might actually develop into a more productive relationship. This sense was strengthened by Obama's 2009 Norouz message to the Iranian people and leaders in which he talked about the strained relation of the two countries and promised a new beginning. He ended by wishing everyone '*Eid-e Shoma Moborak*' (A happy new year)![3]

Ahmadinejad: Clenched Fist in a Tightening Grip

Despite the potential for a new relationship with the USA, Ahmadinejad revealed little changes in his external posturing nor in his tight grip over domestic politics. If anything, the spring of 2009 was worse than ever for free speech, free media and face-to-face politics.

Just a week after the Iranian New Year, a number of activists were arrested, among them Delaram Ali, Leila Nazari, Khadijeh Moghaddam, Farkhondeh Ehtesabian, Mahboubeh Karami, Baharah Behravan, Ali Abdi, Amir Rashidi, Mohammad Shourab and Arash Nasiri Eghbali. Sadly in April 2009 Omid Reza Misayafi become the first known Iranian blogger to die in jail. Roxanna Saberi, the Iranian-Japanese journalist, was arrested and only released after a strong international campaign. Others arrested included Alireza Saghafi, the editor of the magazine *Rah Ayandeh*; journalist Kaveh Mozafari, who wrote for two websites *FeministSchool* (www.feministschool.com) and *Wechange*, also known as *Change for Equality* (www.4equality.info); Jelveh Javaheri, who also wrote for *FeministSchool*; Amir Yaghoubali, who wrote for the daily *Etemad* and *Wechange*, and Nikzad Zangane, who maintained a blog (www.nik-nevesht.blogspot.com).

Also arrested was Sajad Khaksari, a journalist with the weekly *Ghalam Moalem* (*Teacher's Pen*), for photographing a demonstration by teachers. Two journalists who worked with Nobel peace laureate Shirin Ebadi's Human Rights Defenders Centre – Nargues Mohamadi and Soraya Azizpanah, the editor of the Kurdish magazine *Rasan* – were prevented from leaving Iran on 8 May to attend a conference in Guatemala on women's rights. And there were many others.

Ahmadinejad's regime was tightening even further the spaces for debate and ignoring human rights.

The Presidential Election Campaign

Despite all this activity, it was somewhat without warning that the May presidential election campaign triggered such unprecedented and impassioned involvement inside Iran. Of course, presidential elections are important moments in every country, even in Iran with its bifurcated political structure, and the preceding election in 2005 that had produced Ahmadinejad as the surprise winner had caused much controversy and debate – Karrubi claimed then that he was wrongly denied victory.

Some 475 candidates, including 42 women, put their names forward for vetting by the Guardian Council which announced on 21 May the names of the four candidates allowed to run: the incumbent Mahmoud Ahmadinejad; Mir-Hussein Mousavi, a former prime minister; Mehdi Karoubi, a former parliament speaker; and Mohsen Rezaie, a former head of the *Pasdaran*, Revolutionary Guard. Campaigning was to run until 10 June and stop, allowing 24 hours quiet before the voting on 12 June, so the entire campaign process was only three weeks long.

Mousavi ran as an independent Principled Reformist candidate and put forward a modest, reformist programme that included greater freedom of media and expression, gender equality – devised by his wife and public campaigner, Zahra Rahnavard – and a more tolerant outlook to the rest of the world, including to Israel. Former president Khatami withdrew from the race in support of Mousavi.

From the start of the campaign, Islamic Republic of Iran Broadcasting signalled its intention to broadcast live debates between the candidates. This was a powerful way to drum up interest and to try to ensure high voter turnout, something that the Islamic Republic has always taken seriously. Lots were drawn and the first debate between Karoubi and Rezaie was held on 2 June. But it was the next debate, between Ahmadinejad and Mousavi on 3 June, that opened up the political terrain. It was broadcast live on national television and available for repeat viewing on *YouTube*. Ahmadinejad raised questions about Mousavi's revolutionary commitment and about his wife's academic credentials. He also attacked Rafsanjani – who has been the second most influential man in the entire history of the Islamic Republic and is known as the godfather of liberalisation – for corruption and economic gains made by himself and his family. Suddenly the recent history of the Islamic Republic was being reworked and the credentials of some of its key figures were being maligned.

All candidates opened up pages on Facebook, which had been proscribed and only became accessible in December 2008, and put up photographs and statements. This was particularly important for the reformist candidates who had little access to state radio and television, although they had plenty of press support, including their own papers: *Etemad-e Meli*, owned by Karoubi, and *Ghalam Sabz*, owned by Mousavi.

Ahmadinejad's main site was *emtedademehr.com/* from which his supporters were encouraged to use other new technologies, including social media such as Facebook and Twitter to spread his election messages. His campaign supporters also created a YouTube channel with the same name on 30 April, with videos of his speeches. Another site, aportal.ir, claimed to be the 'Virtual Society of Ahmadinejad Supporters'. On Facebook, Ahmadinejad had a number of supporter pages although the number of anti-Ahmadinejad sites also proliferated, usually starting with 'down with'/'screw'/ 'kill' or equating Ahmadinejad with Hitler, most of which had just a sprinkling of followers. Someone set up a page called 'I bet I can find one million people who dislike Ahmadinejad' (that amassed 26,000 followers by 9 April 2010).

The incumbent's main rival camp, supporting Mousavi, set up *www. ghalamsima.com*, an internet television, as well as Facebook pages for Mousavi and his wife Zahra Rahnavard, whose page garnered 43,000 supporters (by 9.4.2010). The number of Facebook pages supporting Mousavi also grew rapidly.

The same level of passion and excitement was also visible in the blogosphere. Many bloggers who had decided not to boycott the elections actively took sides and supported their preferred candidates.

During the election campaign, Mousavi's supporters started using green as their colour. The 'green' campaign was quickly visible, with supporters devising green scarves and bandanas, posters and flags, holding large rallies and mobilising support via the internet.

Despite the uncertain and ad hoc policies of the state towards online communications and despite regular crackdowns on publications, sites, blogs and Facebook in previous years, the use of these technologies were encouraged by the state and its various factions. As Hamid Tehrani reported on digiactive.org:

> It is very interesting that Iranian authorities allowed Iranians access to Facebook and YouTube just a few months ago and already we see they are really present in the candidates' campaigns. The presence of bloggers as adviser to candidates and/or their campaigners reveal that citizen media has crept its way into mainstream politics. Mohammad Abtahi, former vice president and blogger, is adviser to Karrubi and several bloggers are active in Mousavi's campaign. Just as we now have 'governmental NGOs' in Iran, in the future we will probably have 'state-run citizen media'.[4]

The women's movement utilised their various websites to put out statements demanding women's rights and variously supported Mousavi and Karoubi in the election process, a strategy that many adopted in case one dropped out.

The Iranian diaspora, able to vote, was also hailed and social networking sites like Facebook helped erase the geographic distance between Iran and other homes. *Mowj-e Sabz*, a green wave, was visibly flowing across Iran, not only Tehran but also other cities, and beyond; for example, Lindsay Hilsum, reporter for the British Channel Four described a huge 'green' rally in Isfahan. Ahmadinejad supporters 'wrapped themselves in the flag'.

12 June: A Day of Infamy

The polls opened at 8 a.m. and polling stations were kept open longer than planned in many places to accommodate long queues. Many people reported not being able to vote and driving around Tehran trying to find a polling station without a long queue. Some people voted at the airport on their way out of Iran. The diaspora voted in embassies around the world.

And suddenly, within two hours of the polls closing, the vote was announced: an astonishing 63 per cent vote for Ahmadinejad. And the vote remained constant for all subsequent areas of the country. The overly rapid and unbelievable declaration of a landslide victory for Ahmadinejad was immediately rejected by the other three candidates, including the second 'conservative' candidate Rezaie. The Reformist camp questioned the outcome for the speed of declaration (since it seemed impossible for all votes, including those from abroad, to have been counted so quickly), for the actual figure given (which remained constant) and for the lack of variation by region of Iran. Quickly the slogan of a 'stolen election' spread and 'where is my vote?' become a national outcry of many Iranians who believed that their votes were ignored. The internet was buzzing. As during in the election campaign, the use of technologies was not limited to the reformist camp. Ahmadinejad supporters also relied on blogs and social networking sites to defend the integrity and legitimacy of his victory.[5]

By the Saturday morning, there were street demonstrators protesting the result. And over the next few days the crowds got bigger. On 16 June, Tehran witnessed the biggest demonstration in 30 years, as over a million people marched in the city, the day ending in violence. Demonstrations also took place in a number of other cities, including Isfahan, Mashhad, Shiraz, Tabriz and Rasht.

On the same day, the regime started to ban and throw out foreign reporters: many started saying that they were being confined to their hotel rooms and were simply eking out the visa period until they had to return home. Yet on British television, at least, John Simpson still walked among the crowd and filmed relatively openly, while Hilsum reported from Isfahan.

State television initially paid little attention to demonstrators and reformist candidates. But slowly it was forced to acknowledge the political crisis and unrest, even though it tended to minimise their size and scope and tried to discredit the opposition.

But for many young people, who had already started to refer to themselves as the lost or 'burnt' generation, '*nasle sookhteh*', but who had been mobilised with serious intent to find meaning in this election process, the loss and the denial of their voice was a powerful insult.

Facebook Goes Green

Facebook goes Green, July 2009

One metaphor of the current globalised moment is of 'network society'. For Iranians, their pre-existing social networks of family and friends rapidly became the basis for spreading the political message of the green wave, *Mowj-e Sabz*. Far from the fear that was palpable in Tehran during the autumn of 2008, such networks were already the embodiment of trust relations and were rapidly summoned into something even bigger. Many Iranians on Facebook changed their profile picture to a green square that included the text 'where is my vote?', while many non-Iranians tweaked the icon to 'where is their vote?'. Facebook turned green. It became a space for posting video (sometime culled from YouTube), articles (culled from international media and sometimes the Iranian press), photographs that had been sent by mobile or email attachment from people in Iran. Facebook became an enormous distribution site of new and recycled materials. One could watch a new post be picked up and shared almost instantly, seeing it move across Facebook. Many people were permanently logged in and its 'chat' facility helped many to keep in touch with loved ones and colleagues inside Iran.

More innovatory journalistic set-ups, such as Tehran Bureau, found new vigour as link and liaison between Iranians and the global press, their website hosting articles, images and blogs. Some of the young bloggers mentioned in previous chapters, including some 'returnees' who found themselves outside Iran, became important nodes in a chain of message distribution, using their familiarity with Western media channels to provide these with original user-generated content.

Twitter

Almost instantly, the external network pundits summarised the Iranian protests as a 'twitter revolution'. Comparisons were made with Moldova, when it came to the issue of Twitter (techpresident, 14 June).[6] The colour-coded campaign, particularly the green colour of Mousavi, drew comparison with 'Orange revolution' in Ukraine. Many media organisations, from BBC to CNN to *The Jerusalem Post*, jumped to proclaim the role of new technologies in the election and its aftermath (14 June),[7] and after that headlines such as 'Twitter Revolution', 'Twitter Revolutionaries', 'Revolution will be Twittered', 'The Iranian Twitter-lution', highlighted the alleged significance of technologies in Iran during and after the 12 June presidential election.

As Ari Berman put it in a post on 15 June 2009 called 'Iran's Twitter Revolution', 'Forget CNN or any of the major American "news" networks. If you want to get the latest on the opposition protests in Iran, you should be reading blogs, watching YouTube or following Twitter updates from Tehran, minute-by-minute'. Iranian bloggers were posting information, and Tehran Bureau aggregated a lot. He also mentioned bloggers such as Andrew Sullivan of *The Atlantic* and Nico Pitney of the *Huffington Post* posting round-the-clock updates and often beat the mainstream media to the story.

The Iranian demonstrators provided fascinating case study data for all the analysts now working on networking, new media and politics. And the data told a different story. According to Alexa, the web information company, the ranking of Twitter traffic in Iran is almost zero.[8] Other reports have suggested that there are around 10,000 Twitter users in Iran but only a small number of them, around 100, are active.[9] It is true that some Twitterers had a large following, sometimes as many as 5,000, but it is not clear how many of the followers were based in Iran.

The WebEcology project, linked to Harvard's Berkman Centre, made an almost instantaneous study of the Iran tweeting phenomenon. Their main findings were:

> From 7 June 2009 until the time of publication (26 June 2009), they recorded 2,024,166 tweets about the election in Iran.

Approximately 480,000 users have contributed to this conversation alone.
59.3% of users tweet just once, and these users contribute 14.1% of the total
number
The top 10% of users in the study account for 65.5% of total tweets.
1 in 4 tweets about Iran is a retweet of another user's content.

So much of the tweeting, as is increasingly the case with much media content, is a repost or commentary on previous published material. Twitter functioned mainly as a huge echo chamber of solidarity messages from global voices that simply slowed the general speed of traffic.

There is little evidence that Twitter and Facebook or YouTube played a major role in organising demonstrations. They did became channels through which messages could be sent to international media organisations that had little access and first-hand information about what was happening in Iran. These sites also attracted messages and actions of international solidarity as well as mobilising the Iranian diaspora.

But, as this entire book has shown, part of the move to use new technologies in Iran has been because of the profound difficulties of organising face-to-face politics and peaceful demonstrations. Facebook and Twitter came into their own as other platforms and voices were closed down. However, the 'real' action remained on Iranian streets and rooftops, examples of the powerful 'somatic solidarity' that had also driven the events of 1979 (Sreberny-Mohammadi and Mohammadi, 1994). It is also safe to suggest that the Iranian election wasn't the only significant election or event in the world at that time. Had it not been for the international focus on Iran and the relaying of tweets and other information by the international media, the interest in and coverage of the election in Iran probably would have matched the usually weak interest in and coverage of other elections in the world, barring the USA. It was Michael Jackson's death that pushed Iran down the news agenda. Whatever the outcome of the Iranian protests, it is already obvious, as Andy Greenberg wrote in Forbes, that these have been good for Twitter's business.[10]

So the demonstrators who became the 'green movement' variously used their somatic power, as in the sheer energy and number of bodies in one place; a wide range of new media sites, portals and platforms; and mash-ups of text, image and sound in a wave of political creativity.

They also discovered a piece of software produced by a young British software engineer called Ryan Keely who had developed a page reboot application for ebay that was used against government sites. Such applications target websites and overload them with requests for images and web pages, which exhausts bandwidth capacity and results in a distributed denial of service (DDoS) error message. Some government ministry websites, including leader.ir, Ahmadinezhad.ir, and iribnews.ir, and government news agencies such as Fars News were reported to have been brought down using DDoS attacks. A lengthy debate on the Web was triggered by this use of DDoS, with debates about both its ethics and efficacy; the tag of 'cyber-war' was downgraded to 'net-war' to describe such attacks.

Regime Responses: Violence, Arrests

The authorities' responses included violent attacks against demonstrators, often using the *Basij* (Mobilisation Force, a brutal volunteer paramilitary) on motorbikes. The shooting of Neda Agha-Sultan was the first of many terrible moments. They enforced restrictions on reporters from both international and domestic media. They kept foreign journalists sequestered in hotel rooms until their visas ran out, while the main newspaper of Mousavi's campaign, *Kalameh Sabz* (Green Word) was censored and many people associated with the Green campaign – and many who were not – were arrested. They jammed BBC PTV and other international media channels. This was combined with regular attacks by the conservative daily newspapers and a venomous campaign by Islamic Republic of Iran Broadcasting and its international channels. They periodically cut off mobile telephony, often at considerable financial loss, and blocked SMS facilities, including on the day prior to the election and periodically through the next week. They too used DDoS attacks, especially against *Balatarin* (en.balatarin.com) and several of Mousavi's websites including *ghalamnews*, and also new forms of internet and mobile surveillance, including deep packet inspection, to locate the sources of message distribution. Wasserman's cartoon neatly depicts the problem the regime had – and has – in trying to control this unprecedented avalanche of popular communication.

Ahmadinejad commented that those upset at 'losing' the election were all *khas o khashak*, dirt and dust, as though they had merely lost a football match. This prompted a new slogan, '*khas o khashak to-i*' – 'you are the dirt and dust' – and numerous music videos, based on the original elements of Rumi's poem, were posted on YouTube as anthems for the growing movement. Music videos with mash-ups of images were rapidly produced and countless of these are available on YouTube.

The Supreme Leader's unconstitutional announcement that the election was fair before the ratification of the result by the Guardian Council was an

Dan Wasserman cartoon, *The Boston Globe*, June 17, 2009

attempt to wrap up what was effectively a coup and prevent unrest and further demonstrations. What certainly surprised the authorities was the willingness of millions of ordinary Iranians from all walks of life to dare to dispute the result and demand a recount. Khamenei became the target of general anger and cries of 'down with the dictator' grew louder.

Slogans by demonstrators showed humour and politicisation. One of the first warned '*agar taghalob beshe, Iran ghiamat beshe*', if there is cheating, Iran will be rioting! Another tried to banish fear: '*natarsim, natarism, ma hame ba ham hastim*', don't be frightened, don't be frightened, we are all together. '*Marg bar dictator, che shah bashe, che doctor*', down with the dictator, whether a shah or a doctor, was directed toward Ahmadinejad and his claim to have a doctorate in engineering. Yet another played with Ahmadinejad's religious visions: '*haleye noor-ra dideh, raye ma ra na dideh*', you saw the "light" but you didn't see our votes! After a number of deaths, the anger mounted: '*baradar-e shahidam, raye-to pas migiram*', martyred brother, we will get back your vote. By 30 July, cries of an 'Iranian republic' were heard on the streets. At night, shouts of '*allah o akbar*', God is great, punctuated the night air, which resonated the cries of the 1979 revolution.

As police and revolutionary guards presented a massive security presence on the streets, deaths, injuries and arrests mounted. Images of Neda Agha Sultan dying on a Tehran street made the front page of many of the world's newspapers, while numerous video versions set to music were posted on YouTube and have been watched by hundreds of thousands of people. The British newspaper the *Guardian* established a website,[11] where it tries to log all those killed and imprisoned since the election. Sadly, many names still have no picture and the numbers continue to rise. According to Reporters sans Frontiéres, Iran has surpassed China as the world's biggest prison for journalists.[12]

By 1 August over 100 people were set to face trial for rioting, vandalism and 'acting against national security', trials quickly labelled as and compared with Stalinist 'show-trials'.

The media coverage and analysis of the Iranian election and its aftermath has become a controversial and divisive issue, a kind of Rorschach test of one's political sensibilities. Some have reacted to the immense coverage of the events by mainstream media in the USA and Europe by suggesting that this was merely evidence of the US administration wanting to destabilise Iran. Many, including Seamus Milne[13] of the *Guardian*, claim that there was no fraud and Ahmadinejad was the clear winner. He suggested that 'If Ahmadinejad was in fact the winner, then there is an attempted coup going on in Tehran right now, and it is being led by Mousavi and his western-backed supporters'. When it came to use of new technologies, again there are no shortage of stories linking online activities to the West. A good example is an article published on the Web claiming that there is proof of 'Israeli Effort to Destabilize Iran Via Twitter'.[14] As Al Giordano suggested in an article published on *CounterPunch* the events in Iran have caused schism on the right as well as the left. For him what this alliance between the right and sections of the left demonstrate is 'nostalgia for the Cold War and an inability to break out of its dualist mode of thought: one in which the world is divided between two ideological poles (the dinosaur left and the neo-con right disagree only on which pole is "good" and which is "evil" but the rest of their analyses line up seamlessly together)'.[15]

The Iranian left and progressive forces had no such doubts. The crack that has appeared inside the Islamic Republic was unprecedented in the entire history of the Islamic state. What was also significant was the reformist candidates' unwillingness to back off from their claim of rigged elections. The stakes in 2009 were high. The coup which gave Ahmadinejad a 'landslide victory' was a significant step towards further 'Pakistanisation' of Iran, bringing further aspects of public life under the control of the Revolutionary Guard and homogenising and centralising the Iranian state even further. The direct attacks on Rafsanjani and other leading figures in the Islamic Republic were also clear indications that the electoral game, as far as the Iranian state is concerned, is no longer necessary.

Intense debate centred on whether this political move had been planned or whether it was a desperate scramble to hold on to power. The answers reflected wishful thinking ('they are stupid and even organise a coup stupidly') versus paranoia ('this has been planned and they are so desperate to hold on to power that it doesn't matter how crudely it is done'). But it is important to recognise that since 1979 elections in Iran have had a dual role, both hiding the truly undemocratic nature of a system based on *velayat-e faghih*, rule of the Supreme Jurist, but also allowing various factions of the state to share power. The state has used elections as a kind of public performance of support when it suited, most notably in the 1979 referendum in which the vast majority voted for the sole option of the creation of the 'Islamic Republic'. In the first decade of the Islamic Republic, from 1979 until to Khomeini's death in 1989, when the regime enjoyed popular support and legitimacy, elections were taken seriously and emphasis on the *ray-e mellat*, the nation's vote, covered the undemocratic nature of *velayat-e faghih* as a political system.

Different periods have seen the gradual unravelling of the importance of the popular base of the Islamic Republic. The late 1980s was marked by revising the constitution, and the furthering of the centralisation of the state, including abolition of the post of prime minister and elevating the role of president, putting Islamic Republic of Iran Broadcasting under direct control of the Supreme Leader and above all adding *motlagheh*, absolute, to the *velayat-e faghih*. Under the banner of 'reconstruction' the radical wing of the Islamic Republic was marginalised and efforts were made for the rapid liberalisation of Iranian economy. In this period (in which Rafsanjani served two terms as president) the electoral processes grew paler.

Khatami enjoyed a landslide presidential victory of 1997, but his slogan of the 'rule of law' had little impact. His powers were limited. The publications, journalists and personalities that supported him were attacked, as we have described before, and the Basij was reshaped and reorganised to confront not the Iraqi army but internal dissent. In the final phase under Ahmadinejad, as we have described, the reformists were defeated and marginalised. The Revolutionary Guards with the Basij have increased their control over society; having benefitted from massive divestment of state assets and become huge quasi-public investors, builders and owners of telecoms infrastructure, they now lurk as an Iranian version of the military–industry complex. The workers, women and student movements were suppressed and yet more cultural restrictions were introduced. Already after the unexpected victory of Ahmadinejad in the 2005 election, the issue of vote-rigging was raised, first by Karoubi himself, when he didn't make it to the second round and then by Rafsanjani's supporters.

The manipulation of the presidential election of 2009 clearly demonstrates that the state can no longer risk playing the electoral game. The *ray-e mellat*, the people's vote, no longer matched the interests of the system and had begun to challenge it directly. Elections in Iran have been a useful charade so long as they didn't threaten the *velayat-e faghih*. However, this time, after having been persuaded to participate in a performance of democracy only to have it mean nothing, the people will not be so readily pacified.

It is this complex history and the role of the Iranian people in the process of democratisation of Iran that has been, rather sadly, reduced to a 'Twitter Revolution', 'Green Revolution', 'Middle-class Revolution'. Most importantly, the inherent tension between the two sources of political support, the popular and the religious, has become apparent after the 2009 election. As many reformist commentators have started to say, the popular 'republican' element is asserting itself over the 'Islamic' element of the Islamic Republic of Iran.

Finally

On 11 August, supporters of Ayatollah Khamenei, who had already maintained a website since 2004, opened a Facebook page for him. That seems like a good moment to end this analysis. Here we see the dilemmas that new information technologies pose for authoritarian governments. They cannot simply dismiss them but have to be part of them, even if they do not fully comprehend how they work or what their impacts might be.

The shouts of '*allah o akbar*' still resounded at night through the winter of 2009–10, but what we might call the first wave of change after the election seems to have run its course for the moment, mutating into other kinds of political forms. The mass arrests, the uncertain number of deaths, the visible presence of armed police and Basij on the streets have extracted their toll. Iranians at home and abroad wait to see if the regime finds a liberal face, reprimands those in custody and lets them go, or whether it will exact an even bloodier price for this cleaving of Islam and Republicanism that will not be easily stitched back together. Certainly, the demands for a free press, freedom to organise politically and greater access to the net do not look to be satisfied any time soon. The green wave has shown, however, how much can be achieved within a repressive context. But it has also shown that technologies in themselves are insufficient substitute for political strategy, goals and discourse.

In this book, we have tried to provide a reading of Iran that is nuanced, complex and multidimensional. But we have also tried to present it warts and all, to show the paradoxes and contradictions in state policy, the arbitrariness of much of its practice and the limitations of its development policies. Iran is large in territory and population, potentially wealthy on the back of its oil revenues, young and libidinous, creative and curious. Yet an approach based solely on the 'exceptionalism' of the world's only theocracy or 'Islamic communications' only constructs a 'single case' approach to Iran. It is both like and unlike other places and sorting the elements out is vital to fully understand how it functions and what it might be.

We have also tried to provide an analysis of blogging that moves away from a technologically driven understanding of ICTs and their associated practices and genres towards a historically located and sociopolitical reading of blogging. We would argue that there is no single 'internet', as there is no single 'society', and that books that purport to analyse 'the internet and society' do nothing of the sort. Universalising approaches overlook everything that is relevant to the way actually existing societies, their media and ICT environments behave. Yet theories of exceptionalism are inadequate also. Serious analytic work on the development of the media and communications environments of the global south have to work in between these two radical theoretical poles, both of which offer glib solutions to the real problems of analysis and comprehension that we face. Perhaps between the general and the specific we can excavate the vernaculars used in particular places and their modes of engagement with freedom, expressivity, the changing nature of politics and the shifting relationship between the personal and the public that all societies have to face.

The events of the summer of 2009 have helped to reinforce the general argument of the book – that Iran is seething with politics, that these take many forms and that new media are, once again, central to understanding the dilemmas of contemporary Iranian history. The long march towards freedom and equality continues.

We end with a provocative cartoon from the RSF website. Democracy is an endless performance and Iran surely has a lot more political theatre to come.

'Iran – Do not let the curtain close', Reporters Sans Frontieres, 16 August 2009

Notes

All web addresses were correct at the time of writing.

Introduction

1. See http://www.youtube.com/watch?v=MChlT0GvFPM.
2. Earlier and different versions of some of the chapters have appeared elsewhere. Some of the issues raised in Chapter One were rehearsed in a chapter in a book edited by Gerard Goggin and Mark McLelland (2008). An earlier version of Chapter Two appeared in a special edition of *Comparative Studies of South Asia, Africa and the Middle East*. (Khiabany and Sreberny, 2007). A version of Chapter Five appeared in *British Journal of Middle Eastern Studies*. (Sreberny and Khiabany, 2007). Some of the materials on citizen journalism in Chapter Seven appeared in Stuart Allen and Einar Thorson's volume on citizen journalism (2009).

CHAPTER 1   The Internet in Iran: Development and Control

1. See http://www.internetworldstats.com/stats.htm.
2. US Department of Commerce (2002) 'A Nation Online: How Americans are expanding their use of Internet', www.ntia.doc.gov/ntiahome/dn/anationonline2.pdf.
3. See http://iran-daily.com/1386/3056/html/economy.htm.
4. 'Performance record: Telecommunication Company of Iran', December 2007, http://irantelecom.ir/pdfs/amar/gozaresh__2007.PDF.
5. See http://irantelecom.ir/eng.asp?sm=35&page=17&code=5.
6. See http://www.bbc.co.uk/persian/iran/story/2007/02/070209_oh_internet_itc.shtml.
7. 'Performance record: Telecommunication Company of Iran', December 2007.
8. For full list and details of US sanctions see US Department of Treasury, Office of Foreign Asset control, http://treas.gov/offices/enforcement/ofac/programs/iran/iran.shtml.
9. See http://treas.gov/offices/enforcement/ofac/legal/eo/12170.pdf.
10. The *Guardian*, 2002.
11. See http://www.bbc.co.uk/persian/science/030510_h-banned-sites.shtml.
12. See http://www.bbc.co.uk/persian/business/story/2006/07/060703_he-privatization.shtml.

13. *Ibid.*

14. According to *Iran Daily*, in 2006, the Iranian telecom industry's revenues were estimated at $1.2 trillion or approximately 3 per cent of the gross world product. See 'Privatization of Telecom Company', 9 October 2006, http://www.iran-daily.com/1385/2681/html/focus.htm.

15. See http://irantelecom.ir/pdfs/amar/gozaresh_2007.PDF.

16. See http://www.iran-daily.com/1385/2681/html/focus.htm.

17. *Hambastegi*, 2001.

18. Ahmadi, 2001.

CHAPTER 2   The Politics of and in Blogging

1. See http://www.globalpersian.com/salman/weblog.html.

2. See http://i.hoder.com.

3. See http://www.bbc.co.uk/persian/iran/story/2004/11/041107_mj-mb-iran-web-log-anniv.shtml.

4. See http://www.eyeranian.net.

5. See http://www.badjens.com/rediscovery.html.

6. See http://www.blogherald.com/2005/10/10/the-blog-herald-blog-count-october-2005.

7. See http://weblogcrawler.blogspot.com/2005/08/blog-post_112812672727486398.html.

8. See http://www.blogherald.com/2005/10/10/the-blog-herald-blog-count-october-2005.

9. See http://dijest.com/bc/2004_08_01_bc.html.

10. See http://www.favanews.com/default.aspx/news_17034.htm.

11. See http://www.blogherald.com/2005/04/14/number-of-blogsnow-exceeds-50-million-worldwide.

12. See http://www.blogherald.com/2008/02/11/how-many-blogs-arethere-is-someone-still-counting.

13. See http://www.ariagostar.com.

14. Persianblog.com recently announced that two Iranian IT companies are in negotiation with the Blogfa management over the sale of its blog services, something that was immediately denied by Blogfa. In an announcement, the Blogfa management suggested such rumours were a sign of unhealthy competition, while also claiming that such news is a clear indication of its company's success and acknowledged that the company has received a number of offers, including one from its main competitor PersianBlog, http://news.blogfa.com/post-79.aspx.

15. See http://www.itna.ir/archives/news/003711.php.

16. See http://technorati.com/weblog/2007/04/328.html.

17. See http://www.bbc.co.uk/persian/iran/story/2004/11/printable/041115_mj-en-iran-web-log-anniv.shtml.

18. See http://www.webstats4u.com/catalogue/top1000?id=1255303&country=IR.

19. A meeting organised by womeniniran.org to celebrate International Women's Day on 8 March 2004 attracted a large number of Iranian journalists, academics and activists from inside and outside of the country. Participants in the meeting were secular feminist activists inside and outside Iran, including the granddaughter of Khomeini, Zahra Eshraghi.

20. See http://weblog.ccwmagazine.com/2004_01_01_ccw_archive.asp #107425233892335854.

21. See http://www.weblogfestival.com/introduction.htm#intro-en.

22. See http://www.weblogfestival.com/news/news_67.htm.

23. See http://mazrooei.ir/2005/03.

24. See http://drmoeen.ir.

25. See http://hoder.com/weblog/archives/cat_weblog.shtml.

26. See http://www.alternet.org/mediaculture/21316/?page=1.

27. A much celebrated Persian blog (http://z8un.com/) has listed more than 350 blogs/sites under the title of *dostan* (friends).

28. The case of Derakhshan is interesting in another way. Facing a $2-million defamation suit for critical comments about Mehdi Khalaji, a visiting Iranian scholar at the Washington Institute for Near East Policy, clearly shows the downside of being an editor. See 'The Blogfather: Times are hard for Iran's online free-speech pioneer NN', in *The Ottawa Citizen*, 2 November 2007, http://www.canada.com/components/print.aspx?id=83f9c3fd-dd92-4cef-8028-4e458a5721b2.

29. See http://www.bbc.co.uk/persian/iran/story/2004/11/041114_mj-asa-iran-web-logs-anniv.shtml.

30. See http://ashouri.malakut.org/archives/005873.shtml.

31. See http://debsh.com/rule.

32. Khatami's first landslide victory came on 2Khordad (23 May 1997).

33. See http://farjami.debsh.com.

34. See http://news.gooya.eu/politics/archives/047389.php.

35. See http://mebaily.com/archives/001268.html.

36. See http://ashpazbaashi.blogspot.com/2006/04/blog-post.html.

37. See http://herlandmag.com/about.

38. See http://www.iftribune.com.

39. See http://herlandmag.com/weblog/06/03.

40. See http://farnaaz.com.

41. See http://(www.commentisfree.com.

42. See Behnod's report (Symbolic Action of Persian Bloggers) on BBC Persian, http://www.bbc.co.uk/persian/interactivity/debate/story/2004/09/040920_h_emrooz.shtml.

43. See http://www.rooznegar.com.

44. 'Not about Sina', http://www.eyeranian.net/archives/000021.html.

45. See http://www.petitiononline.com/sina.

46. 'Weblogs Unite to Protest Detained Iranian Blogger', http://www.ojr.org/ojr/glaser/1051148901.php.

47. See http://raminj.iranianstudies.ca.

48. See http://releaseraminjahanbegloo.blogspot.com.

49. See http://en-democratiranian.blogspot.com/; http://releaseganji.net.

50. See http://penlog.blogspot.com.

CHAPTER 3 Web of Control and Censorship: State and Blogosphere in Iran

1. See http://www.genderit.org/upload/ad6d215b74e2a8613f0cf5416c9f3865/A_Report_on_Internet_Access_in_Iran_2_.pdf.

2. Full text of the document (in Persian), www.iranispassociation.com/etelaiye/mosavabeh1.htm.

3. IT Iran, 2002.

4. See http://stop.censoring.us/archives/2005_02.php.

5. Opennet Initiative, 2005.

6. See http://stop.censoring.us/archives/2005_01.php.

7. See http://www.securecomputing.com/index.cfm?skey=85.

8. See http://stop.censoring.us.

9. See http://stop.censoring.us/archives/2003_12.php.

10. See http://www.rsf.org/article.php3?id_article=7268.

11. See http://www.bbc.co.uk/persian/science/030510_h-banned-sites.shtml.

12. See http://news.bbc.co.uk/1/hi/technology/3312841.stm. Transcript of Khatami's interview, http://www.dailysummit.net/english/archives/2003/12/11/the_iranian_president.asp.

13. See http://stop.censoring.us.

14. See http://www.rsf.org/article.php3?id_article=10733.

15. See http://www.opennetinitiative.net/bulletins/004/#10.

16. See http://www.opennetinitiative.net/bulletins/004/globallist.html.

17. See http://stop.censoring.us/archives/2003_12.php.

18. See http://itiran.net/archives/001260.php.

19. See http://stop.censoring.us/archives/2005_01.php.

20. See http://www.itiran.com/?type=news&id=6911.

21. See http://www.farsnews.com/newstext.php?nn=8507240053.

22. See http://www.itna.ir/archives/news/005618.php.

23. The *Guardian*, 'Iran bans fast internet to cut west's influence: Service providers told to restrict online speeds Opponents say move will hamper country's progress,' 18 October 2006, http://technology.guardian.co.uk/news/story/0,1924637,00.html.

24. See http://www.itna.ir/archives/news/005577.php.

25. See http://www.bbc.co.uk/persian/science/story/2006/10/061020_fb_rsh_adsl.shtml.

26. See http://weblog.shaar.com/archives/2006/10/000949_.php.

27. See http://www.salehoffline.com/archives/002131.html.

28. See http://weblog.andia.ir/1385/07/20/adsl128.

29. See http://asemannet_1.mihanblog.com/post-83.aspx.

30. See http://www.dci.ir/english/moarefi.htm.

31. See http://www.more-speed-more-progress.ir.

32. See http://opennet.net/research/profiles/iran.

33. The two arrested were Babak Ghafoori Azar (http://www.ghafooriazar.com) and Shahram Rafi Zadeh (http://yeknoon.blogsky.com).

34. See http://omidmemarian.blogspot.com.

35. See http://opennet.net/research/profiles/iran http://opennet.net/research/profiles/iran.

36. The full text of Cyber Crime Law, http://www.itc.ir/aeenname/rayane.htm.

37. See http://www.rsf.org/article.php3?id_article=21052.

38. See http://www.payvand.com/news/07/feb/1292.html.

39. See http://www.opennetinitiative.net/bulletins/004/blacklist.html.

40. See http://jadi.civiblog.org/blog/censorship.

41. See http://www.farsnews.com/newstext.php?nn=8412130053.

42. See http://freekeyboard.net/node/spip.php?article196.

43. See http://iraniandiaries.blogspot.com/2004/06/filter-filter-everywhere.html.

44. See http://www.samandehi.ir/help.php for the Ministry's Guide to how to register only in Persian.

45. See http://news.bbc.co.uk/1/hi/talking_point/6252737.stm.

46. A blogger from Iran who after his release from prison moved to the USA and continues blogging in his weblog *Iran Prospect*, http://omidmemarian.blogspot.com.

47. See http://weblog.parastood.ir/. In March 2006 Parastoo launched her blog in English calling it *Remains of the Day*: 'I just want to give it a try and write a weblog in English; that is, after four years of keeping one in Persian – and feeling great about it. Here you can find my notes on almost everything: daily life, movies, books, as well as my views on social and political issues. The name of the blog comes from a book written by Kazuo Ishiguro, a well-known British-Japanese author. It's simply what I'd be doing: writing every night about what remains of the day. I love the book and its great translation into Persian by Najaf Daryabandari. By the way I gotta work more on my writing. Do encourage me please!'

48. See http://kamangir.wordpress.com/2007/01/01/a-law-not-even-obeyed-by-the-president.

49. See http://www.khorshidkhanoom.com/archives/2007_01.php.

50. See http://femirani.com/weblog/?p=138.

51. See Khiabany and Sreberny, 2007, CCESSME.

52. See http://cobraweblog.blogspot.com.

53. See http://www.osyan.net/2007/01/post_900.php.

54. See http://etravelog.blogfa.com/post-227.aspx.

55. See http://www.manionline.org/1385/10/14/yalda-and-censorship.

56. See http://rozmaregi.blogfa.com/post-130.aspx.

57. See http://www.cloob.com.

58. See http://www.persianpetition.com/sign.aspx?id=dd937e14-aebf-4ee5-9335-6f6af724282d.

59. See http://eistgah.blogfa.com/post-172.aspx.

60. For a full responses to new law, see http://www.iranianpep.com/2007/01/samandehi_links.html.

61. See http://nikick.blogspot.com.

62. See http://iranpoliticsclub.net/club/viewtopic.php?t=51.

63. See http://jadi.civiblog.org/blog/archives/2006/12/25/2595792.html.

64. See http://www.reuters.com/article/technologyNews/idUSDAH83913820070428.

65. See http://www.bbc.co.uk/persian/iran/2008/11/081119 mg basij filtering.shtml.

66. See http://cyber.law.harvard.edu/publications/2008/Mapping_Irans_Online_Public.

CHAPTER 4   Gender, Sexuality and Blogging

1. See Mitra Bagherian, 'Economic analysis of women journalistic activities', *Zanan*, 1/3 (1993); Masoumeh Keyhani, 'How women-oriented issues are reflected in the Tehran newspapers', *Rasaneh*, 13/2 (2002); Omid Massoudi, 'A glance at the early experience of Iranian women journalists', *Rasaneh*, 9/1 (1998).

2. Keyhani 'How women-oriented', p. 67.

3. See Mohammad Sadr-Hashemi, '*History of Iranian Press and Magazines*' Vol. 2 (Isfahan, 1985):181–185.

4. Keyhani 'How women-oriented'.

5. See Farid Qasemi, '*Iranian Press in Twentieth Century*' (Tehran, 2001).

6. Bagherian, 'Economic analysis'.

7. Keyhani, 'How women-oriented'.

8. Parvin Ardalan, 'Zanan introduces women's press: Zan-e Rouz', *Zanan*, No. 52, pp. 2–6.

9. Centre for Cultural and International Studies, '*The Cultural Viewpoints of the Leader of the Islamic Revolution of Iran Ayatollah Seyed-Ali Khamenei*' (Tehran, 2000).

10. Maryam Poya, '*Women, Work & Islamism: Ideology and Resistance in Iran*' (London: 1999).

11. Noushin Ahmadi Khorasani, '*Women under the Shadow of Patriarch's*' (Tehran, 2001), p. 166.

12. Nira Yuval-Davis, '*Gender and Nation*' (London, 1997).

13. Oliver Roy, '*The Failure of Political Islam*' (London, 1994).

14. Asghar Schirazi, '*The Constitution of Iran: Politics and the State in the Islamic Republic*' (London, 1998), pp. 141–143.

15. Ali Barzegar, 'Who are in search of civil society?', *Political & Economic Etelaat*, 13/135–136 (1999), pp. 28–33.

16. Haleh Afshar, 'Competing interests: democracy, Islamicisation and women politician in Iran', *Parliamentary Affairs* No. 55 (2002); Poya, '*Women, Work & Islamism*'.

17. Valentine Moghadam, '*Women, Work and Economic Reform in the Middle East and North Africa*' (Boulder, CO, 1998); Poya, '*Women, Work & Islamism*'.

18. Kian, 'Women and politics'; Afshar, 'Competing interests'; Poya, '*Women, Work & Islamism*'; Mir-Hosseini, Ziba, 'Feminist movements in the Islamic Republic', http://www.hamta.co.uk/feminist.htm.

19. Azar Tabari and Nahid Yeganeh (eds.), '*In the Shadow of Islam: The Women's Movement in Iran*' (London, 1982).

20. Poya, '*Women, Work & Islamism*'.

21. Kian, 'Women and politics'.

22. Kian, 'Women and politics'; Afshar, 'Competing interests'.

23. Valentine Moghadam, 'Islamic feminism and its discontents: Towards a resolution of the debate', *Sign: Journal of Women in Culture and Society*, 27/4 (2002).

24. Janet Afary, 'The war against feminism in the name of the almighty: Making sense of gender and Muslim fundamentalism', *New Left Review*, No. 224 (1997); Haleh Afshar, 'Islam and feminism: An analysis of political strategies', in Mai Yamani (eds), '*Feminism & Islam: Legal and Literary Perspectives*' (New York, 1996); Kian, 'Women and politics'.

25. Mir-Hosseini, Ziba, 'Stretching the limits: A feminist reading of the Shari'a in post-Khomeini Iran' in Mai Yamani (ed.), '*Feminism & Islam: Legal and Literary Perspectives*' (New York, 1996).

26. Shahrzad Mojab, 'Theorizing the politics of 'Islamic feminism', *Feminist Review*, No. 69 (2001); Moghissi, *Populist Feminism and Islamic Feminism: A Critique of Neo-Conservative Tendencies among Iranian Feminists in the West*.

27. Moghadam, 'Islamic feminism', p. 1165.

28. Mir-Hosseini, Ziba, 'Feminist movements'.

29. Lily Farhadpour, '*Berlin's Women*' (Tehran, 2000).

30. The main firms in Iran are regarded as 'public property', and their managing directors are selected and appointed by the Supreme Leader.

31. Mohammad Ghouchani, '*Godfather and the Young Left: The Struggle for Critique of Power*' (Tehran, 2000).

32. Ardalan, 'Zanan introduces'.

33. Elham Gheytanchi, 'Civil society in Iran: Politics of motherhood and the public sphere', *International Sociology*, 16/4 (2001), p. 563.

34. Ziba Mir-Hosseini, 'Feminist movements'; Ziba Mir-Hosseini, 'Stretching the limits'; Haleh Afshar, 'Islam and feminism'.

35. The 'Iran after the Elections' conference was held April 7–9 in Berlin by the Heinrich Boll Institute, an organisation associated with the German Green Party. It aimed to promote understanding and informed political opinion and intended to bring together critical voices from both secular and Islamic reformists groups. Some prominent writers, publishers and well as reformist politicians and journalists were invited to speak. A large demonstration of some Iranian political groups in exile, however, disrupted the proceedings and a woman danced in her underwear to protest the Islamic dress code in Iran. Rafsanjani later condemned these people for shameful conduct. Iranian national television, controlled by the supreme leader Ali Khamenei, showed a highly biased and selective film of the conference, cynically skewed to inflame religious opinion and paint the participants in an anti-Islamic light. A number of participants, including two women, Mehrangiz Kar, a human rights lawyer, and Shahla Lahiji, an independent publisher; together with Alireza Afshar, secretary of the Office of Consolidation of Unity, the largest student association, and Akbar Ganji, a reformist and well-known investigative journalist, were all arrested and sent to jail and charged with acts against national security by making propaganda against the Islamic Republic of Iran.

36. See http://www.badjens.com/fourthedition/kar.htm.

37. Elaheh Rostami Povey, 'Feminist contestations of institutional domains in Iran', *Feminist Review*, No. 69 (2001).

38. See http://www.pbs.org/adventuredivas/iran/divas.

39. Ardalan, 'Zanan introduces women's press: Farzaneh', *Zanan*, No. 69 (2000a).

40. Shadi Sadr, '*Justice from the Point of View of Third Person*' (Tehran, 2000).

41. Ahmadi Khorasani, '*Women Under the Shadow of Patriarchs*'. pp. 158–165.

42. Parvin Ardalan, 'Zanan introduces women's press: Payam-e Zan', *Zanan*, No. 62 (2000b).

43. Parvin Ardalan, 'Zanan introduces women's press: Neda', *Zanan*, No. 55 (1999b).

44. See www.iranwomen.org.

45. See Parvin Ardalan, 'Zanan introduces women's press: Faslnameh', *Zanan*, No. 80 (2001).

46. Ahmadi Khorasani published the journal without a licence. It was published in a book format by Ahmadi Khorasani's own publication firm. The regime was alarmed when *Jens-e Dovom* appeared with numbers and ordered the editor, who was hoping to get away with it, by pretending that the journal was a book, to close it.

47. Poya, '*Women, Work & Islamism*'.

48. See http://www.badjens.com/fourthedition/lahiji.htm.

49. Cinema is of course another area in which Iranian women have made a strong headway. In contrast to only two women directors in pre-1979 period, there are at least 11 women directors in Iran now. Some are internationally known and well-received in international film festivals and despite the limitations imposed by the Islamic Republic have managed to produce movies of astonishing quality dealing with 'women's questions' with spectacular effect. See Hamid Naficy, 'Veiled vision/powerful presence: Women in post revolutionary Iranian cinema', in Afkhami, Mahnaz and Erica Friedl (eds.), '*In the Eye of Storm: Women in Post-Revolutionary Iran*' (London, 1994). Some – for example, Tahmineh Millani – have even been imprisoned for their movies. According to one report, in the years before the revolution only three women made a feature film in Iran, one in 1956 and the other two in the late 1970s. Of 11 women film directors in post-revolution Iran, the majority have made more than one film and four have made at least 4 or 5 movies, and what makes them distinct is their focus on gender issues. Reza Tahami, 'Iranian women make films', *Film International Quarterly*, 2/3 (1994).

50. See http://www.irandokht.com/irandokhtstory.

51. See http://herlandmag.com/weblog/06/03.

52. See http://www.meydaan.com/aboutus.aspx.

53. Notably depicted in Jafar Panahi's film *Offside*.

54. See http://www.meydaan.com/campaign.aspx?cid=45&pid=0.

55. See http://www.iftribune.com.

56. See http://www.womeniniran.com.

57. See http://irwomen.net.

58. See www.herlandmag.com.

59. See http://www.irwomen.org.

60. See http://www.irwomen.org/spip.php?article2.

61. See http://www.irwomen.org/spip.php?rubrique14.

62. See http://herlandmag.com/about.

63. See http://www.iftribune.com.

64. See http://asre-nou.net/pnav1/zanan.html.

65. See http://www.akhbar-rooz.com/section.jsp?sectionId=105.

66. See http://www.dw-world.de/dw/article/0,2144,3172932,00.html.

67. See http://www.zigzagmag.com/categories/women.

68. For analysis of the Iranian political structure, see http://news.bbc.co.uk/hi/english/static/in_depth/middle_east/2000/iran_elections/iran_struggle_for_change/who_holds_power.

69. As stated in Article 99 of constitution, the Guardian Council 'has the responsibility of supervising the elections of the Assembly of Experts for Leadership, the President of the Republic, the Islamic Consultative Assembly, and the direct recourse to popular opinion and referenda'. The Council has the power, exercised regularly, to veto candidates in election to Parliament, local councils, the presidency as well as the Assembly of Expert (*Majles Khebreghan*).

70. See http://weblog.parastood.ir/archives/2002_06.php.

71. See http://ladysun.wordpress.com.

72. See http://www.khorshidkhanoom.com.

73. See http://ladysun.wordpress.com/2003/04/29/why-an-english-weblog.

74. See http://www.we4change.info/english.

75. See http://www.mehrangizkar.com/english.

76. See http://www.cappuccinomag.com.

77. See http://ladysun.wordpress.com/2007/08/05/low-profile-confessions.

78. See http://www.khorshidkhanoom.com/archives/2007_08.php.

79. See http://www.khorshidkhanoom.com/archives/2004_02.php. Lady sun plays with a Persian name. Fuker in Persian means someone who thinks, a wise person.

80. See http://beingdoxtare.blogspot.com/2006_07_01_archive.html.

81. See http://beingdoxtar.blogspot.com/2008_03_01_archive.html.

82. See http://pagard.ayene.com.

83. See http://gistela.blogspot.com.

84. See http://gistela.blogspot.com/search?updated-max=2004-08-29T08%3A10%3A00%2B04%3A30&max-results=50.

85. For detailed analysis of some of these discussions, see Ziba Mir-Hosseini (1996).

86. See http://www.payvand.com/news/08/feb/1131.html; http://www.bbc.co.uk/persian/arts/story/2008/01/080128_bd-zanan-close.shtml; and Asieh Amini's report in *Rooz Online*, http://www.roozonline.com/archives/2008/01/post_5936.php.

87. For campaign outside Iran see Human Right First campaign, http://action.humanrightsfirst.org/campaign/Zanan?qp_source=ga%5fadv; and International Petition in Support of Zanan Magazine, which attracted the support of more than 150 activists and academics in Europe and United States, http://www.petitionforzanan.com/; In Iran a campaign against the closure is organised by Associations of Iranian Journalists, http://aoij.ir/001335.php; for a photograph of gathering of Associations in Tehran see http://www.meydaan.org/Showarticle.aspx?arid=456.

88. See http://varesh.blogfa.com/post-624.aspx.

89. See http://razeno.com/2008/02/the_order_to_close_zanan.php.

90. See http://blog.ahmadnia.net/spip.php?article1201.

91. See http://www.mimnoon.com/mana/archives/000504.html.

92. See http://femirani.com/weblog/?p=290.

93. See http://www.fahimehkh.com/2008/01/694.php.

94. See http://nilofarrostami.blogfa.com/post-2.aspx.

95. See 46 http://4zanan.blogfa.com/8611.aspx.

96. Sadeq Mojtahedi in an article published in Baztab regards this as a result of spread of 'Western' tradition of courtship of engaged couples before marriage, and as one solution offered to deal with the sexual dilemmas and needs of youths. See

'Temporary marriage or justifying prostitution?', http://www.baztab.com/news/
68639.php.

97. See http://movaghat.blogsky.com.

98. See http://movaghat.blogsky.com/?PostID=7.

99. See http://movaghati.com.

100. See http://panahjoyan.blogspot.com/2007/06/blog-post_15.html.

101. See http://omidmemarian.blogspot.com.

102. See http://www.roozonline.com/archives/2007/06/005031.php.

103. See http://badhijab.blogfa.com/post-28.aspx.

104. See http://yardabestani-1.blogfa.com/post-46.aspx.

105. See http://inroozhaaa.blogfa.com/post-94.aspx.

106. See http://www.forequality.info/english.

107. See http://www.meydaan.com.

CHAPTER 5   Becoming Intellectual: The Blogistan and Public Political Space in the Islamic Republic

1. M. Borujerdi, *'Iranian Intellectuals and the West: The Tormented Triumph of Nativism'*
   (Syracuse: Syracuse University Press, 1996); H. Dabashi, *'Theology of Discontent:
   The Ideological Foundation of the Islamic Revolution in Iran'* (New Brunswick and
   London: Transaction Publisher, 2006); A. Gheissari, *'Iranian Intellectuals in the 20th
   Century'* (Austin, TX: University of Texas Press, 1998); A. Mirsepassi, *'Intellectual
   Discourse and the Politics of Modernization: Negotiating Modernity in Iran'* (Cam-
   bridge, MA: Harvard University Press, 2000); M. Tavakli-Targhi, *'Refashioning
   Iran: Orientalism, Occidentalism and Historiography'* (New York: Palgrave, 2001);
   F. Vahdat, *'God and Juggernaut: Iran's Intellectual Encounter with Modernity'* (Syra-
   cuse: Syracuse University Press, 2002).

2. M. Kamrava, *'The New Voices of Islam: Reforming Politics and Modernity'* (London:
   I.B.Tauris, 2006); F. Khosrokhavar, 'The new intellectuals in Iran', *Social Compass*,
   51:2 (2004a), pp. 191–202; F. Khosrokhavar, 'The Islamic Revolution in Iran:
   Retrospect after a quarter of a century', *Thesis Eleven*, 76 (2004b), pp. 70–84; C.
   Kurzman, 'Critics within: Islamic scholars' protests against the Islamic State in
   Iran', *International Journal of Politics, Culture and Society*, 15:2 (2001), pp. 341–359;
   K. Tabari, 'The rule of law and the politics of reform in post-revolutionary Iran',
   International Sociology, 18:1 (2003), pp. 96–113; A. Sadri, 'The varieties of religious
   reform: Public intelligensia in Iran', *International Journal of Politics, Culture and
   Society*, 15:2 (2001), pp. 271–282.

3. B. Ghamari-Tabrizi, *'Islam and Dissent in Post-revolutionary Iran: The Religious Pol-
   itics of Abdolkarim Soroush'* (London: I.B.Tauris, 2000); Z. Mir-Hosseini, and R.
   Tapper, *'Islam and Democracy in Iran: Eshkevari and the Quest for Reform'* (London:
   I.B.Tauris, 2006).

4. A. Gramsci, *'Selections from the Prison Notebooks'* (London: Lawrence & Wishart,
   1971), p. 10.

5. N. Garnham, 'The media and narratives of the intellectual', *Media, Culture and Society*, 17 (1995), p. 360.

6. N. Alavi, '*We are Iran*' (Washington, DC: Soft Skull Press, 2005).

7. R. Jacoby, '*The Last Intellectuals*' (New York: Basic Books, 1989).

8. M. Castells, '*The Rise of the Network Society*' (2nd ed), (Cambridge, MA: Blackwell, 2000).

9. D. Kellner, 'Intellectuals and new technologies', *Media, Culture and Society*, 17, (1995), pp. 427–448.

10. E. Eisenstein, '*The Printing Press as an Agent of Change*' (Cambridge: Cambridge University Press, 1979).

11. W. Benjamin, '*Illuminations*' (New York: Schocken Books, 1968).

12. B. Brecht, 'Radio as a means of communication: A talk on the function of radio', *Screen*, 20:3/4 (1979), p. 25.

13. P. Alizadeh, '*Iran's Economy: Dilemma of an Islamic State*' (London: I.B.Tauris, 2003); M. Karshenas, '*Oil, State, and Industrialization in Iran*' (Cambridge, Cambridge University Press, 1990); J. Foran and J. Goodwin, 'Revolutionary outcomes in Iran and Nicaragua: Coalition fragmentation, war, and the limits of social transformation', *Theory and Society*, 22:2 (1993), pp. 209–247.

14. A. Bayat, '*Workers & Revolution in Iran*' (London: Zed, 1987).

15. *Ibid.*

16. This is rather in contrast to the USA/UK where the 'democracy deficit' means less than half the population participating in the formal politics of elections.

17. N. Garnham, 'The media and narratives of the intellectual', *Media, Culture and Society*, 17 (1995), p. 376.

18. C. Mouffe, '*On the Political*' (London: Routledge, 2005), p. 18.

19. G. Khiabany, and A. Sreberny, 'Internet in Iran: The battle over an emerging public sphere', in M. McLelland and G. Goggin (eds.), '*Internationalising Internet Studies: Beyond Anglophone Paradigms*' (New York: Routledge, 2010).

20. G. Khiabany, and A. Sreberny, 'The Iranian press and continuing struggle over civil society 1998–2000', *Gazette*, 63:2/3 (2001), pp. 203–223.

21. D. Lerner, '*The Passing of Traditional Society: Modernizing the Middle East*' (New York: Free Press, 1958), p. 363.

22. See http://www.radiozamaneh.org/nilgoon/2007/02/post_39.html.

23. See http://www.nilgoon.org/pdfs/dustdar_roshanfekri_piramooni.pdf.

24. See http://www.radiozamaneh.org/nilgoon/2007/02/post_38.html.

25. A. Dirlik, 'Global modernity? Modernity in an age of global capitalism', *European Journal of Social Theory*, 6:3 (2003), pp. 275–292.

26. The article is entitled 'Public Intellectuals and Farsi Language' and posted on http://www.radiozamaneh.org/nilgoon/2007/02/post_41.html.

27. N. Alavi, 'We are Iran' (Washington, DC: Soft Skull Press, 2005).

28. See http://www.bbc.co.uk/persian/iran/story/2005/08/050802_mj-mkhalaji-internet-qom.shtml.

29. Ahmadinejad has also joined the long list of officials with their own blogs, see http://www.ahmadinejad.ir.

30. CNN, 1997.

31. Rahimi, 2003.

32. Ayatollahs with their own sites include Ali Khamenei, Javadi Amoli, Mousavi Ardebili, Safi Golpayegani, Fazel Lankarani and Mesbah Yazdi. Among sites presenting seminaries and religious institutions there are http://www.hawza.net; http://www.balagh.net ; http://www.j-alzahra.org and http://www.shareh.com.

33. See http://www.diniblog.parsiblog.com.

34. See http://saeed623.persianblog.com.

35. See http://www.menbar.persianblog.com.

36. See http://www.quranblog.org.

37. See http://www.velayatefaghih.parsiblog.com.

38. See http://shiashenasi.parsiblog.com.

39. See http://hamedtalebi.blogfa.com.

40. See http://www.muslimbloggers.ir.

41. See http://www.webneveshteha.com.

42. See http://www.webneveshteha.com/media.asp?id=2146308279.

43. See http://mohajerani.maktuob.net.

44. See http://kadivar.maktuob.net.

45. See http://www.drsoroush.com/index.htm.

46. Afshin Matin-Asghari, 2005, 'The rise of modern subjectivity in Iran', Critique, Vol. 14(3):333–337.

47. See http://blogs.law.harvard.edu/idblog/2009/02/12/mapping-change-in-the-iranian-blogosphere.

48. See http://www.globalvoicesonline.org/2006/10/31/hugo-chavez-in-the-iranian-left-wing-blogs.

49. See http://www.newleft.blogfa.com/post-56.aspx.

50. See http://naslefarda.blogfa.com/post-122.aspx.

51. See http://havari.blogfa.com/post-25.aspx.

52. See http://www.takravi.blogfa.com/post-26.aspx.

53. See http://khak82.blogfa.com.

54. See, for example, Coordinating Committee to Form Workers' Organisation (http://www.komiteyehamahangi.com/index.htm); Iranian Teacher Association-Tehran (http://www.ksmt.blogfa.com); National Union of Sacked and Jobless Workers (http://www.ettehade.com); Workers Action Committee (http://www.kargari.blogfa.com); and Syndicate of Workers of Tehran and Suburbs Bus Company (Sherkat-e Vahed) (http://www.syndicavahed.com).

55. See http://www.kosoof.com.

56. See http://www.webneveshteha.com/media.asp?id=2146308279.

57. See http://www.kaargar.blogfa.com.

58. See http://kaargar.blogfa.com/post-1104.aspx.

59. See http://www.itfglobal.org/transport-international/ti29-osanloo.cfm.

60. See http://www.syndicavahed.com/english.htm.

61. See http://www.kargari.blogfa.com.

62. See http://www.ksmt3.blogfa.com.

62. See http://www.ksmi.ir.

63. See http://www.ksmi.ir/showpage.asp?file=فادها&pagename=فادها.

64. See http://www.ksmi.ir/showpage.asp?file=مرابرد20%نوناك&
pagename=نوناك20%مرابرد.

65. See http://www.shorayehamkari.com/darbareyema.htm.

66. See http://takravi.blogfa.com.

67. See http://www.nowaroniran.org.

68. See http://elenazi.blogfa.com.

69. See http://kanoon.mooo.com/DOCuments%20(htm)/080314Evin.htm.

70. See http://www.salam-democrat.com.

71. See http://www.militantmag.blogfa.com/post-127.aspx.

72. See http://militantmag.wordpress.com.

73. See http://www.javaan.blogfa.com.

74. See http://www.khak82.blogfa.com.

75. See http://armane-no.blogspot.com.

76. See http://www.gavaznhamag.blogspot.com.

77. See http://shoramag.blogfa.com.

78. See http://toloomag.blogfa.com.

CHAPTER 6 English Language/Diasporic Blogs: Articulating the Inside and the Outside

1. See http://www.eterazonline.com.

2. Annabelle Sreberny declares an interest: 'My younger daughter Leili went to stay in Iran in November 2007 and started a blog, "kebabandtwoveg". She had not blogged before and hadn't appeared particularly interested in blogging. She started partly as an easy way of keeping a large number of people informed about what she was doing, in a detailed and thoughtful way that blends writing with photography'.

3. This turns out to be a former student. Indeed, looking at English blogging about Iran, I find a strong 'small world' phenomenon.

CHAPTER 7   Journalism, Blogging and Citizen Journalism

1. See http://zigzagmag.net.
2. See http://www.aoij.ir/en.

CHAPTER 8   The Summer of 2009

1. See http://globalvoicesonline.org/2008/06/09/iran-judicial-investigator-publically-accuses-ayatollahs-ofcorruption.
2. See http://globalvoicesonline.org/2008/06/19/iran-citizen-media-sex-scandal.
3. See http://www.youtube.com/watch?v=HY utC-hrjI.
4. See http://www.digiactive.org/2009/05/12/presidential-candidates-go-virtual-in-iran.
5. See http://globalvoicesonline.org/2009/06/17/iran-islamist-bloggers-react-to-protest-movement.
6. See http://techpresident.com/blog-entry/engaging-iran-contested-election-twitter-and-response-inside-and-out.
7. See http://cgis.jpost.com/Blogs/persianabyss/entry/iranian_reactions_from_across_social.
8. See http://www.grandestrategy.com/2009/06/alexa-rankings-confirm-that-twitters.html.
9. See http://www.businessweek.com/technology/content/jun2009/tc20090617_803990.htm?chan=top+news_top+news+index+-+temp_news+%2B+analysis.
10. See http://globalvoicesonline.org/2009/06/17/iran-islamist-bloggers-react-to-protest-movement.
11. See http://www.guardian.co.uk/world/interactive/2009/jun/29/iran-election-dead-detained.
12. See http://www.rsf.org/Repression-stepped-up-yet-again-as.html.
13. See http://www.forbes.com/2009/06/16/twitter-iran-election-markets-equity-dissent.html.
14. See http://www.guardian.co.uk/commentisfree/2009/jun/18/iran-elections-us-foreign-policy.
15. See http://www.chartingstocks.net/2009/06/proof-israeli-effort-to-destabilize-iran-via-twitter.
16. See http://www.counterpunch.org/giordano06192009.html.

Bibliography

Abdo, Geneive and Jonathan Lyons (2003) 'Answering Only to God: Faith and Freedom', *Twenty-First-Century Iran*. New York: Henry Holt and Company.

Abrahamian, Ervand (1982) *Iran Between Two Revolutions*. Princeton: Princeton University Press.

Abrahamian, Ervand (1993) *Khomeinism: Essays on the Islamic republic*. Berkeley: University of California Press.

Ahmadi, Babak (2001) 'Internet, Mobile and Satellite in Iran', *Norouz*, Sep. 27, p. 10.

Alavi, Nasrin (2005) *We are Iran*. Washington: Soft Skull Press.

Alinejad, Mahmoud (2002) 'Coming to terms with modernity: Iranian intellectuals and the emerging public sphere', *Islam and Christian-Muslim Relations*, Vol. 13(1):25–47.

Alizadeh, Parvin (ed.) (2000) *Iran's Economy: Dilemma of an Islamic State*. London: I.B.Tauris.

Allan, Stuart and Thorsen, Einar (2009) *Citizen Journalism: Global Perspectives*. New York: Peter Lang.

Amir-Ebrahimi, Masserat (2004) 'Performance in Everyday Life and the Rediscovery of the "Self" in Iranian Weblogs', http://www.badjens.com/rediscovery.html.

Ansari, Ali (2006) *Iran, Islam & Democracy – The Politics of Managing Change*. London RIIA, London: RIIA.

Arabshahi, Payman (1997) 'The Internet in Iran: A survey', http://www.iranian.com/WebGuide/InternetIran.

Ardalan, Parvin (2001) 'Zanan introduces women's press: Faslnameh', *Zanan*, No. 80. Pool, Ithiel de Sola (1983) *Technologies of Freedom*, Cambridge, MA:Belknap Press.

Arjomand, Said Amir (2000) 'Civil society and the rule of law in the constitutional politics of Iran under Khatami', *Social Research*, Vol. 67(2):283–301.

Ashraf, Ahmad and Ali Banuazizi (2001) 'Iran's tortuous path toward "Islamic Liberalism"', *International Journal of Politics, Culture and Society*, Vol. 15(2): 237–256.

Bagheri, M. (1997) 'Iranian Press: From early days to 1943', *Research Papers on History of Iranian Press*, Vol. 1(1):389–428.

Bayat, Asef (2007) 'A women's non-movement: What it means to be a woman activist in an Islamic state', *Comparative Studies of South Asia, Africa and the Middle East*, 27:3, p. 169.

Bayat, Asef (1987) *Workers & Revolution in Iran*. London: Zed.

BBC (2003) 'Iran steps up net censorship', http://news.bbc.co.uk/go/pr/fr/-/1/hi/technology/3019695.stm.

Behdad, Sohrab (2000) From populism to economic liberalism: The Iranian predicament, in P. Alizadeh (Ed.) *Iran's Economy: Dilemma of an islamic state.* London: I.B.Tauris.

Benjamin, Walter (1968) *Illuminations.* New York: Schocken Books.

Borujerdi, Mehrzad (1996) *Iranian Intellectuals and the West: The Tormented Triumph of Nativism.* (Syracuse: Syracuse University Press).

Burkhart, Grey (1998) 'National Security and the Internet in the Persian Gulf Region', http://www.georgetown.edu/research/arabtech/pgi98-4.html.

Castells, Manuel (2000) *The Rise of the Network Society* (Second Edition). Cambridge, MA: Blackwell.

CNN (1997) 'Islam, Iran and the Internet', www.cnn.com/WORLD/9705/22/iran.tech.

Couldry, Nick and Curran, James (2003) *Contesting Media Power*, Rowman and Littlefield.

Curran, James & Myung-Jin Park, (Eds.) (2000). *De-Westernizing Media Studies.* London: Routledge.

Dabashi, Hamid (2007) *Iran: A People Interrupted.* New York: The New Press.

Dabashi, Hamid (2006) *Theology of Discontent: The Ideological Foundation of the Islamic Revolution in Iran.* New Brunswick and London: Transaction Publisher.

Dirlik, Arif (2003) 'Global modernity? Modernity in an age of global capitalism', in *European Journal of Social Theory*, Vol. 6:3:275–292.

Downing, John (1996) *Internationalizing Media Theory*, London: Sage

Ebadi, Shirin (2006) *Iran Awakening: Memoir of Revolution and Hope*, New York: Random House.

Ebrahimian, Laleh (2003) 'Socio-economic development in Iran through information and communications technologies', *Middle East Journal*, Vol. 57(1):93–111.

Egherman, Tori and Kamran, Ahstary (2007) *Iran: A View from Here.* Available at: http://ashtarydesign.com/book/book nl.htm

Eisenstein, Elizabeth (1979) The Printing Press as an Agent of Change. Cambridge: Cambridge University Press.

Foran, John, and Jeff Goodwin (1993) 'Revolutionary outcomes in Iran and Nicaragua: Coalition fragmentation, war, and the limits of social transformation', *Theory and Society*, 22:2:209–247.

Garnham, Nicholas (1995) 'The media and narratives of the intellectual', *Media, Culture and Society*, 17, pp. 359–384.

Garnham, Nicholas (1997) 'Amartya Sen's 'Capabilities' Approach To The Evaluation Of Welfare And Its Application To Communications', *Javnost/Public*, Vol.4,(4)

Ghandi, H. (1998). Expert personnel in press. Collection of articles of Second Seminar in *Analysis of Iranian Press* (vol. 2). Tehran: Centre for Media Studies and Research.

Ghamari-Tabrizi, Behrooz (2000) *Islam and Dissent in Post-revolutionary Iran: The Religious Politics of Abdolkarim Soroush*. London: I.B.Tauris.

Gheissari, Ali (1998) *Iranian Intellectuals in the 20th Century*. Austin: University of Texas Press.

Gillmore, Dan (2004) *We the Media: Grassroots Journalism by the People, for the People* (http://oreilly.com/catalog/wemedia/book/).

Goffman, Erving (1959) *The Presentation of Self in Everyday Life*, New York: Anchor Books.

Gouldner, Alvin (1979) *The Future of Intellectuals and the Rise of the New Class*. London: Macmillan.

Gramsci, Antonio (1971) *Selections from the Prison Notebooks*. London: Lawrence & Wishart.

Hallin, Dan and Mancini, Paolo (2005) Comparing media systems, in J. Curran & M. Gurevitch (Eds.) *Mass Media and Society* (Fourth Edition). London: Arnold.

Hambastegi (Daily) (2001) 'Iran will have 1,326,000 Internet users in 2002', April 29, p. 7.

Harris, Mark Edward Harris and Kiarostami, Ahmad (2008) *Inside Iran*, Chronicle Books.

Henry, Clement (2003) The clash of globalizations in the middle east, *Review of Middle East Economics and Finance* 1(1):3–16.

Hermida, Alfred (2002) 'Web gives a voice to Iranian women', June 17, http://news.bbc.co.uk/1/hi/sci/tech/2044802.stm.

IT Iran (2002) A committee of High Council of Cultural Revolution will supervise the Internet', December 19, http://www.itiran.com.news.

International Telecommunication Union (2003) ITU. (2003). *World Telecommunication Development Report*. Available at http://www.itu.int/wsis/tunis/newsroom/stats/WorldTelecomDevelopmentReport-2003_E.pdf

Jacoby, Russell (1989) *The Last Intellectuals*. New York: Basic Books.

Kamrava, Mehran (2006) *The New Voices of Islam: Reforming Politics and Modernity*. London: I.B.Tauris.

Karbasian, Akbar (2000) Islamic revolution and the management of the Iranian economy, *Social Research* 67(2):621–640.

Karshenas, Massoud (1990) *Oil, State, and Industrialization in Iran*. Cambridge, Cambridge University Press.

Kasravi, Ahmad (2006) *History of the Iranian Constitutional Revolution*. Costa Mesa, California, Mazda Publications.

Keddie, Niki (1991) 'Introduction: Deciphering Middle Eastern women's history', in Nikki Keddie and Beth Baron (eds), *Women in Middle Eastern History*. New Haven and London: Yale University Press.

Kellner, Douglas (1995) 'Intellectuals and new technologies', *Media, Culture and Society*, 17, pp. 427–448.

Khajepour, Bijan (2000) Domestic political reforms and private sector activity in Iran, *Social Research*, Vol. 67(2):475–518.

Khaniki, H. (1997) 'First constitution and Reza Shah period: Comparative content analysis of newspapers in two periods', *Research Papers on History of Iranian Press*, Vol. 1(1):378–388.

Khiabany, Gholam (2010) Iranian Media: The Paradox of Modernity. New York: Routledge.

Khiabany, Gholam (2007) 'Iranian Media: The Paradox of Modernity', *Social Semiotics*, Vol. 17(2):479–501.

Khiabany, Gholam and Annabelle, Sreberny (2001) 'The Iranian Press and the Struggle over Civil Society 1998–2000', *Gazette*, 63:2–3.

Khiabany, Gholam and Annabelle, Sreberny (2004) 'The Women's Press in Iran:Engendering the Public Sphere', in N. Sakr, (ed.), *Women and Media in the Middle East*, London: I.B.Tauris.

Khiabany, Gholam and Annabelle, Sreberny (2007) 'The Politics of/in Blogging in Iran', special issue, 'Mediated Politics of the Middle East', *Comparative Studies of South Asia, Africa and the Middle East* (CSSAAME), 27, 2, 2007, pp. 563–579.

Khiabany, Gholam and Annabelle, Sreberny (2008) 'Internet in Iran: The Battle over an Emerging Public Sphere', in Mclelland, M. and G. Goggin (eds), *Internationalising Internet Studies: Beyond Anglophone Paradigms*. New York: Routldege.

Khosravi, Shahram (2008) *Young and Defiant in Tehran*. Philadelphia: University of Pennsylvania.

Khosrokhavar, Farhad (2004a) 'The new intellectuals in Iran', *Social Compass*, 51:2, pp. 191–202.

Khosrokhavar, Farhad (2004b) 'The Islamic Revolution in Iran: Retrospect after a quarter of a century', *Thesis Eleven*, 76, pp. 70–84.

Kian, Azadeh (1997) 'Women and politics in post-Islamist Iran: The gender conscious drive to change', *British Journal of Middle Eastern Studies*, 24:1:76.

Kian-Thiébaut, Azadeh (2005) 'From motherhood to equal rights advocates: The weakening of patriarchal order', *Iranian Studies*, Vol. 38(1):45–66, 22p.

Kurzman, Charles (2001) 'Critics within: Islamic scholars' protests against the Islamic State in Iran', *International Journal of Politics, Culture and Society*, Vol. 15(2): 341359.

Lebowitz, Frank (2001, May 17). *Internet cafes closed in Iran*. Digital Freedom Network.

Lerner, Daniel (1958) *The Passing of Traditional Society: Modernizing the Middle East*. New York: Free Press.

Livingstone, Sonia (2005) 'Critical Debates in Internet Studies: Refelections on an Emerging Field', in Curran J and M Gurevitch (eds.) *Mass Media and Society* (Fourth Edition). London: Arnold.

Mahdi, Ali Akbar (1999) 'The Students Movement in the Islamic Republic of Iran', *Journal of Iranian Research and Analyses*, Vol. No. 15:5–46.

Mahdavi, Pardis (2008) *Passionate Uprising: Iran's Sexual Revolution*. Stanford, CA: Stanford University Press.

Main, Linda (2001) 'The global information infrastructure: empowerment or imperialism?' *Third World Quarterly*, Vol. 22(1):83–97.

Mansell, Robin (2002). From Digital Divides to digital entitlements in knowledge societies. *Current Sociology*, 50(3), 407–426.

Matin-Asghari, Afshin (2005) 'The Rise of Modern Subjectivity in Iran',*Critique: Critical Middle Eastern Studies*, Vol. 14(3), pp. 333–337.

McQuail, Denis (2000) Some reflections on the western bias of media theory, *Asian Journal of Communication* 10(2):1–13.

Mir-Hosseini, Ziba (1999) Feminist Movements in the Islamic Republic, Ehsan Yarshater (ed) (1999), *Encylopaedia Iranica*. Vol. IX:498–503.

Mir-Hosseini, Ziba (1996) 'Stretching the limits: A feminist reading of the Shari'a in post-Khomeini Iran', in Mai Yamani (ed.), *Feminism & Islam: Legal and Literary Perspectives*. New York: New York University Press.

Mir-Hosseini, Ziba (2002) 'The conservative-reformist conflict over women's rights in Iran', *International Journal of Politics, Culture & Society*, Vol. 16(1):37–53.

Mir-Hosseini, Ziba and Richard Tapper (2006) *Islam and Democracy in Iran: Eshkevari and the Quest for Reform*. London: I.B.Tauris.

Mirsepassi, Ali (2000) *Intellectual Discourse and the Politics of Modernization: Negotiating Modernity in Iran*. Cambridge, MA: Harvard University Press.

Mohsenian-Rad, M. (2001) 'A permanent image of one exceptional period in Iran's press history', *Rasaneh*, Vol. 12(2):10–27.

Motamed Nejad, Kazem (1998) Analysis of the condition of independent and pluralistic press, *Collection of Articles of Second Seminar in Analysis of Iranian Press*, Vol. 1. Tehran: Centre for Media Studies and Research.

Mouffe, Chantal (2005) *On the Political*. London: Routledge.

Mouffe, Chantal (2006) 'Hegemony, democracy, agonism and journalism', interviewed by N. Carpentier and B. Cammaerts, *Journalism Studies*, 7:(6) 964–975.

Mousavi Shafaee, Seyed Masoud (2003) 'Globalization and contradiction between the nation and the state in Iran: the Internet case', *Critique*, Vol. 12(2): 189–195.

Opennet Initiative (2005) Internet Filtering in Iran 2004–2005, http://www. opennetinitiative.net.iran.

Qasemi, F. (1994) *Directory of Iranian Press 1979–1993*. Tehran: Centre for Media Studies and Research.

Qasemi, F. (2001) *The history of Press in Iran*. Tehran: Centre for Media Studies and Research.

Qazi-Zadeh, Ali-Akbar (2000) *Fallen Journalists*. Tehran: Rasaneh.

Rahimi, Babak (2003) 'Cyberdissent: the Internet in revolutionary Iran', *Middle East Review of International Affairs*, Vol. 7(3):101–115.

Reporters San Frontières (RSF). (2007). 24 Internet cafés closed and 23 arrests as government steps up online crackdown. 17 December 2007 available at: http://www.rsf.org/24-Internet-cafes-closed-and-23.html

Rezvani, M. (1997) 'Circulation of Iranian Press from beginning to 1941', *Research Papers on History of Iranian Press*, Vol. 1(1):373–376.

Rifkin, Jeremy (2000) *The Age of Access*, London: Penguin

Rouhani, Farhang (2000) 'The spatial politics of leisure: Internet use and access in Tehran, Iran', http://nmit.georgetown.edu/papers/frouhani.

Saba, Sadeq (2005) 'Iran bans parliamentary reporter', http://news.bbc.co.uk/2/hi/middle_east/4414895.stm.

Sadri, Ahmad (2001) 'The Varieties of Religious Reform: Public Intelligensia in Iran', *International Journal of Politics, Culture and Society*, Vol. 15:(2):271–282.

Samii, Abbas (1999) 'The contemporary Iranian news media, 1998–1999', *Middle East Review of International Affairs*, Vol. 3(4):1–10.

Saul, John (2004) 'Globalization, Imperialism, Development: False Binaries and Radical Resolutions', in *Leo Panitch, Colin Leys (eds)* Socialist Register 2004. London: Merlin.

Schuh, Trish (2008) 'Iranians: They're Just Like Us!', *Esquire*, March 12, http://www.esquire.com/the-side/blog/iranians-like-us-031208#ixzz0jxQ1h4se.

Shahidi, Hossein (2007) *Journalism in Iran: From Mission to Profession*. London and New York: Routledge.

Siavoshi, Sussan (1997) Cultural policies and the Islamic republic: Cinema and book publication, *International Journal of Middle East Studies*, 29:509–530.

Sreberny-Mohammadi, Annabelle & Mohammadi, A. (1994) *Small Media, Big Revolution: Communication, Culture, and the Iranian revolution.* Minneapolis: University of Minnesota Press.

Sreberny-Mohammad, Annabelle and Mohammadi, Ali (1987) 'Post-revolutionary Iranian exiles: A study in impotence'. *Third World Quarterly*, 9(1):108–129.

Sreberny, Annabelle and Khiabany, Gholam (2011) *Media Power, People Power: The Green Movement and Digital Politics in Iran*, Boulder: Paradigm Publishers.

Sreberny, Annabelle and Khiabany, Gholam (2007) 'Becoming Intellectual: The Blogestan and Public Political Space in the Islamic Republic' *British Journal of Middle Eastern Studies*, 34:267–286.

Statistical Centre of Iran Yearbook (2001–02) Annual Statistics, http://www.sci.org.ir.

Tabari, Keyvan (2003) 'The rule of law and the politics of reformin post-revolutionary Iran', *International Sociology*, Vol. 18:(1):96–113.

Tabatabai-e Naini, S. (1999) *Directory of Iranian Press (1925–1979)*. Tehran: Centre for Media Studies and Research.

Tarock, Adam (2001) 'The muzzling of liberal press in Iran'; *Third World Quarterly*, Vol. 22(4):585–602.

Tavakli-Targhi, Mohammad (2001) *Refashioning Iran: Orientalism, Occidentalism and Historiography*. New York: Palgrave.

The Global Diffusion of Internet (1998) 'Iran', http://mosaic.unomaha.edu/ GDI1998/7CIRAN.PDF.

The *Guardian* (2002) 'Iran nets another revolt', February 21, http://www.guardian. co.uk/online/story/0,3605,653282,00.htlm.

UNESCO (2000). World Information and Communication Report. Paris: UNESCO.

UNDP (1999) Human Development Report. International cooperation at a cross-roads: Aid, trade and security in an unequal world, http://hdr.undp.org/ reports/global/2005/.

UNDP (1999) Human Development Report: Globalization with a Human Face, http://www.undp.org/hdro/99.htm.

UNDP (2001). Arab Human Development Report. Washington, D.C.

UNDP (2001). Human Development Report. Washington, D.C.

UNDP (2005). Human Development Report. Washington, D.C.

Vahdat, Farzin (2002) *God and Juggernaut: Iran's Intellectual Encounter with Modernity*. Syracuse: Syracuse University Press.

Wilhelm, Anthony (2000). *Democracy in the digital age: Challenges to political life in cyberspace*. New York: Routledge.

Williams, Raymond (1974) *Television:Technology and Cultural Form*, London: Fontana

Winston, Brian (1998) *Media, Technology and Society*, London: Routledge

Index